The
FIVE HUNDRED YEAR REBELLION

Indigenous Movements and the
Decolonization of History
in Bolivia

The
FIVE HUNDRED YEAR REBELLION

Indigenous Movements and the
Decolonization of History
in Bolivia

BENJAMIN DANGL

The Five Hundred Year Rebellion:
Indigenous Movements and the Decolonization of History in Bolivia

© 2019 Benjamin Dangl
© 2019 AK Press (Chico, Edinburgh)
ISBN: 978-1-84935-346-5
E-ISBN: 978-1-84935-347-2
Library of Congress Control Number: 2018961639

AK Press
370 Ryan Ave. #100
Chico, CA 95973
USA
www.akpress.org
akpress@akpress.org

AK Press
33 Tower St.
Edinburgh EH6 7BN
Scotland
www.akuk.com
ak@akedin.demon.co.uk

The above addresses would be delighted to provide you with the latest AK Press distribution catalog, which features books, pamphlets, zines, and stylish apparel published and/or distributed by AK Press. Alternatively, visit our websites for the complete catalog, latest news, and secure ordering.

Cover design by John Yates | www.stealworks.com
Cover photo: Thousands of President Evo Morales's supporters gather in the Plaza Murillo in La Paz, Bolivia, on December 15, 2007, to show their support for the country's new constitution. Photographer: Bear Guerra.

Printed in the USA on acid-free, recycled paper

Contents

List of Abbreviations

COB–Bolivian Workers' Central, *Central Obrera Boliviana*

CONAMAQ–National Council of Ayllus and Markas of Qullasuyu, *Consejo Nacional de Ayllus y Markas de Qullasuyo*

CSUTCB–Unified Syndical Confederation of Rural Workers of Bolivia, *Confederación Sindical Única de Trabajadores Campesinos de Bolivia*

MAS–Movement Toward Socialism, *Movimiento al Socialismo*

MNR–Nationalist Revolutionary Movement, *Movimiento Nacionalista Revolucionario*

PMC–Military-Campesino Pact, *Pacto Militar-Campesino*

THOA–Andean Oral History Workshop, *Taller de Historia Oral Andina*

Map of Bolivia

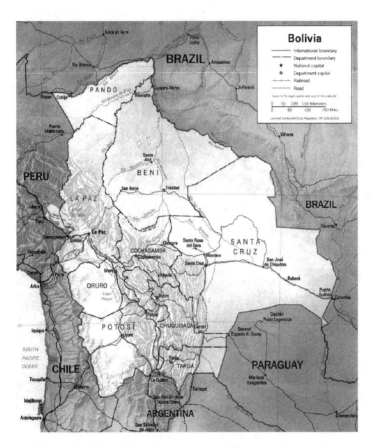

Map of Bolivia courtesy of the University of Texas
Libraries, The University of Texas at Austin

The indigenous March for Land and Territory enters La Paz from El Alto on September 26, 1996, crossing the same terrain Túpac Katari's army used to seize La Paz in 1781. The march began among indigenous communities in the eastern lowlands of the country and grew in size as it reached La Paz. Photographer: Museo Nacional de Etnografía y Folklore. Courtesy of the Archivo Central del Museo Nacional de Etnografía y Folklore.

A caravan of buses, security vehicles, indigenous leaders, and backpackers with Che Guevara T-shirts wove their way down a muddy road through farmers' fields to the precolonial city of Tiwanaku. Folk music played throughout the cool day of January 22, 2015, as indigenous priests conducted complex rituals to prepare Bolivia's first indigenous president, Evo Morales, for a third term in office. His ceremonial inauguration in the ancient city's ruins was marked by many layers of symbolic meaning. "Today is a special day, a historic day reaffirming our identity," Morales said in his speech, given in front of an elaborately carved stone doorway. "For more than five hundred years, we have suffered darkness, hatred, racism, discrimination, and individualism, ever since the strange [Spanish] men arrived, telling us that we had to modernize, that we had to civilize ourselves. . . . But to modernize us, to civilize us, first they had to make the indigenous peoples of the world disappear."[1]

Morales had been reelected the previous October with more than 60 percent of the vote. His popularity was largely due to his Movement Toward Socialism (MAS) party's success in reducing poverty, empowering marginalized sectors of society, and using funds from state-run industries for hospitals, schools, and much-needed public works projects across Bolivia. "I would like to tell you, sisters and brothers," Morales continued, "especially those invited here internationally, what did they used to say? 'The Indians, the indigenous people, are only for voting and not for governing.' And now the indigenous people, the unions, we have all demonstrated that we also know how to govern better than them."

For most of those in attendance, the event was a time to reflect on the economic and social progress enjoyed under the Morales administration and to recognize how far the country had come in overcoming five hundred years of subjugation of its indigenous majority since the conquest of the Americas. "This event is very important for us, for the Aymara, Quechua, and Guaraní people," said Ismael Quispe Ticona, an indigenous leader from La Paz. "[Evo Morales] is our brother who is in power now after more than five hundred years of slavery. Therefore, this ceremony has a lot of importance for us. . . . We consider this a huge celebration."[2]

For critics on the political left, the Tiwanaku event embodied the contradictions of a president who championed indigenous rights at the same time that he silenced and undermined grassroots indigenous dissidents, and who spoke of respect for Mother Earth while deepening an extractive economy based on gas and mining industries. Indeed, the way the MAS used the ruins of Tiwanaku for political ends, as it had in past inaugurations, appeared shameful and opportunistic to some critics.[3] But such uses of historical symbols by Morales were part of a long political tradition in Bolivia. From *campesino* (rural worker) and indigenous movements in the 1970s to the MAS party today, indigenous activists and leftist politicians have claimed links with indigenous histories of oppression and resistance to legitimize their demands and guide their contested processes of decolonization.

When Evo Morales walked through the doors of Tiwanaku amid smoking incense and the prayers of Andean priests, for many Bolivians it was a profound moment marking the third term in office for the country's first indigenous president. It was also just another day in a country where the politics of the present are steeped in the past.

The Morales government typically portrays itself as a political force that has realized the thwarted dreams of eighteenth-century indigenous rebel Túpac Katari, who organized an insurrection against the Spanish in an attempt to reassert indigenous rule in the Andes. This was underlined in the recent naming of Bolivia's first satellite, Túpac Katari (also known as TKSat 1). The launching of the satellite was broadcast live in the central Plaza Murillo in La Paz, an event accompanied by Andean spiritual leaders who conducted rituals to honor Mother Earth. The government has also named state-owned planes after Katari. As Bolivian air force commander Tito Gandarillas told the president at a celebration marking the official use of a new plane, "There you have it in front of you, our legendary 727-200 Boeing, that we are going to name Túpac Katari; he has returned converted into millions [of people] and this airplane is going to transport millions of Bolivian men and women, people with few resources."[4] That Katari's legacy could be put to use in such a way speaks to the enduring political capital of the indigenous leader.

Over two hundred years before the Morales government launched a satellite bearing his name, the Aymara indigenous rebel Katari led a 109-day siege of La Paz that rattled Spanish colonial rule. Katari's revolt was part of an indigenous insurrection across the Andes launched in 1780 from Cuzco and Potosí, and spread by Katari to La Paz in March 1781. The essential demand of the revolts led by Tomás Katari (no relation) in Potosí, Túpac Amaru in Cuzco, and Túpac Katari in La Paz was that governance of the region be placed back into indigenous hands.

An Aymara commoner born in the town of Sica Sica roughly thirty years before the 1781 siege, Túpac Katari lived in the community of Ayo-Ayo, spoke only the Aymara language, and was one of the many itinerant coca and cloth traders in the region.[5] His birth name was Julián Apaza, but he took on the name Túpac Katari to tie his legitimacy as a leader to the rebels in Cuzco and Potosí. Accounts from the era describe Katari as a poor man who was not necessarily handsome, "but his eyes," one scribe reported, "though small and sunken, along with his movements demonstrated the greatest astuteness [*viveza*] and resolution; of slightly whiter color than most of the Indians from this region."[6] Bartolina Sisa, Katari's wife and close ally during the rebellion, said that her husband's goal was to establish indigenous self-rule. She explained that Katari inspired troops with the promise that "they would be left as the ultimate owners of this place, and of its wealth." Rebels, she said, fought for a time in which "they alone would rule."[7]

On March 13, 1781, the residents of La Paz awoke to an assault of roughly forty thousand indigenous men and women entering the valley from the surrounding high plains of El Alto. The rebels planned to seize the city, cutting it off from its main access and trade routes. The geographical setting lent itself to this strategy, as El Alto, where the rebels were based, is located along the rim of the deep valley that is home to La Paz, making it easy to cut the city off from the highlands.[8] The siege was held from various points, and Katari's army descended to make regular assaults and incursions against the Spanish in La Paz. Water sources were cut off by the rebels, and a lack of food forced city residents to eat mules, dogs, and cats.[9] Katari presided over his insurrection from the heights of El Alto, surveying the city below from a busy encampment out of which messengers, soldiers, and spies came and went. Staged to inspire fear among the Spanish in the valley, this hive of constant activity was the logistical and symbolic heart of the siege. Each morning, Katari's troops descended into La Paz, barraging the city with drums, mortar fire, flutes, and traditional *pututo* horns made of conches or cow horns.[10]

By the end of the siege, fifteen thousand people, roughly a third of the city's population, had died. On July 1, Spanish reinforcements arrived in the city. As the army approached, Katari ordered his forces to retreat.[11] He fled to the nearby town of Peñas and then to Achacachi to reorganize the resistance, but was captured. On November 14 in Peñas, Katari's limbs were tied to the tails of four horses and he was quartered alive. To inspire fear among his followers, the Spanish put his separated limbs on display throughout the region. The dismemberment of Katari represented the destruction and death of the rebellion, morbidly displaying the power of the Spanish over the defeated rebels. Katari's head was exhibited in La Paz's main plaza, near Quilliquilli, where the rebel leader had hung his own enemies from the gallows.[12] It is widely understood that moments before his execution, Katari promised, "I will return as millions."[13] Indeed, though his dream of overthrowing the Spanish and gaining indigenous self-rule was crushed, during the hundreds of years that have passed since his execution, this martyr and his struggle have been taken up as symbols of indigenous resistance by countless movement participants, activist-scholars, and union leaders in Bolivia. Activists have erected Katari statues, his name and portrait have graced placards and the titles of campesino unions, and his legacy has fueled dozens of indigenous ideologies, manifestos, and political parties. Katari's street barricade strategies have been taken up again by twenty-first-century rebels, and the satellite named after him circles the globe.

Katari's symbolism travels well. In April 2000, the specter of Katari returned in the form of a series of Aymara-led protests against water privatization and neoliberal policies. The protests involved road blockades that cut off La Paz from the rest of the country.[14] Marxa Chávez, an Aymara sociologist with rural roots, became involved in the uprising. She said that activists took turns maintaining the barricades and established vigils along the highways to signal when locals, visitors, and the military were arriving. The very act of blockading roads to strangle La Paz recalled Katari's struggle. "The blockade is a form of remembering the siege," Chávez explained. The movement's organization of road blockades utilized practical knowledge that had been "transmitted basically by oral memory."[15] For example, "there was a form of convening people in the Túpac Katari uprising which was to light bonfires in the hills so that other communities would see them, and it was a symbol of alert." In the blockades of 2000, activists used the same style of fires to summon people. "That's why hundreds of people later arrived in [the highland town of] Achacachi to face off with the military, because they had seen the smoke." She placed the origins of the technique in the "unwritten memory in the communities."[16] Three years later, another siege would rock La Paz, this time led by the same highland communities and spreading to El Alto. For weeks on end, Aymara activists maintained barricades surrounding La Paz to protest government repression and a plan to privatize and export Bolivian gas. The protests ousted the neoliberal president Gonzalo Sánchez de Lozada and ushered in a new phase of grassroots organizing and leftist politics that paved the way for Morales's election in 2005.[17]

As a journalist, researcher, and activist, I have witnessed firsthand many of the dramatic political and social changes Bolivia has experienced since the turn of the twenty-first century. From the tumultuous Gas War protests in 2003 to the political roller-coaster ride of the Morales years, I have been continually struck by the discursive power and presence of historical narratives and symbols in Bolivia's social movements and political realm. I had to return time and again to the country's history to begin to understand the constant references made in street protests and presidential speeches to preconquest civilizations, Katari's siege, and the hopes and betrayals of the 1952 National Revolution. Historical consciousness forged out of protests, oral histories, and popular depictions of the past coursed through these intense years of social and political transformation.

What explains history's hold on Bolivia? How did the country get to the point of celebrating indigeneity and five hundred years of resistance with its first indigenous president in Tiwanaku? Why was the dream of a return to a preconquest indigenous civilization shared by so many people? Why was Katari widely embraced as a symbol of the indigenous struggle for justice and political power? How were these histories made to be so alive and to have so much relevance in the social and political sphere, in spite of the silences in the academy and official histories of the country? Who produced and maintained these historical discourses, collective memories, and oral histories at the street barricades, marches, and political rallies? These questions were raised again and again in conversations with activists and politicians in my fifteen years of work in the country. *The Five Hundred Year Rebellion* is an attempt to provide some answers.

This book argues that the grassroots production and mobilization of indigenous people's history by activists in Bolivia was a crucial element for empowering, orienting, and legitimizing indigenous movements from 1970s postrevolutionary Bolivia to the uprisings of the 2000s. For these activists, the past was an important tool used to motivate citizens to take action for social change, to develop new political projects and proposals, and to provide alternative models of governance, agricultural production, and social relationships. Their revival of historical events, personalities, and symbols in protests, manifestos, banners, oral histories, pamphlets, and street barricades helped set in motion a wave of indigenous movements and politics that is still rocking the country.

The book focuses primarily on Aymara-based indigenous movements and groups in the Andean highlands of Bolivia, largely in and around the capital city of La Paz. Aymara activists, leaders, and intellectuals in this region are highlighted here because of their striking production and use of history in indigenous movements and political thought. This research therefore focuses on how the Kataristas, the Confederación Sindical Única de Trabajadores Campesinos de Bolivia (Unified Syndical Confederation of Rural Workers of Bolivia, CSUTCB), the Taller de Historia Oral Andina (Andean Oral History Workshop, THOA), and the Consejo Nacional de Ayllus y Markas de Qullasuyo (National Council of Ayllus and Markas of Qullasuyu, CONAMAQ) drew from and produced histories and symbols to guide and strengthen their struggles.

Over the more than three decades examined here, indigenous movements and intellectuals dramatically reshaped the political landscape of the country. The Kataristas, a group of indigenous activists and intellectuals operating largely in La Paz in the wake of the National Revolution, helped launch an indigenous resurgence in the 1970s. They did so through manifestos, rural organizing efforts, and small publications that championed indigenous identity, historical consciousness, and the political model of past indigenous martyrs and preconquest utopias. The Kataristas sought to overturn what they saw as the paternalistic and racist yoke of state hegemony in the countryside and to forge an independent campesino union movement that served the needs and values of the indigenous majority.

One of the Kataristas' greatest legacies was their role in the 1979 founding of the CSUTCB, an indigenous campesino union made up of small-scale farmers who promoted indigenous culture and identity, and pressured government officials for access to land, technical and financial support, and a direct role in rural policy development. As part of their work, the CSUTCB produced and mobilized indigenous histories through speeches, rallies, and political proposals. The CSUTCB highlighted the centuries-long roots of their struggle in public statements released in the midst of road blockade campaigns, and they used blockade tactics that drew specifically from Katari. Their rhetorical and physical evocation of the eighteenth-century siege underscored the CSUTCB's power as they toppled dictatorships and fought to revolutionize land reform.

The use of the past by these groups as a tool for mobilizing their members and fighting for social change was echoed in the work of the THOA, which was founded in 1983 by a group of primarily Aymara scholars and students who met at the Universidad Mayor de San Andrés in La Paz. The THOA used oral history practices to gather testimonies and produce pamphlets, books, and radio programs on little-known histories of indigenous resistance. It then distributed these materials throughout the rural highlands. The THOA's innovative research methods and accessible publications strengthened indigenous historical consciousness and contributed to the rise of a new generation of indigenous movements.

One of the THOA's most influential historical productions was on the indigenous rebel Santos Marka T'ula, a *cacique apoderado*, the title for leaders chosen by their communities to legally represent them in court and in government in defense of their rights and land claims. T'ula and other caciques apoderados fought large landowners' dispossession of indigenous lands in the early twentieth century. The THOA produced a booklet and nationally broadcasted radio program in Aymara on T'ula's struggle, bringing the largely unknown history of the caciques apoderados to life.

The THOA expanded its work in the 1990s by accompanying the national indigenous movement CONAMAQ and its effort to reconstitute and strengthen Bolivia's *ayllus*, a centuries-old form of community organization in the Andes. Key ayllu traditions that survived over the centuries include systems of rotational leadership, ethics of mutual aid, communal labor organization, and archipelago-like agricultural production spanning various ecological zones in the Andes. The CONAMAQ and ayllu activists, with the help of the THOA, conducted their own historical research on ayllu history, principles, traditions, and customs, which led to the development of a national network of ayllus that collaborated to promote indigenous and ayllu community rights, autonomy, and political power.

In the midst of this process of ayllu reconstitution, the Bolivian government pushed forward a series of neoliberal policies that undermined workers' rights and unions, privatized services and resources, and enacted austerity measures. This economic overhaul of the country led to a wave of protests in the early 2000s. The ayllu networks, along with many other indigenous organizations, unions, neighborhood councils, and social movements, filled the streets in uprisings that overturned the neoliberal model in Bolivia and led to the election of Bolivia's first indigenous president in 2005.

The indigenous historical production and discourses examined here took on further importance at the start of the twenty-first century. Protesters resisting corporate globalization and state repression once again raised the symbol of Katari at the barricades, renewing the legacy of his eighteenth-century siege. Under Bolivia's first indigenous president, indigenous histories, symbols, and consciousness gained more prominence through the rewriting of the country's constitution, rescuing the model of the ayllu and indigenous justice, championing a state-led process of decolonization, and elevating the works of prominent indigenous historians and thinkers. The seeds of these twenty-first-century political uses of the past can be traced to the twentieth-century postrevolutionary movements and organizations discussed here. As contemporary Bolivian politics and movements demonstrate, the struggle to wield people's histories as tools for indigenous liberation is far from over.

A WORLD SHAPED BY COLONIZATION AND CONQUEST

The Western conquest and colonization of what is now Latin America and the Caribbean is a story of blood. It is a story of genocide. It is a story of the colonizers' attempt to completely destroy and enslave a continent of people and to crush cultures that were thousands of years old. After Columbus famously "discovered" the Americas, Hernán Cortés defeated the rulers of the Aztec empire in 1521. The Spanish conquistador Francisco Pizarro captured Incan emperor Atahualpa in 1532, brutally massacring his followers and looting Incan gold. At the time of the Spanish invasion, the Incan empire—and its Quechua language—spanned the Andes, and the Aztec capital had a larger population than Madrid.

The Spanish conquest was a turning point for the region. In the Andes, the Incan empire was destroyed, and the ayllus were broken up into smaller, centralized communities to facilitate the extraction of taxes, land, and labor. Thousands were sent to the mines in Potosí (in modern-day Bolivia) for the silver that empowered the Spanish empire. Though indigenous resistance continued, the great civilizations of the Aztec, Maya, Inca, and countless other indigenous communities spanning the hemisphere were all but vanquished under the boot and plunder of colonization; the Americas would never be the same.[18]

We live in a world shaped by conquest. For much of modern history, Western powers conquered, colonized, and controlled the global south. Edward Said writes that by 1914, "Europe held a grand total of roughly 85 percent of the earth as colonies, protectorates, dependencies, dominions, and commonwealths. No other associated set of colonies in history was as large, none so totally dominated, none so unequal in power to the Western metropolis."[19] The overarching goal was the extraction of labor and profit from Africa to Asia, from Brazil to Cuba.

These centuries of exploitation have had their victims. But they have also had their rebels. For as long as Western powers have been occupying and colonizing the global south, people have been rebelling against this conquest, sometimes violently, sometimes peacefully. They have met guns with guns, slave labor with insurrections, plantation and factory exploitation with strikes and flight, as well as everyday forms of resistance in the streets, in the home, and in the government palace.

Over time, the colonized rose up against colonial powers, overthrew them in revolutions, and built independent and sovereign nations. This global political process of recovering sovereignty following colonial rule has been called "decolonization." As a political process, decolonization has generally involved forming an independent nation-state, constitution, flag, set of laws, and political system based on the dreams and beliefs of that nation's local people. The global road toward decolonization has been anything but simple. Indeed, it has been one of the most dramatic and consequential processes in modern history.

One of the first waves of decolonization took place between the late eighteenth century and early nineteenth century in the Americas. During this time, the British were forced out of what is today the United States, and revolutionaries ousted the French from Haiti and abolished slavery in that new nation. In the early 1800s, independence wars against Spain raged throughout Latin America. Those conflicts led to the birth of new, independent nations, from Venezuela and Colombia to Argentina and Bolivia. The second wave of decolonization took place in Europe between 1917 and the 1920s, after the collapse of the Russian and Habsburg empires. Following World War II and into the late 1970s, freedom from European colonial rule was won among colonies throughout Asia, Africa, and the Caribbean.[20]

"Let us leave this Europe which never stops talking of man yet massacres him at every one of its street corners, at every corner of the world," the great decolonial thinker Frantz Fanon wrote.[21] For many, decolonization was a process of self-determination, of leaving Europe behind rather than trying to build a society in its image. As Fanon wrote, "The Third World is today facing Europe as one colossal mass whose project must be to try and solve the problems this Europe was incapable of finding the answers to."[22]

Yet in many new nations, once the old oppressors were ousted from power, new ones quickly filled their places. Elites in newly founded countries quickly seized power and used the vestiges of the colonial system to continue exploitation under a new flag. Meanwhile, foreign and national companies continued the colonization of the globe with their conquest of natural resources, cheap labor, land, mines, and oil reserves. Indigenous people were still sent to the mines; the poor were sent to the factories and sugar plantations—and often massacred or jailed when they refused to obey. In the Americas, THOA member and Aymara historian Carlos Mamani explains, "The colonies, now converted into republics, developed processes of ethnic cleansing through 'Indian wars,' which were no more than raids that cleared out certain territories for the settlement of colonists brought in from Europe. This was the crude, cruel, and bloody history up until the first decades of the 1900s."[23] Colonization continued for the dispossessed of the earth.

From the Maya of Mexico to the Mapuche of Chile, indigenous communities are still resisting. Today they are against mega-dams and soy plantations that displace their communities, the mines that poison their rivers and land, and the local and foreign military repression that riddles their communities and lives with bullets and violence. After facing a genocidal conflict from the 1960s to the 1990s that left two hundred thousand dead, the Maya of Guatemala continue to resist further displacement and violence.[24] The Mapuche of Chile continue to organize against mega-dams and dispossession.[25] The indigenous people of Brazil face down enormous deforestation and displacement as cattle ranchers, loggers, and soy farmers continue their conquest of the Amazon.[26] The politics of extraction—linked to global capitalism and imperialism—requires the ongoing oppression of Latin America's indigenous people.

Colonialism robbed indigenous people of their land, gold, culture, and political institutions, but also of their histories. "The indigenous have always been treated as 'savages,' as non-men, as people without history and without collective memory," according to Bolivian sociologist Pablo Mamani.[27] The colonization of the Americas was an erasure of indigenous historical narratives and worldviews, a silencing of indigenous voices, a forced amnesia. "Since the beginning of the European invasion until today, social groups affiliated by descent or by circumstance to Western civilization have sustained historical projects in which there is no room for local [indigenous] cultures to flourish," theorist Javier Sanjinés explains.[28] "The coloniality of power and the coloniality of knowledge, cognitive expressions inherited from the conquerer, do not permit one to see or to invent any other path."[29] In the eyes of the colonizer, the indigenous peoples' inferiority was unquestionable; they were a people without a future or a past.

Today Bolivia is home to over thirty-eight different indigenous groups. The largest among them are the Quechua, Aymara, and Guaraní. Indigenous people make up roughly half of the population; historically, roughly that same percentage lived under the poverty line.[30] This disparity reflects the apartheid in the nation, where a small elite of European descent ruled over the majority of indigenous people, leading to the perception of "two Bolivias"—one oppressed indigenous nation and one made up of the elite holding political and economic power. "The official nation is the modern one that the mestizo-criollo elite endeavors to create," Sanjinés writes. "It is the Western nation *from* which the world is described and known. The entire Bolivian educational system corresponds to this epistemological position. The other nation, the postponed nation, is the one *upon* which epistemological power is exercised."[31]

Such a system of racial oppression and control speaks to the legacy of colonialism in Bolivia. Following the Spanish conquest, colonized peoples were "condemned to orality" and could only express themselves "through the cultural patterns of the rulers," explains theorist Aníbal Quijano.[32] Literacy was wielded and monopolized by colonial elites as a tool to rule over the indigenous masses; to read and write in the language of the colonizers was to control the historical account. "The means used to legitimate and cover up crimes has primarily been through the monopoly of writing; whoever has the ability to write, print reports, newspapers, and books has the capacity to impose their own truth," explains Carlos Mamani. "Colonial states require policies of cover-up and forgetting, *not talking about their own crimes*, genocide, just as the unjust Indian wars are conveniently hidden behind celebrations such as the bicentenaries of national independence."[33]

The national leaders that replaced colonial authorities often promoted their own official histories of independence, highlighting the key role of the country's founding fathers and constructing historical narratives that bolstered the image of government legitimacy—often while maligning those who challenged the new rulers from below.[34] After independence in the Andes, political elites constructed myths and histories of a utopian indigenous past in preconquest Latin America to build their own "imagined communities" of new republics while at the same time disinheriting contemporary indigenous people from their own past. Historian Rebecca Earle has shown how state-sanctioned histories positioned political elites as carrying on the legacy of a preconquest utopia, while those in the poor indigenous majority were portrayed as having fallen from their former glory, thus justifying their continued exploitation and marginalization in the new nation.[35]

Following Katari's insurrection in the late eighteenth century, colonial authorities tried to undermine the forces that had led to the erosion of colonial rule by silencing histories of indigenous civilizations and royalty. "Their main objective was to eradicate any symbolic representation associated with the Inca past and any preeminence extended to their putative descendants, the indigenous aristocracy," historian Sergio Serulnikov writes. "Thus paintings of Inca emperors were removed from public view, and the use of ancient Andean garb was forbidden. Theatrical representations of the Inca past and the conquest were banned."[36]

Katari's rebellion was further silenced when it was convenient for political leaders to do so in the twentieth century. Carlos Montenegro's book *Nacionalismo y coloniaje*, published in 1944, was an influential text for leaders in the 1952 National Revolution.[37] His survey of Bolivian history and his argument for a populist, national revolution against the ruling class positioned only the Bolivian creole and mestizo elite as the vanguard of the revolution, sidelining the indigenous majority. Historian Sinclair Thomson points out how Montenegro's narrative of Bolivian history barely mentions Katari's revolt at all, and quickly moves on to the nineteenth-century independence struggles against the Spanish. "The actual anticolonial content of Indian struggles was erased and replaced by a nationalist narrative," Thomson explains.[38]

Combating such erasure and silencing, and recuperating knowledge of the precolonial past, has been a central part of the wider process of decolonization. As Fanon writes, the "passionate quest for a national culture prior to the colonial era can be justified by the colonized intellectuals' shared interest in stepping back and taking a hard look at the Western culture in which they risk becoming ensnared. Fully aware they are in the process of losing themselves, and consequently of being lost to their people, these men work away with raging heart and furious mind to renew contact with their people's oldest, inner essence, the farthest removed from colonial times."[39]

DECOLONIZING HISTORY, MOBILIZING THE PAST

The decolonization of history has long been a fundamental part of indigenous people's five hundred years of resistance in Latin America. This was a struggle against forgetting, against the silencing, maligning, and marginalization of indigenous histories of resistance, of histories begun long before the arrival of the Spanish. Decolonization meant recovering these histories, strengthening them, and using them as tools to fight the oppressor. For many indigenous Bolivians, remembering was resistance.

The decolonization of history in Bolivia has involved indigenous activists challenging the elites' version of history and decentering historical authority from the university, professional historians, and political leaders so activists can build their own narratives of the Andean past. These indigenous scholars looked to oral history, myths, and collective memory as sources to fill in the gaps left by the official account. They decolonized history by looking to each other, to community elders and ancestors, for histories that had been passed down from generation to generation but were not accounted for in the libraries and archives of the nation.

History was decolonized by these indigenous protagonists through their transformation of historical discourses of indigenous inferiority and victimhood—narratives used to suppress indigenous identity, assimilate indigenous people, and silence their past—into stories of glorious preconquest civilizations, traditions, and political philosophies kept alive for centuries, and into histories of rebellion and defiance. In these stories, indigenous people were not victims without a past; they were heroes and the heirs of Andean utopias.

Indigenous activists took history out of the dry textbooks, the condescending political speeches, the ivory tower, and put it to use in the street, where it was made to be something alive and popular, for political uses, for indigenous liberation. It was produced by indigenous historians in Aymara, Quechua, and Guaraní, and published in accessible pamphlets; histories of Katari and other rebels were broadcast in indigenous languages over the radio. Historical knowledge was decolonized by recovering indigenous traditions and governance models in order to bring back the centuries-old networks and political organization of the ayllu. Indigenous histories of resistance were deployed by activists in street barricades, banners, protest symbols, speeches, and manifestos. Decolonized history was on the march.

"*Coming to know the past* has been part of the critical pedagogy of decolonization," Linda Tuhiwai Smith, a Maori indigenous scholar, writes. "To hold alternative histories is to hold alternative knowledges. The pedagogical implication of this access to alternative knowledges is that they can form the basis of alternative ways of doing things."[40] In Bolivia, this process constituted, as one example, an alternative way of organizing political power through the ayllu and rotational leadership and an alternative set of social relations based on Aymara practices of reciprocity. The past provided raw materials to postconquest indigenous communities for imagining a different world, for developing new ways of thinking and talking about alternatives, and for creating a lens through which to critique and understand the present.

"Decolonization must offer a language of possibility, a way out of colonialism," Smith writes. This language, which "allows us to make plans, to make strategic choices, to theorize solutions imagining a different world, or reimagining the world, is a way into theorizing the reasons why the world we experience is unjust, and posing alternatives to such a world from within our own world views."[41] A first step in Bolivia was recovering indigenous histories. The gathering of oral history provided powerful resources to Bolivian indigenous activists building such alternatives.

For the THOA and other groups examined here, oral history offered a bridge between generations, a way to share stories of oppression and resistance and, as a result, move people to take action.[42] It was an avenue for the recovery of indigenous voices and histories that were not accounted for in the existing written histories.[43] The written record typically favors the elite, those with power, while oral history, writes oral historian Paul Thompson, "makes a much fairer trial possible: witnesses can now also be called from the under-classes, the unprivileged, and the defeated."[44]

As the THOA demonstrated, oral history's strength is typically not in the facts it provides but in its window into the meanings, motives, and emotions behind historical experience and how it was lived. Indeed, oral historian Alessandro Portelli argues that oral history's departure from fact may be one of its strengths, "as imagination, symbolism and desire emerge" from the oral testimony.[45] For the THOA, this aspect of oral history provided a way to explore the relevance of myths within oral accounts of indigenous resistance.[46] The organization's embrace of oral history could be linked directly to oral traditions in rural Bolivia, Aymara conceptions of cyclical time, and the relevance of historical consciousness to the era's indigenous movements. The group's methods filled in silences and gaps in the historical record in a process of decolonizing history. As Humberto Mamani, a THOA member, explained, their organization's recovery of indigenous histories of resistance "was like gathering different parts of a letter torn into many pieces, and when it was put together, we could read all of them and say, 'This is our history.' This is the history that we did not know, that was divided in many parts."[47]

The work of the THOA and indigenous movements examined here was part of a larger international project of decolonization and liberation. Indeed, indigenous and political movements across Latin America have utilized the past to build bonds between communities and strengthen movements' claims and legitimacy.[48] Much like Katari's rebellion and the indigenous movements that strengthened his legacy in Bolivia, Augusto Sandino, who fought a guerilla war in Nicaragua from 1927 to 1933, was used by the Nicaraguan thinker Carlos Fonseca in the intellectual building of the Sandinista National Liberation Front (FSLN). Sandinistas "worked on" the history of Sandino, pulling him out of obscurity and writing him into the trajectory of the FSLN, which positioned itself as the rightful heir of Sandino's legacy and unfulfilled struggle.[49] Similar to the ways Bolivian indigenous activists challenged the narrative of "two Bolivias," in which indigenous people felt as though they were "foreigners in their own country," indigenous movements in Ecuador in the 1990s onward sought to "rewrite narratives of national belonging" through social mobilization.[50] And just as Aymara publications produced largely in La Paz served as a space of political debate and agitation, Fernando Garcés, writing about a Quechua newspaper in the Bolivian lowlands, explained that the paper itself served "as the repository of memory and as an instrument of reflection for the peasant political movement."[51]

The Zapatistas in Chiapas, Mexico, appropriated the history of Mexican Revolution leader Emiliano Zapata as their own symbol of struggle and positioned Maya peoples as protagonists, rather than victims, who were united through a pan-Mayan identity.[52] Indeed, the first Zapatista declaration from the Lacandon Jungle in 1994 began with a reference to this past, placing the Zapatistas within a long arc of resistance: "We are a product of 500 years of struggle: first against slavery, then during the War of Independence against Spain led by insurgents, then to avoid being absorbed by North American imperialism, then to promulgate our constitution and expel the French empire from our soil. . . . We are the inheritors of the true builders of our nation."[53]

Histories of resistance have been widely used by movements and activists seeking to wield historical narratives and symbols as tools in their struggle to build a better world. Historian Howard Zinn wrote of his own approach toward writing people's histories that shed light on injustices and the "unreported resistance" of indigenous people, the antislavery activists, and workers' movements. "To omit these acts of resistance is to support the official view that power only rests with those who have the guns and possess the wealth."[54] He continued, "To think that history writing must aim simply to recapitulate the failures that dominate the past is to make historians collaborators in an endless cycle of defeat. If history is to be creative, to anticipate a possible future without denying the past, it should, I believe, emphasize new possibilities by disclosing those hidden episodes of the past when, even if in brief flashes, people showed their ability to resist, to join together, and occasionally to win."[55]

The various groups examined in this book strengthened Bolivia's collective indigenous identity and constructed a historical discourse out of a shared culture and a history of oppression and resistance.

According to Bolivian social movement scholars Álvaro García Linera, Marxa Chávez León, and Patricia Costas Monje, this process helped to "bring the group together, legitimate their actions, identify their opponents and define their demands."[56] In the cases of the Kataristas, the CSUTCB, and the CONAMAQ, the movements deployed shared visions of history in their speeches, organizational rituals, and collective actions that united movement members in their efforts toward a common goal. For these movements, a past struggle—most notably that of Katari—did not simply exist statically in history but was a "productive symbolic force" for the future as well, something that could return through action in the present. In this way, "the past is living history which pushes toward the fulfillment of an emancipated future."[57] A "memory of rebellion" constantly orients the movements' identities, actions, and goals. "This memory," the authors write, "is permanently ritualized" in speeches, banners, placards, portraits of historical rebels in marches, and posters in movements' offices, as well as demands and manifestos.[58]

Sociologist Pablo Mamani similarly points to the ways in which sacred sites, symbols, and rituals have oriented collective memory and identity during moments of indigenous rebellion. The birthplace of Katari, the geographic site of his siege in El Alto, checkered rainbow *wiphala* flags (representing indigenous nations of the Andes), pututos, and banners of indigenous martyrs all help indigenous activists "define who we are."[59] Activists' assertion of indigenous identity also helps to strengthen the wider indigenous community as a basis for mobilization, as well as to counter government denigration of indigenous people and culture.[60]

These movements also notably used the idea of a preconquest Andean utopia as tools in their struggles.[61] Bolivian indigenous philosophers championed the recovery of this civilization in their postrevolutionary writings and political propaganda. Kataristas called for a return to preconquest ideals and knowledge in their 1973 Manifesto of Tiwanaku. The CSUTCB sought to implement ancient indigenous agricultural models in their 1984 proposal for agrarian reform. Similarly, the ayllu reconstitution efforts of the 1990s sought to rescue and strengthen traditions of communal governance and labor production that predated the Incan empire.[62]

Dreams of a return to a preconquest utopia were based on historical facts with concrete names and places, such as the crushed Incan civilization and the network of surviving ayllus, which had historically spanned the region. As Peruvian scholar Alberto Flores Galindo writes, when the concept of an Andean utopia was recovered for a renewed vision of the future among indigenous people in Peru during the colonial period, "the ideal city did not exist outside history or at the remote beginning of time. On the contrary, it was a real historic fact that had a name [Tawantinsuyo—the Incan empire], and a ruling class (the Incas); and a capital (Cuzco). Andean people changed the particulars of this construction to imagine a kingdom without hunger, without exploitation, and where they ruled once again. It represented the end of disorder and darkness. Inca became an organizing idea or principle."[63] He continues, "For people without hope, the Andean utopia challenges a history that condemned them to the margins."[64]

Indigenous movements' recovery and championing of Andean utopias and histories of resistance increased their numbers and appeal, provided a way to analyze and understand neocolonialism, and offered strategies and potent symbols for revolts. Their historical production and analysis fed into a collective vision for indigenous liberation. Such a vision was renewed throughout five hundred years of resistance, in marches and street barricades, in the dreams of Katari's return, and by indigenous rebels mobilizing the past to change the future.

CHAPTER ONE

KATARI'S RETURN

Indigenous Resurgence in the Shadow of the National Revolution

A statue of Túpac Katari constructed by Kataristas in Ayo-Ayo in 1969. Photographer: Diego Pacheco. Courtesy of the Archivo Central del Museo Nacional de Etnografía y Folklore.

The small K'illi K'illi park sits at the top of one of the hillsides cradling the valley home to La Paz, providing a striking view of the city below. To the east lies Illimani, a towering, snow-covered mountain. Below and to the west is the tree-lined Plaza Murillo, home to the seat of government and the site of dozens of coups and countless protests. Across the valley, set on the sweeping plains of the altiplano, is El Alto, a booming home to millions of largely Aymara working-class people. La Paz itself is a dense mass of winding streets, high-rise apartments, and colonial-style buildings with orange tile roofs. The sounds of the city—car horns, the buzz of construction,

and fireworks echoing from daily marches—reach K'illi K'illi. At nearly thirteen thousand feet, the valley and the plains surrounding it bear
the dramatic weather of high altitude. The powerful sun can scorch the
city in one moment, and a windy storm of hail and rain can rip through
the next, giving way to a brilliant blue sky or clear canopy of stars.

The hills hold the rich past of this city in the clouds. Túpac Katari
launched crucial assaults on La Paz from K'illi K'illi during his army's
1781 siege. After his brutal quartering by the Spanish, Katari's head
was put on display on this same hill to terrorize his followers. On a
moonlit night over a century later, in 1952, rebels crisscrossed the
hillsides to launch the National Revolution. A short walk up from the
K'illi K'illi park is the home of indigenous philosopher Fausto Reinaga. An unassuming gate opens from the street to a steep stairway,
lush with bushes and flowers. At the landing, a small pathway, bor-
dered by gardens and a grassy yard where dogs leap and bark, leads
up to his office and library. In the mid-1960s, dozens of indigenous
union leaders and Aymara youth from the militant province of Aroma
met here with Reinaga, who was older than them, to discuss indigenous history, government paternalism toward indigenous people, and
the development of an independent indigenous movement and political force. The roots of the pro-indigenous philosophy of Katarismo
can be traced back to the rural province of Aroma, a short bus ride
from the city. But it was in La Paz that many young Aymara students
became Kataristas.

Katarismo was a current of political thought and campesino movement organizing created in the late 1960s and 1970s by
young Aymara union leaders in Aroma, in the department of La Paz.
Kataristas maintained that colonialism had never ended and that the
National Revolution and the military regimes that followed it constituted not liberation from empire and colonialism but rather a new
form of neocolonial domination. They worked to build a campesino
union that was independent from the state and directly empowered
the rural, indigenous sector rather than the Nationalist Revolutionary Movement (MNR) and military governments of the 1960s and
1970s. A lasting result of such Katarista efforts was the 1979 founding
of the Unified Syndical Confederation of Rural Workers of Bolivia
(CSUTCB), a national independent union.

Tracing the birth and development of Katarismo requires examining the events, policies, and pitfalls of the National Revolution in regard to the indigenous sector from 1952, at the dawn of the revolution, to 1964, at the revolution's institutional close with the military coup of General René Barrientos. From 1964 to 1978, the Bolivian government was controlled by a string of repressive military regimes that were disastrous for the indigenous majority, the wider Left, and workers' movements in the country. Kataristas played a critical role in resisting these dictatorships with strikes, blockades, and political pressure, helping to bring the country back to democratic rule.

Throughout this period, Kataristas lifted up indigenous identity, history, traditions, and culture, and positioned a politically empowered network of multicultural indigenous peoples at the core of their vision for a new society. These efforts expanded historical consciousness around past indigenous rebellions, popularized the cultural use of indigenous symbols such as the wiphala, and championed preconquest indigenous societies as agricultural and political models. A profound contribution of Katarismo, writes Bolivian intellectual and politician Álvaro García Linera, was the "reinvention of indigeneity, but now not as a stigma, rather as a subject of emancipation, as historical model, as political project."[1]

THE SHADOW OF THE REVOLUTION

The political arena in which Katarismo emerged was shaped by the National Revolution, an event that made a dramatic entry onto the Bolivian stage in 1952. Leading up to the revolt, the MNR party ran Víctor Paz Estenssoro, a popular pro-worker congressman and party leader who was then in exile, as its presidential candidate in 1951.[2] He won a resounding victory at the ballot box, but the military placed General Hugo Ballivián in the presidential palace instead. The MNR decided that their only option for taking power was armed revolution.[3] On April 10, 1952, Ballivián called for the lights to be put out in La Paz in order to impede the advance of the MNR rebels—many of whom were factory workers—as they descended into La Paz from the neighboring city of El Alto. Yet a full moon lit the way, providing the rebels with guidance in their march down the steep hills from El Alto into the capital city. Many MNR rebels were members of the working-class neighborhoods in El Alto and so knew the terrain well. These forces, with miners from Oruro providing crucial support, effectively cut off Ballivián's troops by blocking key routes and rail lines on the outskirts of the city. Conflicts flared up in the night, leaving wounded and dead on both sides. But news of the MNR rebels' advances in La Paz spread throughout the countryside, inspiring similar uprisings across the nation. Three days later, with over six hundred dead from the battles, the MNR vanquished the Ballivián regime and took power.[4]

Euphoria was high in the early days of the MNR's leadership. Paz flew into the El Alto airport from exile in Argentina on April 15, 1952. When he entered La Paz he was met by a crowd of some seven thousand people waving signs that read "Nationalization of the Mines," "Agrarian Reform," and "Welcome, Father of the Poor." The crowd was so massive that it took Paz a full thirty minutes to arrive at the presidential palace half a block away. He greeted the assembled people in Aymara, the language most members of the crowd spoke: "Jaccha t'anta uthjani," he said. "There will be much bread."[5] Soon after, largely as a result of pressure from labor organizations and miners, the MNR signed a decree on October 31, 1952, that nationalized the country's tin mines. In August 1953, the MNR passed the Agrarian Reform Law, which sought to abolish *pongueaje* (a form of obligatory servitude hacienda owners forced on indigenous tenants of hacienda land), expropriate hacienda land and redistribute it to landless farmers and indigenous communities, support agricultural development, and ensure the recognition of indigenous communities' labor and organizational traditions.[6] The reform was limited, however, as it ultimately affected only 28.5 percent of large landowners.[7]

While the 1953 reform did grant significant parcels of land to small producers, these plots were divided over the years among generations of family members, making tracts progressively smaller—now just roughly three hundred square meters in many areas. Such limited land resources contributed to mass migrations to urban areas.[8] Most of the rural Bolivian peasantry at this time lived in the highland, Andean areas, with high density in La Paz (where roughly one-third of the total lived, most of whom were Aymara), Potosí, and Cochabamba. A majority of people in these areas were subsistence farmers producing crops for daily consumption, with some links to the wider market. Another part of this group, primarily in Cochabamba, was more directly inserted into the region's market, with some subsistence activity. Peasants in the other sector, roughly 20 to 25 percent, were entirely dependent on the market, particularly in areas closer to urban centers, such as the semitropical Yungas region, outside of La Paz.[9]

The National Revolution made historic gains with expanded rights for Bolivian workers, land reform, and national economic sovereignty, but the effect was less positive for indigenous identity, culture, and political inclusion. In fact, the MNR government sought to erase indigenous identity, recategorizing this segment of the population as peasants or workers to be incorporated as a base of party support and included in the MNR's economic vision for the development of Bolivia. The government brought indigenous people into the fold as part of its attempts to create a more egalitarian and modern society, but the MNR's mission to integrate indigenous people into the revolutionary state and nation required them to give up their indigenous identity.[10] Such policies involved replacing ayllus with unions, promoting Spanish-language education over indigenous languages, and repressing the use of ponchos and indigenous dress, which were considered by the MNR to be symbols of life on the hacienda. Beginning with cooptation and assimilation, this paternalistic government treatment of indigenous people gave way, over time, to state-led massacres.[11] This oppression of dissident indigenous movements and leaders pushed indigenous activists further from the MNR.

In President Paz's address announcing the MNR's land reform law to some two hundred thousand indigenous people in Ucureña on August 2, 1953, he told the crowd, "From now on you will no longer be Indians ('indios') but rather peasants!"[12] The MNR saw the erasure of indigenous identity as progress, as doing away with an oppressive social structure based on the subjugation of indigenous people through the hacienda and the formerly oppressive Bolivian political system. They hoped to transform this history of oppression through land reform, rural education, and indigenous voter enfranchisement. As Javier Hurtado, noted Bolivian scholar of Katarismo, explains, "The MNR had an unrealistic and inappropriate image of peasants in blue overalls driving tractors within the new social and economic order they were setting out to construct. They wanted the indigenous to stop wearing ponchos and turn their backs forever on traditional agriculture."[13] Politically, this translated into forcing indigenous communities to forsake communal landholdings and the ayllu in exchange for individually held land managed through the MNR rural union structure.

CAMPESINO UNIONS AND MILITARY REGIMES

The interests and demands of the rural sector during this period were articulated largely through the Confederación Nacional de Trabajadores Campesinos de Bolivia (National Confederation of Rural Workers of Bolivia, CNTCB), which was founded in La Paz on July 15, 1953, by the MNR government as part of the agrarian reform program. The CNTCB was the coordinating body of a national network of unions based in small rural communities of farmers throughout Bolivia. Its members were from the MNR's impoverished and largely indigenous rural base. The union channeled the government's land distribution to campesino families, provided an avenue of political representation for the campesino sector, and concentrated and managed MNR support in the countryside on the government's behalf. From the beginning, MNR functionaries held high positions in the CNTCB, underlining the union's adherence to MNR power.[14] The MNR replaced ayllu governing structures with the CNTCB, establishing the state union as the central place to manage agricultural production and rural education.[15] While coopting political structures in the indigenous communities, the MNR won rural support through the agrarian reform's redistribution of land. The government gave out food coupons, established schools, and offered faithful peasants positions in rural unions—all of which contributed to the consolidation of support in the countryside. As the agrarian reform progressed, very few in the rural sector questioned the MNR.[16] In this way, campesino communities were used by the MNR as a faithful voting mass from 1953 to 1964.[17] Katarista protagonist and longtime CSUTCB leader Genaro Flores recalled how, as a boy, he witnessed MNR officials replacing indigenous leaders of the community with younger, less experienced, and less respected union leaders. Anti-indigenous perceptions of modernization were translated into blatant acts of racism by MNR government officials, which included cutting the braids off indigenous men and spraying indigenous people with the chemical DDT (ostensibly to prevent the spread of lice) before they were able to attend government meetings. Rural schools provided an education at odds with indigenous culture and focused on spreading Spanish while blatantly discouraging indigenous languages.[18]

To many indigenous people, this constituted a continuation of the policies of oppressive pre-MNR governments. Indeed, in the decades leading up to the revolution, the Bolivian state had used rural schools primarily as a space to teach indigenous youth basic skills to enter the labor force.[19] Rural education initiatives thus emphasized manual labor over literacy, producing what historian Brooke Larson terms an "unlettered Indian"—an ignorant but efficient worker.[20] Such classes involved instruction in soil work, brick making, work with textiles, and carpentry. The educational projects emphasized loyalty to the Bolivian state and nation. The central goal, Larson writes, was to erase "indigenous communal memories, traditions, political culture, and mobilizations" for the sake of shaping subjects to contribute to the modern Bolivian nation.[21]

The National Revolution abolished rural servitude on haciendas and so freed up time for young people in the rural sector to actually attend school. The MNR expanded access to education, and school attendance did rise in rural areas. From 1950 to 1970, national literacy rates rose from 31 percent to 67 percent.[22] However, indigenous language, history, traditions, knowledge, and values were left out of public school curricula. The schools served as a key avenue for spreading the MNR's historical narrative of Bolivia as one common nation with a homogenized culture, leaving indigenous identity and traditions firmly in the past. Like the spread of the MNR's rural unions as a tool of control and subjugation of indigenous ayllus and autonomy, the government used educational reform to transform indigenous people into Spanish speakers and campesinos, suppressing indigenous identity and culture.[23] In addition to excluding indigenous languages from the classroom, the MNR's educational code maintained past policies aimed at converting indigenous students into workers, emphasizing that in rural education, a key objective was, according to Manuel E. Contreras, to "teach him [the student] to be a good agricultural worker." At the same time, higher school attendance did create a new generation of formally educated indigenous Bolivians. This, in turn, contributed to their rising enrollment in the country's university system.[24]

The various military regimes that succeeded MNR rule in 1964 marked a shift in the relationship between the state and the rural sector, articulated largely through the CNTCB. From 1960 to 1964, MNR President Paz increased the power of the military, putting General René Barrientos on the campaign ticket as his vice president in 1964. Just a few months after Paz won the August 1964 election, Barrientos led a brief coup that overthrew Paz, beginning an era of military power that lasted until 1982. Barrientos moved the government further to the political right, working actively to eradicate leftist sectors, particularly the mining movement and the Central Obrera Boliviana (Bolivian Workers' Central, COB), the country's main labor union. The COB was created by union leaders after the National Revolution and brought together the militant mining sector with workers in manufacturing. The COB had representatives in the MNR government for over a decade following the revolution. Under Barrientos's watch, the COB and the wider workers' movement suffered constant assaults, including the infamous massacre of San Juan in June 1967, during which government troops surrounded and murdered mining families in Catavi in the middle of one of the community's celebrations.[25]

In order to prevent the development of an organized leftist bloc, Barrientos aimed to drive a wedge between the labor movement, largely organized by the COB, and the campesino sector, still under the auspices of the state-controlled CNTCB. While repressing the labor movement, Barrientos strengthened his ties with the campesino sector through the CNTCB. As a military leader in the MNR government, he developed ties between the MNR state and rural communities, connections he used to prop up his own military rule.

Barrientos deepened the government's grip on the countryside through the Military-Campesino Pact (PMC), a formal political alliance between the military regime and the CNTCB that was made on April 9, 1964, in Ucureña, also the site of the announcement of the MNR's Agrarian Reform Law in 1953.[26]

The success of the PMC as a tool of Barrientos's subjugation can be credited to three factors. First, the campesino sector tended to see the relationship as an avenue to ensure the distribution of land to small farmers. Indeed, land redistribution, a cornerstone of MNR popularity in the countryside, continued under Barrientos. Second, the hegemonic presence of the state established through the CNTCB under the MNR remained intact under Barrientos, creating a foundation for the PMC. And finally, Barrientos himself maintained strong ties to the countryside. He spoke Quechua fluently, drank *chicha* beer (a corn-based alcoholic drink disdained by upper-class Bolivians) with rural communities, participated in festivities, handed out gifts (such as televisions, bicycles, and soccer balls), and rewarded allies with rural union posts. In this way, Barrientos consolidated the regime's hold over the countryside through the PMC, even while violently crushing organized labor in the mines.[27]

However, Barrientos's hegemony in the rural sector began to reveal some considerable cracks that prefigured the development of a campesino union movement independent of the state. Campesino dissent against Barrientos emerged after the president announced the imposition of an unpopular tax on individual land titles, including those redistributed to small farmers as part of the MNR's agrarian reform and under Barrientos. Campesinos from La Paz, Oruro, and the eastern province of Santa Cruz organized protests against the tax. This discontent led to the formation of the Independent Campesino Bloc (BCI), which allied with the COB. The BCI was the first articulation of an organized campesino movement that sought to break with the PMC under Barrientos.[28] However, the BCI was an organization essentially wed to the COB and did not emerge out of mass campesino demands: the majority of the campesino sector still supported Barrientos and the PMC at this time.[29]

Barrientos's death in a helicopter crash in April 1969 heralded a shift in Bolivian politics. From 1969 to 1971, two different military leaders created new openings for the Bolivian workers' movement and, to a limited extent, for the campesino sector. These administrations revived the national sentiment and policies of the early MNR rule but largely continued the subjugation of the campesino movement through the CNTCB.[30] General Alfredo Ovando Candía took power in a military coup on September 26, 1969. Ovando and his successor, General Juan José Torres, were military leaders under the MNR government and brought back some of the discontinued leftist policies of the revolution. For example, Ovando nationalized Gulf Oil in Bolivia and strengthened ties with leftist groups and the COB.[31] However, he did not have the national or military support he needed to remain in power and was replaced by General Torres, Ovando's former chief of staff. The leftist Torres ran the country from October 1970 to August 1971, encouraging, rather than repressing, leftist labor unions, building a tin smelter to lessen reliance on US and European smelters, accepting aid from the Soviet Union, and ending US mining contracts.[32]

In June 1971, Torres organized the Popular Assembly, a leftist gathering of representatives from unions, political party leaders, and peasant organizations from around the countryside who were convened to develop a leftist policy agenda for the government. Roughly 218 delegates were present, largely from labor unions, with only 23 delegates from campesino confederations. Though no clear project emerged from the gathering, it underlined the Torres government's efforts to break with the right-wing tendency that had dominated Bolivian politics for nearly a decade.[33] With the death of Barrientos and the openings provided by the leftist governments of Ovando and Torres, a new generation of campesinos began replacing union leaders allied with the PMC and Barrientos. This wave of leaders struggling to build an independent campesino union formed the backbone of the rising Katarista movement.

KATARISMO'S ROOTS

A combination of political and social factors contributed to the rise of Katarismo. The frustrations of the revolution and the PMC pushed Kataristas to fight for campesino unions that were independent from the state. In addition, as migration from the countryside to the cities increased, the urban-rural ties that developed in the indigenous communities and La Paz allowed for crucial exchanges of experiences as well as solidarity between the city and the countryside. Many Kataristas of the time were children of the 1952 National Revolution: their parents had typically been hacienda laborers before the MNR took power and were protagonists of the revolution, while the new generation benefited from recently expanded rights and access to education.[34]

The indigenous peoples of this new class and era were empowered by MNR policies but frustrated by the incomplete land reform and assimilationist government, which encouraged indigenous people to leave their traditions. Examples of such policies included the government imposition of state-controlled unions over ayllu community structures and the denigration of indigenous languages in rural public schools. This friction fed the development of resurgent indigenous politics from the 1960s onward. Because the gains of the revolution were incomplete, Bolivian historian Esteban Ticona writes, "they generated a frustration which revived the long memory of a centuries-old confrontation with the state."[35] The dissatisfaction with unfinished agrarian reform among rural communities was articulated in part through urban-rural connections.[36] Younger Aymara migrants to La Paz had a foot in both worlds. They were aware of the revolution's failures through their parents' experience of agrarian reform, as well as through their own confrontation with structural racism in the city embodied by low-paying jobs and racial oppression in the educational system. In the countryside, discontent toward the assimilationist state and the PMC was articulated most notably through the development of an autonomous rural union.[37]

Young Aymara migrants in La Paz experienced discrimination more acutely in school and work than their rural counterparts did, and they came into direct contact with what they perceived as a neocolonial, racist society—challenges that had supposedly been overcome by the revolution but which were still very much present. By 1976, roughly 48 percent of the population of La Paz was Aymara. Some had been born in the city, some had moved to the city many years earlier, and about 25 percent were recent migrants from the countryside. At the same time that young Aymara people confronted racism in La Paz in the workplace and at primary school, many also attended university as a part of a new generation of indigenous students, thanks to the educational reforms of the National Revolution. This access to education, writes Bolivian sociologist and THOA cofounder Silvia Rivera Cusicanqui, "permitted the rise of a strata of intellectuals who [sought] to give ideological expression to this sentiment of acute frustration that accompanie[d] their urban experience."[38] The potent encounters with urban racism, university education, and networks among Aymara students in La Paz contributed to the formation of new indigenous currents and organizing. Aymara youth from the countryside attending high school and university in La Paz developed groups that provided space for them to reflect on the shortcomings of the MNR government, structural racism in the schools, the PMC, and the limits of the National Revolution. These groups constituted the early networks that gave rise to Katarismo.

The frustrations and hopes of young urban and rural Aymara activists and the critics of Bolivia's neocolonial, postrevolutionary society were expressed through an array of small publications, cultural centers, Aymara radio programs, and organizations that emerged in the late 1960s and early 1970s. Places in La Paz such as the Mink'a Center for Peasant Coordination and Promotion and the Túpac Katari Campesino Center created spaces for cultural activities, indigenous music performances, historical research, and the discussion of indigenous issues on the radio.[39] The Mink'a Center (the term *mink'a* refers to a form of Andean reciprocity) was founded in 1969, largely by people from rural communities, including Mario Gabriel, Genaro Flores's brother-in-law.[40] These organizations aided the clandestine work of Aymara political activists and provided safe haven during periods of government repression. According to its organizers, the Katari Campesino Center had some ten thousand volunteer members in the early 1970s and generated funds out of small membership dues, helping to fund its radio station, among other activities.[41]

The Kataristas' historical analysis held that the oppressive political and economic system of colonialism continued for indigenous people and had been perpetuated by creole elites throughout the nineteenth century and into the MNR era of the 1950s and 1960s.[42] The contemporary failures of the National Revolution were thus understood as a continuation of centuries of oppression, in which, Rivera writes, "the collective memory of the 1952 revolution signifie[d] only just a partial rupture with the past." She explains that "short memory," based in the "revolutionary power of the campesino unions and militias since 1952," oriented the indigenous struggle at this time. Kataristas combined short memory with "long memory," a view toward "anticolonial struggles [and a] pre-Hispanic ethical order."[43] The alchemy of long and short memory, Rivera writes, took hold among Kataristas seeking to build an independent union movement.

The Kataristas wanted to reform the CNTCB, the state-dominated campesino union founded by the MNR in 1953, and make it autonomous from the state. But the union also served as an important space for the development of local and political leadership. Through the union, young people came to learn more about Bolivia's leading politicians, the details of state policy, the art of making union speeches, and the relationship between the union and the state. It also notably operated as a channel for political ambition within the campesino sector.[44] Aside from this educational and professional purpose, the union already served as a tool for the Katarista cause. As Esteban Ticona explains, Kataristas used the "campesino union as a special instrument of struggle. Even though it belong[ed] to the State of 52 [the postrevolution MNR government] and was created in the new form of state domination, the Kataristas had the ability to extend their influence and spread their ideas through the union."[45]

The union was one of the wider indigenous movement's "instruments of struggle." Another was the strengthening of indigenous histories, community governance and organizational models, and knowledge of preconquest Andean societies.

ANDEAN UTOPIAS: THE WORK AND INFLUENCE
OF INDIGENOUS INTELLECTUALS

A portrait of indigenous philosopher Fausto Reinaga in his library
and office in La Paz where he wrote most of his work. Photographer:
William Wroblewski.

Alongside Katarismo, a parallel political and intellectual current
among indigenous activists called Indianismo took a different tack,
focusing less on class-based domination and more specifically on
racial oppression. Indianistas were a group of intellectuals and activists in La Paz who organized almost exclusively through small political

parties. Unlike the Kataristas, who focused on the development of an independent campesino union allied with the wider Left, Indianistas refused to join with the "mestizo-creole" Left, arguing that doing so perpetuated the neocolonialist, racist relationship that existed between the MNR, subsequent military regimes, and the indigenous people of Bolivia.[46] However, Indianismo was an important current of thought that influenced Kataristas as they empowered the indigenous movement in the 1970s and 1980s.

One critical Indianista source for the rise of Katarismo included the writings and influence of indigenous intellectual Fausto Reinaga. Though Reinaga is more identified with the Indianista current, early Katarista activists met regularly with Reinaga in La Paz in the 1960s.[47] This prolific author was known as a great orator and debater. Portraits of him give the impression that he was a deep thinker with a philosophical bearing. Reinaga's books were widely read and referenced throughout his lifetime and continue to be popular to this day, selling in street bookstalls across Bolivia.[48] Born in 1906, Reinaga grew up in a poor indigenous farming family and, through personal sacrifice and the aid of his parents, was able to attend school and university while working various jobs. Through an integration of Marxist and indigenous worldviews, his writing reflected his own lived experience as an indigenous man living through the tumultuous periods of the Chaco War of 1928 to 1935 and the National Revolution.[49] Reinaga's thinking and writing influenced his contemporaries and subsequent generations; dozens of leading Aymara youth activists from Aroma, many of whom would go on to become key campesino union leaders, met regularly with Reinaga in the 1960s and 1970s. Aymara youth who arrived in La Paz to attend secondary school and university came together at Reinaga's home to discuss and develop a contemporary project for indigenous liberation. This group dug into their own indigenous people's history and launched several initiatives linked to Reinaga's thought.

Hilda Reinaga, the writer's niece, described various conferences and talks given in the 1960s by her uncle Fausto. Aymara students from the countryside studying in La Paz would often arrive at these gatherings. In addition to participating in the discussions taking place with Reinaga at his home, the students also used his vast library.

According to Hilda Reinaga, the books her uncle authored were widely circulated among rural campesino unions during this period. Campesino readers would arrive at Reinaga's home, and "they would bring potatoes, eggs, and exchange them for books."[50]

Following their meetings with Reinaga, some indigenous youth at the Gualberto Villarroel secondary school began the November 15 Student Movement (named after the date members then understood Katari to have been executed) in secondary schools, and students at the public Universidad Mayor de San Andrés in La Paz began the Julián Apaza University Movement (MUJA).[51] Reinaga himself launched the Partido Indio Boliviano (Bolivian Indian Party, PIB), which drew from views of a utopian precolonial past and indigenous culture to envision a new society.[52] Reinaga's most popular book, *La Revolución India* (The Indian Revolution), published in 1970, was at once a comprehensive history of Bolivia, a condemnation of colonialism and neocolonialism, and a call to reconstruct the lost nation of Tawantinsuyo, the preconquest indigenous society spanning the Andes.[53] Such influential texts and thought served as fundamental sparks in the early 1970s to ignite political fires across the indigenous movement. Young activists influenced by Reinaga began to develop a deeper sense of their own identity, political orientation, and a feeling of being "foreigners in their own land."[54] Such a sentiment expressed the view that Bolivia was composed of two nations, divided by race, in which the indigenous majority was historically oppressed.

Reinaga's home and library is still occupied and maintained by Hilda Reinaga, who typed up much of her one-armed uncle's work and provided crucial economic support for him in his later years. In a 2015 interview at the Reinaga library, she emphasized the importance of the preconquest indigenous civilization of Tawantinsuyo to her uncle's philosophy. "This was a civilization in which there was no hunger," she explained, "there was no fratricide."[55] Fausto Reinaga's objective was radical but simple: indigenous power. "This meant taking power and returning to become owners of this land and territory." The goal, Hilda Reinaga explained, was to "introduce Incaic socialism, which is to say, the socialism that our ancestors had already lived; there was a socialism. Therefore, we do have our own system of government, which is the ayllu, the community."[56]

In his 1971 *Tesis India* (Indian Thesis), Reinaga outlines a historical narrative of precolonial society that would take hold decades later
in the CSUTCB and the ayllu reconstruction efforts of the 1990s.
When Pizarro arrived at the indigenous civilization of Tawantinsuyo,
Reinaga writes in his thesis, he found "stocks of food that could last
for hundreds of years; palaces of gold," a place where everyone, from
the "Inca to the last able subject worked in perfect harmony; no one
lied, no one robbed, no one exploited." This vision of utopia, what he
calls the "first socialist republic in the world," inspired a generation of
activists building a new indigenous politics in the 1970s.[57] Reinaga's
philosophy was "forged through a rediscovery of the Inca civilization," explains Andean scholar José Antonio Lucero. To Reinaga and
his readers, this past and place was not imaginary but was, Reinaga
writes, "a stable community, historically formed, and which emerged
from a linguistic, territorial, economic, psychological, and cultural
community."[58]

Reinaga's concept of "two Bolivias," one made up of indigenous
people and the other of those of European descent, took hold among
Aymara activists of the time, as expressed in documents such as the
Kataristas' 1973 Manifesto of Tiwanaku. Within this view of two
Bolivias was the nation of creoles and mestizos, with their own language (Spanish) and the Bolivian national flag. The other nation con-
sisted of indigenous people with various languages and the wiphala
flag.[59] This view, alongside the conceptual rescue of Tawantinsuyo as
a model and rallying cry, was essential for a political revolution led by
and for indigenous people.[60]

While Indianistas focused on developing small political parties
and Kataristas emphasized the construction of an independent campesino movement, both currents shared the objective of recovering
political models from preconquest indigenous societies. Two key
Indianista leaders provide critical examples of this worldview and
political current.

One Aymara activist who met regularly with Reinaga was Constantino Lima. Lima was involved in the Indianista current during
this period, and his life story and historical analysis reflect many of
the debates that took place between Reinaga and younger indigenous
activists and thinkers. Lima carries his history with him. He walks

with a limp resulting from being shot three times while a conscripted soldier in the National Revolution; later, he was imprisoned and tortured under various dictatorships. But the injuries have barely slowed him down. At age eighty-five, he speaks fluently on a wide range of topics, sprinkling jokes and humor into almost every account, emitting a charisma that likely aided him in his many roles as a dissident, politician, and groundbreaking indigenous leader and thinker.

When talking of the racism he and his family faced when he was young, however, he bristles with anger as though the wounds were fresh. "All of the native Indians, we were born amidst thorns because of the terrible racism we faced," Lima recalled. "People would call us *shitty Indians* right to our face; they would beat us up when they wanted to."[61] His mother did not speak Spanish, and, as a child, Lima himself worked taking care of the family's sheep. When he was about seven or eight, he remembered asking his father why racism existed against his family and against indigenous people in general in Bolivia.[62]

> "Why all of this abuse?" I asked my father. "Why is this happening?" And so my father brought all of his children together. I was the youngest, and he made us sit down in a circle, and on the wall he first drew Europe, then the ocean and the Abya Yala continent [indigenous territory spanning Latin America with preconquest roots], which is our continent that is now called America. He explained to us that "people with white skin came from here, from Europe, they are not from here. We are owners of this land, they are not. They came from there [Europe] and invaded us, and so now we are their imprisoned slaves." This lesson, that these people abusing us were not from here, got inside of me and never left, never left my mind or my heart. This is the ideological doctrine that my father imparted to me, and it is why I grew up as a rebel.[63]

As an indigenous activist organizing in the wake of the National Revolution and meeting regularly with Reinaga, Lima's political objective was to rebuild Bolivian society under indigenous self-rule. "With very few variants, nearly everyone has always fought for the reconstitution of our ancestral states," Lima told me of his militant colleagues during an interview in downtown La Paz. He continued,

"The view was that with this power, one day Bolivia could go in a different direction, soon [to] reconstitute itself as the National State of [the ancestral indigenous civilization] Qullasuyu."[64]

Such views generated deep personal reflections among indigenous activists in Bolivia in the 1960s and 1970s, many of whom looked to their own pasts and experiences as guides for political orientation and action. For Luciano Tapia, an Indianista and key protagonist in the indigenous movement during this time, his ideology and identity was tied directly to his challenges as a poor farmer and indigenous dissident who faced marginalization, repression, and poverty. Tapia, born in 1923 in the Pacajes Province, was raised in an Aymara ayllu. He combined lessons from life experience and his view of Andean history to develop an identity-based project for indigenous liberation. As a longtime indigenous leader and politician, he bore witness to the rise and activity of the indigenous movement's resurgence after the National Revolution. His popular autobiography, *Ukhamawa Jakawisaxa (Así es Nuestra Vida): Autobiografía de un Aymara,* written and recorded by Tapia himself starting in 1985 and completed in the mid-1990s, reflects on this political trajectory with an eloquent meditation on rural life in Aymara communities during periods of political transformation.[65]

As Tapia explains, "By creating an awareness of my identity, I understood that the cultural expressions of my ancestry, the personality of my people and its millenary history, were the key on which to base and sustain a struggle for liberation."[66] Tapia's political orientation was a direct result of his lived experience as a self-made intellectual. He writes, "I did not need to read any book or embrace the dogmas of the oppressor as orienting guides, because I myself was an open book with the contents of experiences and lived realities, of irrefutable truths that surpassed all theoretical, alienating, and colonizing fantasy."[67]

He was clear that this past and personal experience helped him feel part of a united, living culture. Tapia explained, "I understood that, far from feeling as though I were a beggar and foreigner in my own ancestral land, rather, I should instead feel proud of being a descendant of the great and glorious civilizations from this part of the world. From this comes the reason to maintain that, beyond being a

simple campesino class, we are fundamentally a living historical reality, a people made of flesh and bone, a real Nation."[68]

Tapia's political objectives were rooted in a push to revitalize
the crushed indigenous movement and strengthen the indigenous
nations of "flesh and bone" in the face of what he saw as structural
racism and neocolonialism. Lima and Tapia's views reflect debates
with Reinaga and Reinaga's own conceptions of an Andean utopia. In
response, Lima founded the Partido Autóctono Nacional (National
Indigenous Party), and Tapia started the Movimiento Indio Tupaq
Katari (Tupaq Katari Indian Movement), political parties that sought
to promote indigenous power through the ballot box.[69]

Meanwhile, young Kataristas took a different approach by
emphasizing the transformation of the campesino union as an instrument of indigenous struggle. The young Aymara activists from Aroma
who met with Reinaga soon emerged as Katarista leaders and focused
on turning the state-dominated CNTCB into an independent campesino union.[70] Operating in the shadow of the National Revolution
and under subsequent military regimes, these young Kataristas successfully challenged the PMC and its allies among the older generation of union leadership.

CHAPTER TWO

KATARISTAS RISING

"We Are No Longer the Peasants of 1952"

Katarista leader Genaro Flores (center) and Indianista leader Luciano Tapia (right). Coca leaves and an Andean staff of authority sit in front of Flores, and a portrait of Túpac Katari holding a rifle hangs in the upper left. Photographer: Roberto Balza. Courtesy of the Archivo Central del Museo Nacional de Etnografía y Folklore.

On a May Day march in 1971 in La Paz, the government handed out posters with portraits of President Torres. In a symbolic act against the state's subjugation of indigenous culture and history, indigenous activists participating in the march hid Torres's pictures beneath their ponchos while displaying publicly, outside the ponchos, portraits of Katari and his wife, the rebel leader Bartolina Sisa. "In this way Katarismo began to convert itself into a mass movement," Javier Hurtado writes. The enthusiasm of the defiant marchers—who also distanced themselves from the president when he sought to lead the march—was so great that they bore Katarista leaders on their shoulders for part of the parade and did not want to stop marching through the streets. These portraits of Katari and Sisa were distributed widely through indigenous organization at the time, appearing in schools and homes next to pictures of the Virgen de Copacabana (the Bolivian apparition of the Virgin Mary) and alongside portraits of the creole heroes of independence distributed by the Ministry of Education. As they had in 1781, the Aymara people, Hurtado writes, "again raised their own flag."[1]

The Katarista struggle was on the march, from Aroma to La Paz. A new generation of indigenous leaders was rising up to build an independent campesino union, develop ties with the wider Left and the workers' movement in the country, and resist the various military regimes that dominated Bolivia in the 1960s and 1970s. As part of their organizing strategies, Kataristas lifted up the indigenous histories of resistance and the symbol of Katari. At the forefront of this movement were young leaders from the province of Aroma—Raimundo Tambo and Genaro Flores.

That the Katarista movement began in Aroma is no accident. In many ways, the province is a national crossroads of campesino movement history. It holds particular geographic importance for campesino-led road blockade campaigns. The Pan-American Highway passes through the region, linking La Paz with Oruro and Cochabamba, and goes through the main provincial towns of Ayo-Ayo, Calamarca, Sica Sica, and Lahuachaca. As a major traffic hub, this province is important as a strategic site for road blockades. These factors contributed to making Aroma a potent site of campesino organizing.[2]

Aroma is also notably the birthplace of Túpac Katari, and his legacy was often evoked by twentieth-century leaders from the province to embolden their claims to prominent positions in union elections. Next to Genaro Flores and other leaders from Aroma, Hurtado writes, "no one could better claim to be the direct heirs of these struggles." In addition, ayllu traditions of rotational leadership were still being practiced by Aroma community members up to 1952 and beyond. In the post-MNR era, such traditions existed alongside the state-led rural union. This a legacy of resistance, based in the actual claim the province had to Katari's legacy, and the endurance of ayllu traditions helped to set Aroma apart from other provinces. As Hurtado explains, "Unlike other Aymara regions, the indigenous campesinos of Aroma have not erased from their memory these traditions of struggle that live on as legends that the elders transmit to the young, as part of their community education."[3]

Raimundo Tambo was one of Katarismo's first advocates. He was born in Ayo-Ayo, the same Aroma community as Katari, and was supposedly a blood relative of the eighteenth-century rebel.[4] He organized against Barrientos's tax on land titles, was closely tied to the union bases in Aroma, and devoted the bulk of his political efforts to the independent campesino union struggle.[5] Like many other Aymara youth from Aroma at this time, Tambo studied in the Gualberto Villarroel secondary school in La Paz, where he was a founder of the November 15 Student Movement. In the mid-1960s he worked closely with Fausto Reinaga and was involved in the early years of Reinaga's PIB.[6] Tambo and other young Kataristas participated in the Julián Apaza University Movement (MUJA) as well. Ramón Conde Mamani, a member of MUJA, recalled that the organization had, at its peak, approximately forty members and was made up primarily of students who had migrated to the city but maintained ties to their rural homes. MUJA sought to spread awareness of indigenous culture and promoted indigenous identity and rights. At the university level, members tried to increase scholarships and shape admissions policies in ways that benefited indigenous students. Their wider activism extended into attending campesino union meetings, where they promoted an indigenous-based analysis aligned with Katarismo in a space where a narrow class analysis and the paternalism of the PMC still reigned.[7] Tambo and others in the MUJA were influenced by Reinaga, circulated his writings, and met regularly with the writer.[8]

Aside from Tambo, one of Katarismo's greatest and most effective proponents was Genaro Flores, also a product of Aroma's vibrant political and historical culture. A moving speaker, Flores was a charismatic union leader who inspired his followers early on with both his soccer skills and political convictions. In union rallies and meetings, the young Flores spoke with the confidence and sharp

analysis of a seasoned union leader.[9] Flores was born in the community of Antipampa in 1942. His mother, who labored on the hacienda of Culli Culli until the hacienda was abolished by the MNR,
was a descendant of the late-nineteenth-century indigenous rebel
Zárate Willka.[10] During Bolivia's 1899 Federal War, the Aymara
cacique apoderado Willka led his indigenous army against the Con-
servatives, who were taking over indigenous land. Before Willka was
betrayed by Liberals, his indigenous revolt spread across the highlands in the most extensive indigenous uprising in the region since
that of Katari.[11] His father was a descendant of caciques, worked
in the Caracoles mines, and was well known for his knowledge of
astronomy and Andean agricultural traditions, including his expertise in planting and harvesting at distinct altitudes. This agricultural
knowledge and notable ancestry contributed to Flores's prestige in
his community.[12]

While these rural roots were necessary for Flores's rise to prominence, the connections he made and the experiences he had in urban
La Paz were also critical for shaping him as a trailblazing campesino
organizer. After he graduated from primary school, Flores's parents
sent him to the Gualberto Villarroel secondary school in La Paz. A
particularly large number of Aymara students from rural areas, especially from Aroma, attended the Villarroel school. Ticona writes
that many Aroma parents sent their children to this school because
the high number of other Aymara students made for an easier transition for their Aymara-speaking children moving to the city from
the countryside. The other likely reason for the Aroma connection
was Hernando Guarita González, a leftist schoolteacher who included indigenous issues and culture in his curriculum. In addition, the
director of the school was from the Aroma town of Ayo-Ayo.[13] It was
here at the secondary school that Flores first came into contact with
other early leaders of Katarismo, most notably Tambo, and became
involved in the November 15 Student Movement. In 1964, the year
of Barrientos's coup, Flores graduated from school and began his
military service, where he served under General Gary Prado Salmón,
who led the military actions against Che Guevara in 1967. Flores also
witnessed a massacre of miners in Milluni. These experiences pushed
him to be more critical of the PMC and the Bolivian military in

general. After leaving military service, Flores entered the Universidad Mayor de San Andrés in La Paz to study law and there made contact with the Julián Apaza University Movement.[14] In 1966, Flores married Nieves Velasco and returned to his home of Antipampa. Shortly after his return, he was hired by a research group from the University of Wisconsin and the National Agrarian Reform Service of the Bolivian government, which was conducting work in Antipampa.[15] The research focused on the relationship between the CNTCB union leaders and their bases at the provincial, departmental, and national levels. Flores's experience in this project informed his critical stance toward the older generation of union leaders, whom he came to see as corrupt and subservient to the state rather than responsible to the campesino bases. This view was fundamental to the Katarista desire to break with the PMC and develop an independent union movement. As Flores recalled, "In all of this research work, the only thing I saw was the corruption of the leaders, who were servants of the bosses, of the landowners, and they received bribes. This is why people said 'the leaders are a bunch of gangsters,' because they were servants of MNR of this era, and in addition, were leaders of the military-campesino pact."[16]

Facing what they perceived as institutional corruption and subservience to the state among the CNTCB leadership, Kataristas such as Tambo and Flores organized for change within the union itself, as well as through public acts that spread consciousness about indigenous history and the legacy of Túpac Katari among rural communities and union members. In their early years, Katarista groups organized public acts to commemorate and lift up indigenous rebel leaders and a history of resistance, and, in the words of Hurtado, "refresh the collective memory of their own past." As part of this process, one Katarista group celebrated Katari and Willka on the anniversaries of their deaths in Ayo-Ayo and Imilla-Imilla in the Aroma Province.[17] Flores explained that he and others constructed a monument of Katari in Ayo-Ayo in 1969 in which broken shackles cling to Katari's wrists and ankles, and his arms reach defiantly into the air. The statue symbolically signaled the shift away from the state domination of the campesinos. As the Kataristas famously claimed, "We are no longer the peasants of 1952."[18]

Meanwhile, gains were being made by Flores and others in their struggle for an independent union movement. Flores was elected the general secretary of the rural union of Antipampa in 1970. His election was partly due to family connections to cacique lineage and his own education, military service, and status as a married man. But his victory also notably had to do with a generational divide. Upon returning to Antipampa, Flores recalled that the youth were in a state of "rebellion" against the older union leaders because the union refused to help purchase more sports and soccer equipment for the community. The youth decided to simply try to replace all of the older generation of union leaders with younger people. As a result, when the election for the local union took place, the young soccer players and sports enthusiasts—as well as the wider community—chose Flores as their local union's leader.[19] This anecdote speaks of a generational divide that would prove critical to Flores's trajectory as a young, rising union leader who came to represent an increasingly militant generation of youth in Aroma.

Flores quickly proved himself as an able union leader and a vocal critic of the CNTCB. After his election to the leadership the Antipampa union, he was chosen as the head of the larger regional union of Lahuachaca. Though the union network was still ostensibly controlled by the state as an avenue for state distribution of land and construction of schools, Flores spoke out against state subjugation and carved out spaces for union activity that better reflected the community bases. For example, his promotion of soccer as a union-organized sport inspired the youth and defied the older generation of leaders. Flores also proved his competency early on by winning lower transportation costs from bus drivers who were abusing their monopoly in the rural areas by demanding high fares.[20] Six months after his election to the leadership in Lahuachaca, Flores attended a provincial union meeting in Ayo-Ayo, where his youth support and critiques of the PMC helped him win the election as a provincial CNTCB union leader for Aroma, an important step in the rise of Katarismo within the state union network.[21]

Flores's direct style of public speaking was marked by his militancy and his proximity to the base. Such a rhetorical approach was demonstrated in a phrase he coined as a provincial leader in Aroma:

"All of the land to the campesinos," which served as both a slogan for his leadership style as well as a call to action. It was a simple but radical demand and harkened back to the early days of the MNR government.[22] The phrase was a rallying cry for Flores's technique of occupying hacienda land, unused land, and land the agrarian reform had not reached and claiming it for campesino use. Such a strategy helped to define Flores as a leader who used the union as a tool to meet the needs of the base and to put land into campesino hands through direct action. Largely because of such bold moves as a leader critical of the PMC, Flores was elected executive secretary of the departmental campesino union of La Paz in March 1971. To mark the La Paz federation's independence, Flores and the congress that had elected him decided to add Túpac Katari to the end of the union federation's name.[23]

POPULARIZING KATARI'S HISTORY AND STRUGGLE

A number of different groups and activists popularized Katari's history and struggle during this time, lifting the martyr up as a symbol of their cause. In this vein, the work of the Kataristas and their allies demonstrates how indigenous activists constructed and mobilized symbols to define their movements. "Symbols are taken selectively by movement leaders from a cultural reservoir and combined with action-oriented beliefs in order to navigate strategically among a parallelogram of actors, ranging from state and social opponents to militants and target populations," social movement theorist Sidney Tarrow argues. "Most important, they are given an emotional valence aimed at converting passivity into action."[24] Indeed, Kataristas recovered Katari's life story as a symbol to mobilize indigenous activists, in this case to encourage their participation in the movement for an independent campesino union. Kataristas consciously constructed and popularized Katari in an example of how, as Tarrow explains, "cultural symbols are not automatically available as mobilizing symbols but require concrete agents to turn them into frames of contention."[25] The development of Katari statues, portraits, and placards, as well as speeches, manifestos, communiqués, and radio programs that evoked the leader, were meant to galvanize supporters, frame indigenous resistance and critiques, and unite indigenous activists in the movement.

A range of actors contributed to the development of Katari as a symbol. Katarista activists benefited from the support of NGOs with international connections. Organizations such as the Instituto de Desarrollo, Investigación y Educación Popular Campesino (Institute of Grassroots Campesino Development, Research and Education, INDICEP), with participation from Chilean and Argentine scholars, offered critical support and funding to Kataristas and their spaces and publications. The Centro de Investigación y Promoción del Campesinado (Center for the Study and Promotion of the Peasantry, CIPCA), a social science research organization, in which Catalan scholar Xavier Albó has been deeply involved to this day, offered critical research help and direct aid to leaders like Flores. Both INDICEP and CIPCA supported the Katarista cause with public events and publications aimed at raising historical consciousness about past indigenous martyrs like Katari.[26] INDICEP itself printed and distributed a portrait of Katari that was widely used by campesino groups in the early 1970s.[27]

The use of Katari was further strengthened by a nexus between activist-scholars and Katarista campesino organizers. Trailblazing Aymara historian Roberto Choque Canqui had regular contact with Flores over this period. Choque, born in 1942, was raised in a poor, rural Aymara family and took on a critical role in La Paz as a historian and archivist who produced indigenous-centered history. He has produced numerous books and countless articles, the most notable being surveys of indigenous oppression and resistance spanning centuries.[28] He is known as a meticulous archival researcher, and his empirically rich works expanded awareness and scholarship regarding the indigenous history of the country. Choque was also involved in the management of a new archive of judicial records of land disputes founded in the 1970s, an archive that later greatly aided the THOA's research.[29]

In the early 1970s, Choque's scholarship took on more explicitly militant aspects as he collaborated with the Kataristas. Choque was a university student in La Paz at this time, was involved with the

Mink'a Center, and provided indigenous movement leaders with the bibliography for the study of Katari and his rebellion.[30] The Aymara historian met with Flores and taught him about Bolivian history, particularly concerning Katari's struggle. "I did try to orient Genaro regarding who Túpac Katari was," Choque stated in an interview. "Because Túpac Katari was also a politician, the struggle is political, the struggle is against Spanish domination, so [Katari was] a political actor." He explained, "Genaro Flores totally identified [with Katari], the struggle, and because of this, Katarismo entered in this way into the [campesino union], it was more *Katarized*." Choque said, "Yes, Katari was mythologized. 'I will return and be millions' becomes the myth. . . . That is more or less oral history. We recovered [Katari]; we utilized the figure as a slogan of the struggle."[31]

Buoyed by such allies and the popularity of his views, Flores reached a new height on August 2, 1971, at the Fourth National Congress of the CNTCB in Potosí. Here, the efforts of the dissident leader and other union activists critical of the PMC were rewarded with Flores's remarkable election as the executive secretary of the CNTCB.[32] In a few short, intense years, Flores had moved through the union ranks at an incredible pace. His election as the leader of the national union marked a high point in the struggle for an independent union. However, the Katarista gains were cut short just weeks later when General Hugo Banzer took power in a military coup on August 21, sending Flores and other rebellious campesino union leaders, leftists, and labor union activists into exile in Chile, where they found temporary safety under the short tenure of Salvador Allende's socialist government.

Banzer's coup was the result of a number of factors. The leftist shift of Ovando and Torres created a backlash within the military and among middle-class and commercial elites of the country, particularly in the Santa Cruz Department in eastern Bolivia. Private business groups in this region in the gas, coffee, and sugar industries banded together to prevent their industries from being nationalized by the Torres administration. This sector organized a right-wing front against Torres, with Banzer as the leader. The so-called Banzerato, the right-wing military rule of Banzer, lasted from 1971 to 1978 and reversed the leftist, nationalist direction of the Torres government.

Banzer's dictatorship coincided with the regional crackdown on leftist dissidents under Operation Condor in Chile, Argentina, Uruguay,
Paraguay, and Brazil. Banzer ignored the needs of impoverished rural
workers and instead awarded land to elites in Santa Cruz, supported
the large-scale commercial agriculture sector of that department, and
offered large government subsidies to the cotton growers association
while small-scale indigenous farmers suffered.[33]

In Chile, Flores, in discussion with other leaders, came to realize
more deeply the importance of an alliance between the campesinos,
the miners, and the COB. He returned to Bolivia in 1972 because
of the death of his father, and alongside Tambo began reorganizing
the Katarista movement underground. During this time, the Túpac
Katari Campesino Center and the Association of Aymara Professors
were critical supporters of the Katarista cause, and through these and
other networks the 1973 Manifesto of Tiwanaku was launched.[34]

THE MANIFESTO OF TIWANAKU:
"WE ARE FOREIGNERS IN OUR OWN COUNTRY"

The wind was strong and the blue sky was cloudless on September 15,
1973, as some thirty-six Aymara men and women dressed in ponchos
and colorful shawls hurried past crowds of tourists and entered the
ancient city of Tiwanaku, an archeological site near Lake Titicaca.
They walked over the ruins, through a courtyard dotted with sculp-
tures, and climbed the stairs of the Gateway to the Sun, a prominent
stone doorway decorated with winged figures including Virocha, the
rain deity. Above the gathered crowd, an Aymara man among the
group read for roughly twenty minutes from the Manifesto of Tiwanaku, a document that denounced neocolonialism and the failures
of the National Revolution and championed the Katarista struggle.
When he finished, the activist crowd cheered and then quickly scattered from the scene.[35]

In this way, Kataristas presented their key document. The participants chose to issue their manifesto for the first time at the ruins
of Tiwanaku because it represented a symbolic center of indigenous
spirituality and culture in the Andes.[36] Though the site itself was

prominent, the creation of the document, much like the hurried reading itself, was the result of many clandestine meetings among Aymara activists in La Paz who organized in secret to avoid repression from the Banzer dictatorship. The police state had been jailing, torturing, and murdering dissidents organizing for democracy, and the indigenous activists involved with the manifesto took every precaution to make sure they could launch their declaration safely. Among those who had helped to create the manifesto were noted indigenous leader Raimundo Tambo and the Catholic priest Gregorio Iriarte, as well as Aymara intellectuals, students, schoolteachers, and farmers involved with the Mink'a Center for Peasant Coordination and Promotion and the Túpac Katari Campesino Center, crucial spaces in La Paz for clandestine indigenous organizing.[37]

The manifesto itself, in just a few pages, analyzes five hundred years of oppression and resistance, neocolonialism, the contradictions of the National Revolution, and the vision of the "Children of 1952." It also notably denounces Banzer's regime and calls for an alliance between the campesino sector and workers' organizations across the country. A central argument weaving throughout the document concerns the persistence of colonialism in the country: "There has been no integration of cultures in Bolivia; it has been a question of imposition and domination."[38] The document critiques the MNR and subsequent military regimes, the PMC, and the paternalism of the state toward the indigenous majority. The Kataristas call for socioeconomic development oriented around indigenous culture and protest the standard approach toward development of the era, stating that government officials sought to "create a type of development based solely on a servile imitation of the development of other countries, while our cultural heritage is totally different." Instead, they call for development that "must spring from our own values," the manifesto continues. "We want an end to state paternalism and we no longer wish to be considered second class citizens. We are foreigners in our own country."

The beating heart of this manifesto is a view of a glorious Andean past. "Even before the Spanish conquest, we were an ancient people whose character developed within a highly socialized environment," the manifesto explains. This culture was repressed, crushed under the boot of colonialism, while Katari is a leader of true independence: "Liberation as embodied in Túpac Katari's struggle for Indian freedom remains shackled." The authors write that the path ahead needs to be shaped by rescuing historical lessons and the legacies and examples of indigenous martyrs. "There has been no revolution in the countryside; it has yet to be achieved. But there must be a revolution, one which holds up once again the banners and ideals of Túpac Katari, Bartolina Sisa, Zárate Willka. . . . The starting point of the revolution should be our people."[39] The authors state that the tools of liberation are in indigenous people's hands, in the rescuing of the ideals of past martyrs, and in the revalorization of indigenous history, culture, and identity.

The manifesto is, in perhaps the most concise terms possible, an indictment of the official history of Bolivia at that time and a rewriting of history from the indigenous people's perspective. The authors glorify a precolonial past with superior civilizations, they portray colonization as totally destructive, and state that Katari's dream "remains shackled." They describe independence from Spain as freedom for but a few as the same system of exploitation continued for the rest. In the manifesto, history and ancestral legacies are used as lenses to analyze both the past and contemporary challenges, and they serve as fodder for building a better future. In the context of postrevolutionary Bolivia, the manifesto's vision was profound. It condemned assimilationist policies and the reduction of social struggles to only class and economic terms, and it placed indigenous culture at the core of its politics.[40]

The manifesto would serve as the cornerstone for indigenous political ideology, parties, and movements for years to come, and is perhaps the best synthesis of Katarista thought and vision. In spite of state repression and the lack of media attention, the document was distributed widely thanks to the help of progressive NGOs, peasant unions, and allies in the Catholic Church. The manifesto was translated into Aymara, Quechua, and Guaraní and circulated throughout the country, particularly in the highland provinces, from Potosí and Oruro to Jesús de Machaca and La Paz.[41] It was also used by Flores and Tambo to develop younger leaders in the movement. Throughout Bolivia, small groups of people would gather to discuss the document secretly. In La Paz, such meetings were often held in the Túpac Katari Campesino Center. The manifesto served as a vehicle for discussing the political and economic problems of the day in terms of the challenges and hopes of the Katarista movement.[42]

KATARI'S SYMBOLIC RETURN

The manifesto reflected other historical consciousness-raising efforts within Katarista publications of the time. For the authors, as with many people involved in these projects, the idea of rescuing and strengthening the model of a precolonial indigenous civilization was critical. This model incorporated the governing structures and social order of a past society, such as the political model of the ayllu and Andean forms of reciprocity.[43] Alongside this recovery stood the objectives of reconstructing a lost indigenous state and rescuing indigenous values, ethical codes, and models for equitable social relationships—many of which had endured for centuries and took on new meaning in this era of clandestine indigenous resurgence.[44] The concepts, traditions, and ethics promoted in the manifesto would be taken up in the following decades in the agricultural models advocated by the CSUTCB and the ayllu reconstruction efforts of the CONAMAQ.

Restoring elements of this social order was central to publications produced by Mink'a, a key Katarista group. A 1973 issue of their magazine, *Mink'a*, had on its cover a photo of the Aymara founders of the first indigenous school in the highland community of Warisata, accompanied by a drawing of a student next to a book opened to a page titled "Freedom."[45] The school was founded on August 2, 1931. Since then, that date has been celebrated in Bolivia as "Indian Day."[46] In one article in the magazine, author René Mario Gabriel A. explains that many ancestral forms of organization among Aymara and Quechua people have been preserved, in spite of colonialism. He lists, among other concepts, that of *ayni*, a form of "direct cooperation," "collective work," and "mutual aid" that was "one of the laws that regulated the life of the Aymara and Quechua people, that signified a form of direct aid, in agricultural and livestock work."[47] These were the building blocks that activists in the 1970s used for their proposal of a renewed political order. Another form of cooperative work, Gabriel explains, is *mink'a*, which is one of the "most advanced laws" guiding cooperation and administration of the Aymara and Quechua people. "It consists in a diversified assistance" in which labor is evenly shared among community members. In this way, "the aid is an equitable form of production exchange."[48]

Such forms of cooperation, Gabriel continues, were based in the ayllu, which used the code of *ama qhilla, ama llulla, ama suwa* (do not be lazy, do not be a liar, do not be a thief), social rules the author says were "destroyed during the colonial period." Gabriel explains that Katari, Sisa, and Willka had tried to build an indigenous government based on these laws, with "a government of our own, like our ancestors built."[49] Here was an example of an ethic of cooperation with a precedent in the Andes that served as one basis to rebuild indigenous politics.

Lifting up Katari took other forms as well. The cover of the first issue of a movement pamphlet called *Ayllu*, published by Mink'a in 1974, includes a drawing of a man in a poncho.[50] An article in this issue by Julio Tumiri A. notably calls for unity among Aymara people, stating that the revolts of Katari and Willka "aren't just left in history; but rather the sleeping giant is awakening with signs of a new form of expression, the pride of being an indigenous Aymara."[51] A need for resurgence after centuries of exploitation is highlighted in another piece, where the author writes, "With our dignified, dirty, and calloused hands, [we] raise the sacred banners of our indigenous and anonymous heroes that died to see us as free and dignified people."[52] The motif of martyrdom and the recovery of lost glory is bound to Katari as a symbol among participants in Mink'a and other similar groups of the era.

In this way, Katari's body itself is transformed by the authors into a metaphor for the political body of indigenous activists who considered themselves the living legacy and spirit of Katari. This theme is continued in a 1977 issue of *Mink'a*, which includes a brief history of Katari's life and struggle. The authors recall Katari's quartering by horses and how he has returned as millions in the forms of the many indigenous peoples fighting together for liberation: "Túpac Katari, without having any stone monument, has remained in the Heart of his people, and his spirit, today more than ever, shines in the four winds of Tawantinsuyo."[53] The labor of activists and intellectuals to resurrect Katari conceptually and popularize his legacy helped make Katari's symbolic return a reality.

THE END OF THE BANZERATO

While Katarista groups struggled clandestinely to organize for an independent campesino union, the Banzer regime clamped down on the countryside with bloody repression and austerity measures that debilitated campesino communities. In January 1974 the Banzer government eliminated government subsidies on basic goods, raising the price of eggs, rice, and meat an average of 219 percent. Protests in La Paz immediately followed the move, with workers in factories and mines launching a nationwide strike. The countryside was hit hard by the measures and responded with massive protests. Beginning with a march organized by workers at the Monaco Shoe Factory in Quillacollo (outside the city of Cochabamba) on January 22, protests spread throughout the region, with blockades set up on the road to Santa Cruz and around the Cochabamba valley. Dialogue between the government and protesters came to a standstill; Banzer refused to meet the activists for negotiations, dismissing their demands. Instead, he sent tanks and armored cars to break down the blockades, resulting in the January 29 Massacre of the Valley, which began in the town of Tolata, outside of Cochabamba. Tanks approached the protesters while military officials ordered the crowds to disperse. A tense silence was broken by a female protester who threw a stone at one of the tanks; the military responded with a brutal ground and air assault that left dozens of protesters dead.[54]

The Massacre of the Valley, as well as ongoing Katarista advocacy for the development of an independent rural union, deepened the fractures in the state's hold on the countryside and reduced the viability of the PMC. In the face of the Tolata massacre and the ongoing resistance to his regime from the labor unions and campesino sector, Banzer sought to further undermine rural union autonomy by replacing union leaders with new leadership selected by his regime, closing the Túpac Katari Campesino Center, and suppressing the public use of Katari's image and name.[55]

The Campesino Thesis produced by a 1976 CNTCB congress convened by Banzer in Tarija toward the end of this reconsolidation of his hold on the union points to the historical battles taking place at the time and underlines key differences between the representations of the past presented by the PMC-dominated union and those of the Kataristas. While the Kataristas promoted Katari and denounced Banzer around the country, the pro-Banzer thesis mentioned Katari only briefly as nothing more than a precursor to the Independence War, a "martyr" to the cause of national independence carried forth in 1809. In addition, Banzer is portrayed in the thesis as a national hero and friend of the campesino sector, and the PMC is cited as a "powerful instrument" for improving the plight of campesinos.[56] In spite of Banzer's efforts to control the campesino movement and the untimely death of Tambo in 1975 in a traffic accident, the Katarista and wider pro-democracy efforts persisted.[57]

On November 15, 1977, Flores publicly appeared at a celebration in Ayo-Ayo commemorating the death of Katari. At the event, Flores was designated as the rightful leader of the CNTCB by other campesino and union leaders. He took the helm of the national organization, in clear defiance of Banzer's repression and cooptation of the union, and added Túpac Katari to the end of the CNTCB's name to signal its Katarista orientation.[58] The leader then organized a series of clandestine CNTCB departmental congresses across the country, galvanizing the campesino union movement as an independent and militant force to topple Banzer.[59]

Pressure for Banzer to step down was mounting. The US government, under President Jimmy Carter, encouraged the Banzer administration to hold elections. Within Bolivia, civic and workers' groups clamored for amnesty for the hundreds of political dissidents exiled from the country by the dictatorship. The wives of four exiled miners began a hunger strike on December 28, 1977, demanding amnesty as well as the withdrawal of the military from the mines. The hunger strike quickly gained wide national support, taking off as a mass movement with more than one thousand participating by January 18,

1978, when Banzer capitulated to the all the strikers' demands except the removal of troops from the mines. This hunger strike proved a crucial breaking point for the Banzer regime and an important step in the wider push toward democracy.[60] Elections were held in July 1978 but were deemed illegitimate because of widespread fraud. Days later, Banzer was forced from office by another military coup, one that initiated a period of instability from July 1978 through July 1980, during which the country went through five presidents and four coups.[61] It was in the crucible of this political chaos and agonizing transition to democracy that the independent union Flores had struggled for was born: the CSUTCB was founded on June 26, 1979.[62]

Under Flores's leadership, Kataristas made considerable gains toward developing an independent campesino union that reflected the needs and demands of the union's base. They defied the PMC and built crucial ties with the COB and wider workers' movement, alliances that proved decisive in battling Banzer and later military governments. In this way, Kataristas were able to organize the largely indigenous rural sector into a national union network that they built into the CSUTCB, a militant union led by Flores for nearly a decade.

THE POWER OF THE PAST IN THE CSUTCB INDIGENOUS CAMPESINO UNION

Members of the La Paz Department's Túpac Katari Federation of the CSUTCB, including leaders Jorge Choque Salomé (third from left), Apolinar Quito Mamani (center), and Ismael Quispe Ticona (second from right) on April 4, 2014. Portraits of Túpac Katari and Bartolina Sisa hang on the wall on top of a wiphala flag. Photographer: Benjamin Dangl.

The offices of the La Paz Department's Túpac Katari Federation of the Unified Syndical Confederation of Rural Workers of Bolivia (CSUTCB) are located on a side street among a steep web of winding roads leading up to El Alto, the rim of the valley from which Katari himself laid siege to La Paz. The well-worn steps and furniture of the federation speak of the building's heavy use over decades as perhaps the most militant organizing space in Bolivia's campesino movement. When I visited the offices in April 2014, confetti left over from Carnival celebrations littered the floor. While a handful of union men in customary fedoras clutched papers as they waited outside the leadership's office, a secretary fielded phone calls and greeted newcomers.

Suddenly, a group of men arrived in a truck and rushed into the building, waving aside the secretary's pleas to wait and pushing open the door into the executive's office. The men waiting patiently outside the offices were as startled as the secretary as a fight quickly broke out in the next room, chairs and tables were knocked over, and sharp words were exchanged. Moments later, in hushed tones, a kind of peace was reached, and the men walked out of the room as breathlessly and quickly as they had entered.

After the men in fedoras conducted their business in the office, the CSUTCB leaders asked me to enter. The attitude with which they welcomed me suggested that the scuffle was nothing out of the ordinary—part of business as usual in a movement marked by conflicts, heightened tempers over political power and strategy, and critical decisions that could affect hundreds of communities across the altiplano. The leaders were dressed in outfits common among Aymara leaders in the La Paz region: leather jackets, brimmed hats, and ponchos.

As Katari and Sisa gazed over the office from portraits hung above the multicolored wiphala flag, the leaders described the role of historical consciousness in their movement. "When colonialism arrived to our continent, we had an Aymara state, as well as a Quechua state, a Guaraní state," said Jorge Choque Salomé, the general secretary of the Túpac Katari Federation. These states thrived, he explained, but the colonizers "arrived and quartered them."[1]

Choque's use of the phrase "quartered" to describe the impact of the conquest on indigenous society is a metaphor, obvious to any member of the movement, directly referencing Spanish soldiers' literal treatment of Katari's body during his execution in 1781. Similar violence was committed by the Spanish authorities and their successors against indigenous societies, Choque explained: their political body was dismembered. Reuniting the quartered indigenous political body in a struggle that renews Katari's dream has been the CSUTCB's objective for over thirty-five years.[2] Positioning Katari at the heart of this struggle for the recovery of indigenous power and identity both evokes the martyr as a potent symbol of resistance, action, and sacrifice and calls various indigenous groups to come together—a reuniting of the indigenous strength of the Andes. This historical analysis as presented by Choque reflects the central role of historical consciousness as an organizing tool in the CSUTCB.

The union emerged during a dramatic period of political transition to democracy, roughly from 1979 to 1983. The CSUTCB, founded in 1979 with Genaro Flores at its helm, was, and remains, an independent union whose members are primarily indigenous campesinos from across the entire country. Over the first years of its operation, the CSUTCB helped overthrow various military regimes and paved the way for a return to democracy. The union championed the interests of small farmers, advanced a radical land reform agenda, and called for more campesino participation in the government's rural policy development, all while promoting indigenous culture and histories of resistance.

Though the Agrarian Reform of 1953 had positive benefits for the campesinos, government rural development from the rise of Banzer in 1971 and onward typically empowered just a small group of wealthy large-scale commercial farmers.[3] In the early 1980s, 44 percent of Bolivia's economically active population was employed in agriculture, most on small plots of land that had been divided into smaller holdings, often around three hundred square meters, over generations following the agrarian reform.[4] The highlands of Bolivia, home to La Paz and a majority of the Aymara communities, depended more on subsistence farming than did other regions of the country. The quality of the land in the hands of small farmers was generally poorer than elsewhere, and this region lacked basic services, schools, and the government's technical and financial aid. The poverty and neglect from the state meant that campesino demands for land and support from the government were a matter of survival as well as economic viability.[5]

This situation led to nearly constant campesino protests. As militant and poor Aymara communities in the highlands were crisscrossed by major highways running into urban centers, blocking roads was a common and effective tactic for pressuring the government and making campesino voices heard. While the CSUTCB membership spanned the country, including the Quechua and Guaraní indigenous populations in the eastern and tropical lowlands, of particular interest here are the concerns and participation of Aymara campesinos in the highlands of Bolivia, as their role in the union was the most critical in this early period.

The centrality of historical consciousness in the CSUTCB can be understood by exploring three key aspects of the union's strategy, analysis, and vision: the reorganization of the union, historical consciousness in road blockades, and the union's 1983 "Political Thesis."

The CSUTCB, immediately after its founding in 1979, was reorganized to reflect the needs and identity of its historically oppressed base of largely indigenous campesinos. This was accomplished through Flores's leadership in the democratization of the union structure and the union's focus on direct action to win concessions, land, resources, and political power from the government for the campesino sector. In addition, the CSUTCB began to celebrate and embrace indigeneity in its meetings, rallies, and marches. Lastly, Kataristas within the CSUTCB developed a unique historical analysis that reflected the makeup and objectives of the union.

Whereas the MNR had tried to erase indigenous identity and hardline Indianistas promoted a vision of the world in purely ethnic terms, Kataristas rejected the reduction of their struggle to a binary class *or* solely indigenous paradigm. With the rise and consolidation of the Katarismo current in the CSUTCB throughout the 1970s and early 1980s, Kataristas analyzed the world with "two eyes," as early Katarista activist and intellectual Víctor Hugo Cárdenas put it, seeing society both as exploited campesinos, members of the wider oppressed working class of Bolivia, *and* as exploited Aymara peoples, connected to the more than three dozen nations of indigenous peoples in Bolivia.[6] This vision is reflected in the Kataristas' organizing strategies within the union, in their alliance with the COB, and in their political analysis as presented in theses and speeches, accounts that documented their identification with the wider working class as well as their defense of indigenous culture and identity.

Historical consciousness played a critical role within the CSUTCB's road blockade campaigns against a 1979 military coup and subsequent economic austerity package. The power of the past was evident in the extent to which CSUTCB actions leveraged their demands and legitimacy by evoking the centuries-long roots of their struggle in public statements released through newspapers in the midst of blockade efforts. The physical and rhetorical evocation of Katari's 1781 siege was also prominent as the intensity and breadth of the blockades echoed that of the eighteenth-century rebellion. In addition, the CSUTCB's very strategies for conducting road blockades drew explicitly from strategies deployed by Katari.

The CSUTCB's 1983 Political Thesis was a distillation of Katarista thought within the CSUTCB that reflected both the political moment of 1983 in Bolivia and the approaching five-hundred-year anniversary of the start of Spanish colonization. In the thesis as well as in other union proposals for agrarian reform, the CSUTCB looked to a preconquest Andean civilization for agricultural models and political orientation. The union's perception of five hundred years of oppression and resistance served members as a measurement of injustice and a reason to continue the struggle.[7]

INDIGENOUS HISTORY, POLITICS, AND CULTURE IN THE CSUTCB

The Kataristas were at the dawn of a new era after the fall of Banzer in 1978. With Flores at the head of the Confederación Nacional de Trabajadores Campesinos de Bolivia–Túpac Katari (National Confederation of Rural Workers of Bolivia–Túpac Katari, CNTCB-TK), the Katarista movement entered a period of intense growth. At this time, Flores and members of the CNTCB-TK were eager to gain acceptance into the COB for the support, solidarity, and legitimacy the country's largest labor union would offer. The new campesino union had proven itself to be an effective organization clandestinely resisting the Banzer regime, breaking with the PMC, and developing a pro-indigenous, leftist union independent of the state and political parties.[8] Their next step would be broadening their base of support by allying with the COB.

On June 25, 1979, the COB organized the First Congress of Campesino Unity in La Paz to bring together a broad-based campesino union movement. In speeches at the start of the congress, leaders heralded the meeting as a historic move toward the critical unification of the campesino sector.[9] In attendance were thousands of campesino representatives, including those with the Katarista current from Flores's CNTCB-TK; the recently formed Julián Apasa Confederation linked to the Revolutionary Nationalist Party of the Left (MNRI), a leftist splinter party of the MNR; and the Independent Campesino Bloc (BCI), a union representing campesinos within the COB but lacking the level of mass support of the CNTCB-TK.[10]

CSUTCB members gathered at the Fourth National Congress of the CSUTCB in Tarija in July 1989. Photographers: Luis Oporto and Diego Pacheco. Courtesy of the Archivo Central del Museo Nacional de Etnografía y Folklore.

The congress resulted in the establishment of the CSUTCB, a union that brought together all of the various campesino unions around the country. Genaro Flores was elected the executive secretary of the CSUTCB, a position he would hold for nearly ten years. Flores's election, as well as the presence of other Katarista leaders in high positions of the CSUTCB, underlined the union's formation as a victory for the Katarista political project. Though Katari's name was left out of the new union name in order to reflect the broader participation of the national campesino sector, Katari's image remained on much of the group's literature and in the name of the La Paz, Oruro, and Potosí CSUTCB departmental federations.[11]

Small-scale indigenous farmers made up the base of the CSU-TCB, and the union was organized around defending the livelihoods of the campesino sector. Members did so through a mixture of political pressure, direct action, and the development of political proposals and policies that promoted their interests. As its leader, Flores restructured the union so that rural communities could directly elect their union representatives rather than having union leaders imposed from outside by the state, military, or central union hierarchy.[12] In the new CSUTCB, military- and state-appointed union leaders were replaced with democratically elected leaders, a move marking the union's new direction as an independent entity guided by its base.[13]

The CSUTCB also indigenized the COB in the sense that, alongside the standard suits and Western dress of the union meetings and offices, there were now members dressed in ponchos and colorful woven *lluch'u* hats with earflaps. Similarly, indigenous dress became more prominent at the annual May Day rallies in La Paz. One interview I conducted pointed to the meaning and significance of indigenous dress at such gatherings. Ismael Quispe Ticona, a leader in the CSUTCB Túpac Katari Federation in La Paz, was dressed in a poncho and lluch'u himself during our interview at the union's offices, and he explained that "the clothing that we are wearing is our armor, our mandate."[14] He said that each community has its own rules and traditions in terms of dress codes, and that for him, and in his community, each piece of clothing has a practical and symbolic purpose. Beyond protection from the elements, wearing the poncho means that "we embrace all of the bases [community members]," he explained. "It is important to take care of them, because anything can happen." He described other pieces of clothing, including his hat, which is like a "shade" or a "blanket." "Someone can be so sad in their life, a shadow. But [the hat] can alleviate it in this way, brother . . . the hat is going to calm them. Now, the whip [carried by many Aymara leaders] is really to purge the crimes that a person has committed." Regarding the style of dress designated in each community in the department of La Paz, Quispe said, "it is our cape which no one can take from us. No one. It is the respect that we have for the twenty provinces that we

comprise."[15] In rural meetings during the early years of the campesino union, when COB members met with CSUTCB members to discuss their common problems, leaders in local communities in some
cases required COB members to speak in Aymara or Quechua. Such
exchanges underlined the impact that the CSUTCB had in expanding
the indigenous presence physically, symbolically, and culturally within wider union activity.[16]

Indigenous culture was also put on display and celebrated by the
union under Katarista leadership through the internal CSUTCB congresses—crucial moments of gathering for major decision-making,
strategizing, organizational elections, and debates. The congresses,
held in cities on both the regional and national levels, typically began
with a boisterous march through the main streets of the city hosting
the event, with loud music, wiphala flags, drumming, pan flutes, and
the sonorous call of Andean pututo horns.[17] Such marches, historian
Esteban Ticona writes, were a "demonstration of the strength of the
indigenous and campesino movement; in addition to a symbolic idea
of the 'taking of the city by asphalt.'"[18] The taking of the city is a reference to the siege of Katari, a figure who permeated the gatherings.
The CSUTCB congresses' "sieges," although peaceful and symbolic,
embodied the power of the indigenous campesino sector and their
concerns as well as the threat Katari posed to his oppressors, a threat
that lingered in the contemporary consciousness of both indigenous
people and elites in the La Paz region.

As one account written by a visitor to a 1988 CSUTCB congress
relates, "When [congress participants] speak of their future, they
always do it with reference to their past and present. The short and
long memory are constant parameters for delineating a future society."[19] Indeed, in an audio recording of one 1987 CSUTCB congress,
Javier Condoreno, then the executive secretary of the Túpac Katari
Federation of La Paz, referred to the past in his argument for a strong
alliance among members within the union. He explained that the
oppression faced by all congress participants points to the need for
unity in resistance, "because we're an exploited nation, humiliated
and oppressed in our own land. And because of this, today more than
ever, compañeros, we should be conscious of our cultural identity, as
a people, as a nation."[20] Drumming and flute music continued in the

background during Condoreno's speech, as attendees cheered, "Glory to Túpac Katari! Glory to Bartolina Sisa!"[21] At the conclusion of the gathering, one unidentified speaker declared that everyone in Bolivia, from the north to the south, should "hear the cry of organization and resistance, that every one of the extremities of our beloved Túpac Katari are joining together to initiate the liberation march toward the second and definitive independence of Bolivia, to create a multinational fatherland that is free and with justice."[22]

Examples of such speeches appear throughout various audio recordings and videos of the CSUTCB gatherings in the 1980s and 1990s. One collection of audio recordings of the 1990 indigenous March for Territory and Dignity provides a view into the historical discourses that wove through calls for unity among indigenous people. This long march from the lowlands of Bolivia for rights and in defense of indigenous territory eventually culminated in a historic arrival at La Cumbre, a peak outside of La Paz that marks a geographic and symbolic arrival to the Andean highlands. This was where many indigenous groups and CSUTCB leaders from La Paz and the highlands greeted the marchers from the lowlands in a momentous coming together of Bolivia's indigenous nations. The jubilant emotion in participants' voices is clear in the recordings. In the speeches made at the event, there were constant references to unity and, as pututo horns and drums sounded, to the common struggles in over five hundred years of indigenous resistance to Spanish and neocolonial rule. As one CSUTCB leader greeted the marching crowd over a loudspeaker: "Brothers, we have been oppressed for five hundred years, five hundred years of resistance. And now we are reunited, as Aymaras, as Quechua, as Tupi-Guaraníes, in the Republic of Qullasuyu, brothers!" As the snow fell, the march continued to La Paz accompanied by the quickened beat of the drums and blasting horns.[23]

The CSUTCB promoted a unique political and historical analysis that permeated its speeches, demands, and theses, and drew from members' identity as indigenous campesinos. The Katarista method of "seeing with two eyes" as exploited peasants *and* exploited Aymara communities, together with their compañeros in the mines and the Quechua communities in the lowlands, was clearly present in the July 26, 1979, Thesis of the Campesinado that was produced by the

CSUTCB under Flores's leadership.[24] The thesis touts the Kataristas' historic role in the development of the independent union, their fights against military regimes, and their breaking ties with the PMC. The document states that indigenous identity within the campesino union has not been, nor will it be, lost. In the months and years that followed, many of the organization's demands on the state were economic or based on rural production issues. However, the union explained in the thesis that their movement was, at its core, indigenous. As the following passage illustrates, the elevation of both indigenous and working-class identity, without focusing on one at the expense of the other, was essential.

> In this liberation struggle, our personality as aymaras, quechuas, cambas, chapacos, tupi-guaraníes, etc. did not and does not disappear. [Our goal is] to achieve our liberation without losing our cultural and national identity, without being ashamed of what we are, and raising on high the restitution of our dignity. Our struggle is not only economic, but rather also the liberation and development of our oppressed nationalities. We do not believe in race war, nor racism, nor the superiority of races, but we do revindicate our cultural identities. We fight so that there will not be exploitation and also so that, as aymaras, quechuas, cambas, tupi-guaraníes, we will not be oppressed by dominant systems. We want to be free as nationalities.[25]

This argument was a repudiation of the MNR's erasure of indigeneity and an embrace of the intersectional identity of the CSUTCB base as both indigenous and working class. The analysis underlined the pragmatic need for unity with the COB in order to create an organizational body capable of exerting the political force necessary to win radical change.

With the charismatic Flores in the leadership, the CSUTCB pressured the government on behalf of the campesino sector, utilizing a toolbox of grassroots strategies.[26] Using protests, hunger strikes, and road blockades as key tactics, the CSUTCB made demands on the state regarding price controls on agricultural products, access to imported seeds, water rights and management, access to education and loans, transportation assistance, and a general extension of services to the rural sector.[27] Moreover, the CSUTCB called for a comprehensive reconstruction of the failed 1953 Agrarian Reform.[28] Campesino-led sit-ins in the offices of public officials were another common CSUTCB strategy used to gain support and attention. A goal of this approach was that campesinos be involved in the management and execution of public policies and projects directed at rural development. Still, the most popular and successful direct action tactic was the road blockade, which involved a massive level of participation from male and female members. This strategy was used as a last resort and was effective in many cases, either to push for the creation of new government policies or to pressure officials into implementing existing ones.[29]

From its founding and into the mid-1980s, the CSUTCB organized to benefit the campesino sector, conducting direct actions in La Paz and surrounding regions. For example, it called for the firing of corrupt officials at the National Agrarian Reform Agency (who had demanded bribes from campesinos for processing their land titles), successfully prevented the hiring of unqualified people for positions within the Ministry of Agriculture and Peasant Affairs, and pressured authorities in charge of the Tiwanaku archeological site to set aside funds for local communities. Other actions pressured government authorities into providing farming equipment to small communities. The CSUTCB occupied offices to protest various World Bank development projects, criticizing the lack of local participation in the projects or clear benefits for rural communities.[30] Flores said of these tactics: "We were protesting the way past development programs and military dictatorships had excluded our participation and [we] wanted the new democracy to begin rural development anew. The functionaries of these official programs not only had little understanding of life in the countryside, but frequently neither spoke our language nor showed any respect for our cultural practices and traditional way of life. It is no wonder then that the programs were mostly failures."[31]

From its early years, the CSUTCB had allies in the Federación Nacional de Mujeres Campesinas de Bolivia "Bartolina Sisa" (National Federation of Women Rural Workers of Bolivia "Bartolina Sisa," FNMBC-BS). This federation's history runs parallel to the story of the CSUTCB. The organization was formed in 1980 as a sister to the

CSUTCB, and it took up the name of Bartolina Sisa, Túpac Katari's wife, in recognition of her legacy. The Bartolinas, as they typically referred to themselves, were wed to the structure and activity of the CSUTCB from the beginning; the women's group operated "in the shadow" of the larger union.[32] Flores was an early proponent of forming a women's federation. The resolutions from the first Bartolinas national meeting in 1980 called for broader women's participation in politics and union activity, protested abuses and injustices against campesina women, and demanded access to better education, health care, and basic services for rural communities.[33] Such demands echoed the fundamental concerns of the CSUTCB to address poverty and the lack of services and political representation for the indigenous rural sector.[34]

Bartolina Sisa Federation leader Sabina Choquetillja speaks at a CSUTCB congress in Potosí on November 7, 1988. Photographers: Luis Oporto, Diego Pacheco, and Roberto Balza. Courtesy of the Archivo Central del Museo Nacional de Etnografía y Folklore.

The Bartolinas positioned themselves as heirs to Sisa's struggle. As the historical analysis of one of the group's foundational documents declared, women "were the most utilized" throughout these centuries of oppression. "Now we find ourselves in the 502nd year of forced colonization," they stated, "but at this time we are conscious of our rights."[35] As with the CSUTCB, members of the Bartolinas who traveled to rural communities to organize their bases recalled the hold Sisa's story had on campesina women. "Because of this, in some provinces they already considered us [union leaders] as the second [reincarnated] Bartolinas who wanted to restart the struggle," one leader recalled.[36]

Some described the Bartolinas' vision of equality between men and women as representative of the Andean concept of *chachawarmi*. As Bartolinas leader Bertha Blanco explained, this term refers to the participation of both men and women alongside each other in the struggle. For the Bartolinas, Katari and Sisa were an example of this concept. Within this vision, Blanco explains, "the woman does not just stay in the kitchen, or just take care of the family—though this as well—but she is also someone who has ideological principles of struggle, of dignity and identity."[37] She said this philosophy was passed down from her ancestors as part of the ethics of "living well" and a "political path of equality, equity, and reciprocity, in which we all grow. Where it's not just a few leaving others behind, but all of us moving forward together."[38]

However, the hegemony of the CSUTCB was evident in recordings of early Bartolinas conferences, where men from the CSUTCB often took over the mic to berate the women in condescending tones about their lack of organization and unprofessionalism as leaders.[39] Contemporary Bartolinas leader Anselma Perlacios commented in a 2014 interview that, in the early years, "the men didn't give sufficient space to the women."[40] Even as they negotiated for fair space and just treatment, the Bartolinas formed an essential arm of the CTSUCB, organizing food and childcare but also maintaining road blockades and adding voices to the organization's demands. The Bartolinas' incarnation of Sisa complemented the CSUTCB's adoption of Katari as their hero. Together, Sisa and Katari symbolized archetypal ancestors whose heroic legacy of resistance was the birthright of movement participants and who union members of both sexes could aspire to emulate.

THE POWER OF THE PAST IN CSUTCB ROAD BLOCKADES

CSUTCB members march in Tarija during the Fourth National Congress of the CSUTCB in July 1989. Photographers: Luis Oporto, Diego Pacheco, and Roberto Balza. Courtesy of the Archivo Central del Museo Nacional de Etnografía y Folklore.

The CSUTCB took to the streets almost immediately after its 1979 founding, mobilizing itself as a union with militant grassroots support representing the indigenous campesino majority. The organization's effectiveness would be put to the test that same year while resisting another military coup and economic policies that assaulted campesinos' livelihoods.

Historical consciousness strengthened campesinos' actions in one critical CSUTCB road blockade campaign against the short-lived military coup of Colonel Natusch Busch in November 1979. During these efforts in the town of Sullkawi, in the province of Aroma, women took charge of the blockades in shifts by day, and the men by night, as blockade participant Lucila Mejía recalled. This rotation allowed some residents to take care of the children and prepare food while others stood their ground on the highway. The social pressure to participate was intense, Mejía explained. If residents of the community refused to engage in the rotational blockade maintenance, they were labeled traitors and ostracized from the community.[41]

Sullkawi was in an important geographical position due to the heavy use of the area's highways and the threat of repression from Busch's military regime. "When the danger [of military intervention] increased, we placed a sentinel on a nearby hill. They alerted us with dynamite," Mejía said. "When the explosion signaled us to action, we ran out from all directions to occupy the road." Activists were well aware of the recent government repression during the Massacre of the Valley in Tolata, and fear coursed throughout their ranks. During periods of heightened risk, the children were kept away from the barricades, and the men and women worked together. "In this way, we shared the danger," Mejía noted.[42]

Throughout their maintenance of the blockade, the activists were inspired by stories they told one another about past rebellions. "At night we had our meetings. In the dark, we remembered other blockades. In 1974 only Raimundo Tambo, Daniel Calle, Antonio Quispe were the storytellers, because they knew," Mejía said. But during this action, there were "radio programs which even the children listen[ed] to. This is why we remembered Túpac Katari, Zárate Willka, and others. This took away our fears. Because the planes can fly overhead, and the swindlers can only come and go, but we are always here."[43]

In a 1990 interview, Mejía affirmed that the participation of women in this blockade was critical. However, she recalled that more was demanded of the women than the men. Speaking of her experience during this blockade campaign, she explained, "We campesina women participated actively day and night, we worked as guards at night, we brought [supplies] to our compañeros, and not so much [was brought] to the women." The men had the support of the women, for food and reinforcements, she explained, but the women did not enjoy the same backing from the men. "So, with our babies, we lined up on the road," Mejía said, "and we fought that way."[44]

The sharing of stories of resistance around the Sullkawi barricades points to the power of the past in the 1979 campaigns. In its

efforts against military regimes and harmful economic policies, the
CSUTCB deployed historical consciousness as a tool in building
morale among its members, in leveraging its demands and legitimacy,
in evoking Katari's siege during blockade campaigns, and in deploy-
ing the blockade itself.

Road blockades and strikes orchestrated by the COB and
CSUTCB were critical to ending the short-lived military coup of Colonel Busch, which lasted from November 1 to November 16, 1979,
during which time the CSUTCB quickly proved itself to be a capable
force through its resistance.[45] Their blockades, coordinated through
the alliance with the COB forged just months earlier, were critical to
Busch's downfall and highlighted the importance of the CSUTCB's
collaboration with the COB in the wider struggle for democracy in
Bolivia. The CSUTCB historically contextualized its protest within the written demands it placed on Busch.[46] In a public statement
released by the CSUTCB parallel to its road blockade campaign,
the union embraced Katarista historical consciousness to leverage
its proposals and defend its legitimacy. The union's statement, published in a newspaper in the midst of the blockade efforts, demanded
that Busch step down, but the union notably devoted the first half of
the statement to establishing its struggle within the longer arc of history since the Spanish conquest. The authors of the statement named
Busch in the list of their "long memory" of colonial and neocolonial
governments that had negated indigenous identity and attempted to
"destroy our customs and our millennial culture, for the sole crime of
being authentically American."[47]

This attempt to demonstrate the CSUTCB's legitimacy as a representative of the historically oppressed, original inhabitants of the
Andes was coupled to a Katarista analysis "with two eyes," shown in
the authors' denunciation of the exploitation suffered by workers in
the mines, in the factories, and on haciendas. Such abuse was met,
they write, with constant resistance as the collective experience of suffering among workers accumulated. "The past and present sufferings,
the blood we have spilled yesterday as we do today, the oppression
itself, have been the fecund fertilizer in which our class consciousness
has germinated and matured."[48] The CSUTCB allied with the COB
to carry on the historic struggle against the yoke of colonialism and

labor exploitation. Their united fight against economic and cultural oppression was expressed in this political moment in their resistance to Busch, with strikes in the mines to cripple export earnings and road blockades to halt transportation of all kinds. In the end, their combined resistance forced the downfall of the regime.[49]

Following Busch's departure, the CSUTCB and its members faced disastrous economic policies enacted by the dictator's successor. Parliament president and MNR party member Lidia Gueiler became Bolivia's interim president. In December 1979 she enacted austerity measures encouraged by the International Monetary Fund and decreed by Busch, and their impact on the campesino sector was severe.[50] The policies froze the prices of basic foodstuffs produced and sold by campesinos while simultaneously raising the price of gas and transportation costs. The CSUTCB protested the measure with widely coordinated road blockades, and the COB organized a two-day strike in solidarity.[51] On December 3, the CSUTCB sent a letter to President Gueiler listing their demands, which included having direct control over the prices and distribution of their agricultural products in order to eliminate costly intermediaries, state funding for technical support and training for farmers, increased funding and credit reserved for the campesino sector, the distribution of land for collective ownership and labor through the CSUTCB, lower transportation costs for agricultural products, and more direct involvement from campesinos in rural development projects.[52] As Bolivia scholar Xavier Albó writes, the CSUTCB's fundamental, unspoken demand was "to have the peasants respected and listened to in reality, as first-class citizens."[53]

Historical consciousness played a notable role in the CSUTCB's rhetoric and actions during the road blockade campaign. The blockades were a response to economic measures that disproportionately affected the campesino sector because of their impact on agricultural product prices and rural transportation costs. For the CSUTCB, the measures pointed to the government's continuing neglect of the campesino sector. The length and intensity of the road blockade raised the specter of Katari's siege among elites, and the union publicly positioned its efforts as a reenactment of Katari's revolt. In fact, the CSUTCB explicitly used Katari's strategies in its blockades.

In its efforts and demands, the CSUTCB made it clear that the economic package it protested was just another sign that the Bolivian government was not concerned with the campesino sector. At an enormous
demonstration of COB and CSUTCB members in the central Plaza
San Francisco in La Paz on December 4, 1979, speakers denounced the
government's austerity measures and pledged their commitment to the
struggle.[54] To the gathered masses, Flores expressed the CSUTCB's
view that "the campesinos are the most exploited, and those who suffer
the most with the latest measures," leading them to deploy a blockade.[55]
In the community of Rio Abajo outside of La Paz, where some thirteen
road blockades were being maintained by local campesinos, CSUTCB
members denounced the low prices set for their goods, which, in this
particular area, included onions, corn, potatoes, cherries, and apples.
Transportation costs had risen, in some cases more than doubling since
the application of Gueiler's economic package.[56] According to one
blockader speaking to the press, the government had forgotten that
the campesinos existed at all, "and one more time, they think that we,
the campesinos, do not need to eat."[57]

The anger of CSUTCB members was matched only by the fear
their blockades inspired among political elites. The physical presence
of the CSUTCB road blockade evoked the memory of Katari's siege
for both blockaders and the blockaded. The CSUTCB coordinated
local affiliates in each department in order to block some thirty roads,
bringing the country to a standstill for a week in what was considered
to be the largest campesino uprising since the National Revolution.[58]
Communication between road blockade participants was maintained
through locally run low-power radio stations, on which broadcasters
used indigenous languages alongside Spanish.[59]

With transportation and the flow of the goods blocked by the
campesinos, major Bolivian cities were literally cut off from the rest
of the world. In addition, dozens of tourists were stranded by the
CSUTCB blockades in Copacabana, a town on the shores of Lake
Titicaca. The drama of the stranded tourists was widely sensational-
ized and reported on by the Bolivian press. The focus on the tourists
trapped by the CSUTCB siege further emphasized the motif of the
indigenous masses rising up against creole elites, in the style of Katari
against the Spanish. When the Red Cross and media asked Flores to

stop the blockades because the travelers had been waiting to leave the town for four days, he replied defiantly, "We have been waiting for four hundred years!"[60] The road blockades also created a notable response in La Paz. Residents in middle- and upper-class neighborhoods in the south of La Paz organized armed defense units to protect themselves from the indigenous protests. Silvia Rivera writes, "What greater evidence of the profound colonial attitude of creoles toward the Indian, than this show of subconscious collective memory trapped in the recollection of the siege of Katari, Willka, and other Indian rebels!"[61]

The legacy of Katari in the road blockade effort was also raised by the CSUTCB in its communiqués. Roughly a week after the action began, the CSUTCB announced a temporary lifting of the blockades during which goods could be transported and the union could negotiate with the government. The communiqué, issued by the CSUTCB leadership to the various road blockades around the country and printed on the front page of the Bolivian newspaper *Presencia*, called for the suspension of the blockades and celebrated the historic nature of the mobilization, linking the struggle to the rebellion of Katari. The revolt, the communiqué explained, was "a new expression of the great struggle for the emancipation of the great national majorities, initiated with the magnificent uprising of Julián Apaza Tupaj Katari in 1781 in order to achieve the liberation of the campesino class and do away with the exploitation that today the privileged minorities subject us to."[62] The CSUTCB road blockades highlighted the union's massive organizational strength and bound its present political struggle to Katari's eighteenth-century rebellion.

In modern-day Bolivia, road blockades remain a key tactic of social movements to force demands on the government. The highway system of Bolivia has historically been very limited, with only roughly 10 percent of the country's roads paved even today; until the 1990s not a single paved road left the nation, so blocking key routes could bring the country to a standstill for weeks.[63] To maintain road blockades over long periods of time against the pressure of the police, military, and bus and truck drivers required a high level of organization. In the highland region surrounding La Paz, nothing evokes the memory of Katari's siege more than a road blockade that circles the city.

According to various CSUTCB leaders, contemporary blockades drew from Katari's techniques and philosophies. "We all know very well that Túpac Katari organized a siege of La Paz," Máximo Freddy Huarachi Paco of the CSUTCB told me in a 2015 interview.[64] "It's the same with us," he explained. "Our weapon is the blockade and hunger strikes, and we always think, in whatever meeting, in whatever gathering having to do with revindicating our interests, we are always talking about strategies that our legendary Túpac Katari and Bartolina Sisa have created." He referenced different contemporary road blockade strategies such as the "plan *quti*," involving moving blockades quickly from one place on the road to the next, and the "plan *taraxchi*," deployed to surround a city with blockades. "Therefore, these kinds of strategies came from our ancestors; no one has brought [us] this kind of strategy, neither from the West nor from anyone."[65]

During moments of insurrection, Katari's legacy took on new meaning and relevance. Felipe Quispe, a former leader of the CSUTCB, explained that blockades rely on memory. He elaborated on techniques used to sustain effective blockades day and night. "The plan *taraxchi* was to invade the cities," Quispe writes, speaking of besieging the cities from the highlands, "entering the cities and taking political power."[66] The call would be sent by leaders through various radio stations to thousands of men and women "so that they would gather near the cities, and, in this way, surround and strangle them." A living memory of historical figures was critical for movement leaders and members in such moments. "Tupaj Katari has educated us, has disciplined us, and Zárate Willka has taught us to take the most honest, most revolutionary, most Aymara, most Qhechua route, and this is the route that we are now taking," Quispe writes.[67] By applying such models in periods of rebellion, the CSUTCB proved itself to be a powerful force in the political landscape of the 1970s and 1980s.

"HUNGER DOESN'T WAIT":
THE CSUTCB AND THE RETURN TO DEMOCRACY

The indigenous sector's anger was palpable on August 2, 1984, Bolivia's annual Indian Day. The date had been celebrated with renewed meaning in the country since the 1953 passage of the MNR's Agrarian Reform. Yet on that August 2, the plazas of the city of Cochabamba were empty. The campesinos of the region declared they had nothing to celebrate. Instead of embracing the legacy of the National Revolution's 1953 Agrarian Reform, campesinos called for an overhaul of the agrarian system, and they demanded as much through road blockades.[68] Bolivia as a whole was experiencing a painful transition back to democracy in the early 1980s. After the progressive Democratic and Popular Union party (UDP) democratically won elections, General Luís García Meza Tejada, who made his career during the Banzerato, led a military coup against the government on July 17, 1980. The regime targeted the wider Left, violently repressing campesino and labor union leaders. García Meza's regime took its lead from the stridently anticommunist Argentine military junta (1976–1983), utilizing paramilitaries and death squads to kidnap, torture, and disappear people as a way to intimidate and silence any opposition, and it was effective in momentarily crushing the Left. García Meza and his interior minister, Luis Arce Gómez, publicly sought the tutelage of former Nazi Klaus Barbie, known as the Butcher of Lyon, and others involved in Italian neofascism to train Bolivian death and torture squads.[69] Washington punished García Meza's government with a fifteen-month boycott, which contributed to the overall decay of the administration as it simultaneously faced a severe fiscal crisis and political disarray.[70]

When García Meza's crackdown on dissidents first focused on urban areas, protests from miners and campesinos flared up far from major city limits. Resistance was particularly fierce around the highland mines of Potosí and Oruro, where workers, armed with dynamite and rifles and with support from the CSUTCB, pushed the army back on numerous occasions. On June 21, 1981, Genaro Flores was shot by García Meza's hit squads. Pressure from Amnesty International and the French government helped to keep him safe, but the García Meza government sent him into exile in critical condition, delaying necessary surgery and leaving him to use a wheelchair for the rest of his life. The injury did not stop Flores from his near-constant union work, and it elevated him as a martyr in the eyes of supporters.[71] Indeed, when Flores returned to Bolivia from exile in 1982, he tied his own martyrdom to that of Katari: "I have returned to continue the struggle of our people and to follow in the footsteps of Túpac Katari."[72] Resistance in the streets and internal divisions within the government deepened, and, to avoid a civil war, the Catholic Church fostered a dialogue that facilitated García Meza's departure from power on August 4, 1981.[73] However, two military regimes linked to García Meza followed the dictatorship. General Celso Torrelio Villa and General Guido Vildoso Calderón held power until October 1982, when protests orchestrated by the COB contributed to their downfall. The Bolivian Congress that had been democratically elected in 1980 then reconvened to choose a president, and it quickly elected the National Revolution leader Hernán Siles Zuazo as president and Jaime Paz Zamora of the UDP as vice president. At this time, Siles was a part of the Revolutionary Nationalist Party of the Left (MNRI), the left wing of the MNR.[74]

The military's power was neutralized and democracy had returned. Siles Zuazo sought alliances with the COB, the CSUTCB, and other leftist party leaders—a great relief to a sector that had been facing ongoing state repression for over a decade. Siles quickly dismantled the vestiges of dictatorship, ridding the military of authoritarian leaders, and deporting Argentine and German officials involved in the García Meza regime.[75] When the new president took office, crowds welcoming him booed any military official present at the event. Siles assumed the presidency to applause, as he had in 1952. The historic significance of the returning National Revolution leader was evident, as it evoked the still-potent memory of the revolution and its ideals.[76] The moment held particular importance for the CSUTCB, which saw Siles's presidency as a crucial opening in which the union could leverage its demands.

After overthrowing military regimes in 1977, 1979, and 1982, the wider Left, including the COB and the CSUTCB, had high expectations for their leftist ally in power.[77] Hope surged as unions, civil society groups, and others on the left made many demands on the government. Such union and civil activity was reflected in the high level of strikes and protests from 1982 to 1985.[78] The democratic opening and possibilities perceived by social movements led the

CSUTCB to pressure the government for agrarian reform. However, Siles struggled with a failing economy and could not enact sufficient changes to placate the demands from the streets. Though civilian rule had returned, Bolivia's economy was in crisis in the early 1980s. At the start of the decade, the ever-important tin industry dropped into a serious decline from which it would never recover. Economic growth in the early 1980s declined by an average of 2.3 percent per year (compared with an average increase of 4.7 percent per year in the 1970s), and inflation skyrocketed at 1,969 percent annually.[79] In his second presidency, Siles proved to be inept at political and economic leadership. Infighting and a lack of consensus dominated his relationships with other politicians, parties, and unions. His economic policies were uneven and ineffective, and his inability to create a strong political front led him to call for early elections in 1985.[80]

In addition to the economic crisis, the altiplano, spanning from La Paz to Oruro and Potosí and home to the base of the CSUTCB, suffered a terrible drought in 1983, the worst seen in the highlands in a century. The situation was so severe that water had to be transported by train to Potosí. Small farmers bore the crisis acutely as the drought ruined both harvests and the soil quality for future crops. The government's inability to confront this crisis in the countryside underlined the ongoing challenges facing campesinos in spite of the return to democracy. The main avenue for campesinos seeking solutions to such calamity was the CSUTCB.[81] In response to the economic crisis and the lack of government support for campesino communities devastated by the drought, the CSUTCB organized eighteen major road blockade efforts between 1982 and 1984, demanding support, services, and a direct role in rural development projects.[82]

While Siles tried to help Bolivia weather the economic crisis, the CSUTCB pressured his administration from the countryside. From April 22 to 26, 1983, in the midst of the drought, a CSUTCB blockade campaign was launched to protest the government's inaction. The CSUTCB stated that the roots of the crisis lay with the rural policies of the Banzer and García Meza regimes, but a lack of attention from the Siles administration forced their union back into the streets.[83] CSUTCB blockaders said they were tired of being ignored by the government and that "hunger doesn't wait, due to the disaster of the drought in the altiplano." In this case, the CSUTCB's familiar list of demands included fair prices for their products, loans and financial support, participation in rural development projects, basic services such as electricity, and land distribution to small farmers. Flores told the government that a solution to the crisis was in their hands, and he again situated the CSUTCB's efforts within a larger struggle spanning centuries: "Since 1825, all the governments have offered solutions to the campesino, but they have never put them in place."[84]

It was in the midst of this agricultural, economic, and political crisis that the CSUTCB produced its 1983 Political Thesis. The document reflects the concerns of the day. It also responds to a longer view of history, encompassing not just the political moment of 1983 but five hundred years of oppression and resistance. Indeed, a dominant argument running through the thesis holds that for much of the rural indigenous majority—then facing disastrous drought, government neglect, political turmoil, and recovery from over a decade of military rule—many of the basic oppressive elements of colonialism remained intact.[85]

The CSUTCB's 1983 Political Thesis is a fifteen-page document outlining the history, struggle, objectives, and political beliefs of the indigenous campesino movement.[86] The thesis provides an account of Andean history, calls for updating the Agrarian Reform of 1953, and promotes the indigenous cultures of Bolivia. The process of developing and ratifying this thesis involved various steps. The document that first placed these ideas together within the framework of the independent campesino union was the Political Thesis of March 1978, which was created at the Seventh National Congress of the CNTCB-TK, then under the leadership of Flores. The document was further discussed and ratified at the First Congress of Campesino Unity, organized by the COB in La Paz in June 1979. The 1983 Political Thesis discussed below was debated, revised, corrected, and expanded at the Second National Congress of the CSUTCB, which took place in June 1983.[87] Approximately four thousand delegates from all departments of the country gathered for the 1983 meeting to ratify the thesis. Participants produced the final version collectively, after a week of meetings. The document defines itself as "the result of the concern, work, and discussion of the campesino workers."[88]

Two elements of the thesis stand out for their allegiance to the Katarista current in the CSUTCB: the first is the use of a preconquest civilization as a source of orientation and legitimacy, and the second is drawing on an indigenous, as opposed to strictly working class-oriented, historical analysis of the centuries of indigenous oppression and resistance in order to highlight injustice and embolden the CSUTCB's struggle.

This political proposal holds that the preconquest Andean civilization was destroyed through colonial oppression. The CSUTCB defined its political program in relation to the rescue of this civilization, with the goal of rebuilding it in the present. As the document explains, "Before the arrival of the Spanish, we were [a] communitarian people. In our land, hunger, robbery and lies were not known."[89] This vision of a past utopia is both a compass and a legitimizing claim for the CSUTCB, whose members are framed as the rightful heirs of their land and as qualified to carry on the promise and work of rebuilding this lost society. "These great civilizations developed high levels of knowledge and productivity in the fields of agriculture, livestock, in engineering projects, goldsmithing, the textile industry and metallurgy." After the conquest, the thesis states, such knowledge was destroyed or ignored. "For that reason, it is necessary to recuperate and refresh these scientific understandings, combining them with modern technological advances to construct a highly productive society, but without hunger or exploitation." The task at hand is therefore to "adapt and renovate our methods of struggle, without losing [touch with] the continuity of our historical roots."[90]

For the CSUTCB, just as the model of a preconquest civilization endured into the present, so too did certain systems of oppression suffered by the indigenous majority. The thesis thus covers the colonial exploitation of indigenous people and their forced labor in the mines, all of which "fractured our society." The revolts of 1781 are highlighted as "demonstrating that the colonial power was not invincible," yet gaining independence from Spain "did not have any benefit for us." The thesis dismisses the customary nationalist, heroic treatment of creoles in charge of the Republican government, describing them as figures who constructed "only . . . the caricature of a republic, maintaining the colonial structures and the same relationships of exploitation and oppression." The authors cite the examples of the tribute taxes indigenous communities were forced to pay and the extension of the *latifundio* system, which took over indigenous lands and forced indigenous people into servitude.[91] The thesis describes the victories and pitfalls of the National Revolution, the PMC, and the Katarista struggle for an independent union. It celebrates Katarista sacrifices in the struggle against Banzer and other military regimes, and the fight for a return to democracy as part of the longer history of the union that became the CSUTCB.[92]

Katarista thought, distilled in this document, had already been put into action by CSUTCB members in their road blockades, political proposals, and activism. In their speeches, communiqués, lists of demands, and public statements, the CSUTCB leaders employed their unique "two-eyed" style of historical and political analysis. Leaders and members placed their struggle not just in the contemporary political moment, against the nightmares of dictators and droughts, but also within a longer struggle that spanned centuries. As the CSUTCB explained in their 1983 thesis, "We are heirs of great civilizations. We are also heirs to permanent struggles against any kind of exploitation and oppression."[93]

Such historical recovery was evident in a subsequent document produced by the CSUTCB: the 1984 Fundamental Agrarian Law. The final version of this proposed law, which highlights past indigenous agricultural and labor practices, was passed in the 1984 CSUTCB national congress in Cochabamba.[94] Echoing the tone of the CSUTCB's 1983 thesis, the document frames its proposals in historical terms: "The indigenous communities are those that since time immemorial occupy lands in the geographic space that constitutes the Bolivian State, living in accordance to their uses, customs, and common law norms."[95] The proposal stresses indigenous traditions of communal labor and land use, explaining that work management in rural communities involves "rescuing their ancestral traditions of reciprocity, redistribution and economic complementarity in a way that gives space to their own forms of agricultural, fishing, artisanal and industrial productive development for the benefit of all their members."[96]

An integral part of this vision is a strengthening of communal bonds and cooperation; caring for the land, forests, and rivers; and empowering communitarian labor and governance.[97] Though the proposal was not ultimately accepted by the government, the document provides a window into the CSUTCB recovery of indigenous traditions and historical consciousness in its vision for rural and agrarian policies. Many of the same proposals in this CSUTCB document would be taken up by the ayllu reconstitution efforts in the 1990s.

The CSUTCB, from its founding through the first intense years of its activity, used historical consciousness as a tool in its organizing efforts. In seeing the world "with two eyes" and promoting indigenous identity and culture, leaders and participants expanded the political horizons of their movement. In evoking Katari's siege both physically and symbolically, the CSUTCB deepened the impact and legitimacy of its blockade efforts. By basing its militancy in a historical view that reached back to a preconquest civilization and indigenous resistance movements spanning centuries, the CSUTCB developed a political project that would orient the campesino and indigenous movements for years to come.

CHAPTER FOUR

THE ANDEAN ORAL HISTORY WORKSHOP

Producing Indigenous People's Histories in Bolivia

Indigenous leader Andrés Jach'aqullu (standing) shares oral histories on the caciques apoderados movement with the THOA in La Paz in 1990. Courtesy of the Andean Oral History Workshop.

At the top of a winding street in La Paz, heading up from the city's downtown toward El Alto, lies an inconspicuous brick building that, at first glance, is exactly like most of the others in this working-class neighborhood. A small metal sign reads: Taller de Historia Oral Andina (Andean Oral History Workshop, THOA). Behind the doors of the building are the organization's offices, libraries, archives, and meeting rooms. A vast mural depicting the altiplano covers one wall, and bags of coca sit on the long table where the THOA holds its meetings. This is the headquarters of a grassroots research group that sought to create an alternative to the standard Bolivian historiography by tapping into the wellspring of oral history in indigenous communities. Founded in 1983, the THOA was formed by nearly a dozen indigenous activist-scholars and still operates to this day.[1] The founders and early members were professors and students at the public Universidad Mayor de San Andrés (UMSA) in La Paz. The majority of the members were indigenous people who had recently migrated from the rural highlands to La Paz for studies. In discussions and readings of Bolivian history, founding members encountered a void when it came to indigenous people's history and sought to correct this by producing histories of indigenous resistance, using oral history as their primary source.

Alongside the resurgent indigenous movements of the period, the THOA challenged prevailing intellectual currents in the university and embraced oral history as a tool for the reconstruction of silenced and fragmented indigenous histories. In both its theory and methodology, the THOA broke new ground in historical research in Bolivia. The THOA's political and social commitment to recovering and promoting indigenous culture and history was reflected in the organization's research, production, and distribution. Not only did its work throughout the 1980s and beyond make use of new research techniques and strategies for gathering oral history, but it also created a previously absent historiography on the majority of the country's people and contributed to transforming historical consciousness in Bolivia.

THOA member Felipe Santos Quispe outlines the organization's intellectual program: "The central objective of the institution framed itself in the accompaniment and empowerment of the indigenous communities, based on the strengthening of indigenous identity through the investigation, dissemination [of the histories], formation [of researchers], and education [based on the histories produced]. The THOA generated a space of reflection on and analysis of hot-button issues about national needs and the indigenous communities. Lastly, the community recuperated the organic model of reciprocity in relation with the communities. This made it easier to implement the oral history method in interactive investigations."[2]

The THOA collected oral histories primarily in rural Aymara communities and complemented this material with archival research to produce booklets and radio programs on indigenous histories of Bolivia. With this work, they filled in the public silences surrounding indigenous pasts, rebels, and uprisings, and in so doing, they strengthened historical consciousness and self-awareness among Bolivia's indigenous people. Many of the THOA's members were from the same rural communities in which they gathered and synthesized histories. In these cases, the act of conducting historical research was, in a sense, one of self-investigation. Researchers worked alongside the communities and developed a process in which the interviewees set up the parameters of the interview, the research, and the historical production.

The THOA's work can be best understood alongside efforts at about the same time by the Kataristas and CSUTCB to use anticolonial indigenous history for political purposes. Protagonists in these currents recuperated and distributed indigenous history to indigenous and working-class Bolivians through unions, speeches, protests, manifestos, and monuments to Katari. Similarly, the THOA promoted the history and cause of the previously unknown caciques apoderados movement of the early twentieth century, the role of women in indigenous movements, and the revitalization of indigenous community politics and identity.

The THOA's work has an important place in the landscape of indigenous organizing in Bolivia during the 1980s. Its historiographical efforts rippled throughout the consciousness of CSUTCB leaders and members. For example, the THOA helped spread awareness about the struggle of Santos Marka T'ula, a key leader of the caciques apoderados indigenous movement. The caciques apoderados were elected by their communities to represent them in the political and legal fight to defend land rights in the face of hacienda expansions. As the early THOA member, UMSA history professor, and Aymara scholar Carlos Mamani wrote in 1989, "Until just a few years ago, the name of Santos Marka T'ula was practically ignored, even in the community and province where he was born. Today the provincial campesino syndical federation carries his name and they are contemplating the possibility of changing the current name of the province [from Gualberto Villarroel] to that of Marka T'ula."[3] Indeed, to this day T'ula's name is regularly referenced alongside Katari and Willka in campesino union and leftist politicians' speeches, a testament to the success of the THOA's work. One of the most notable and lasting impacts of the THOA on the country's indigenous movement was its critical role in the formation of the CONAMAQ, a national ayllu network.

The THOA's emergence onto the sociopolitical scene in the early 1980s was part of a national shift toward indigenous organizing and politics. While activists fought in the streets to change the course of history, the THOA produced indigenous histories and transformed the way the country's indigenous majority saw themselves, their past, and their future in the nation they wanted to rebuild.

Through the collection of oral histories, the THOA sought to recover the silenced indigenous past of the Andes.[4] Members saw the Spanish conquest and colonialism of the Americas as forces that destroyed and fragmented indigenous history. For Carlos Mamani, the long duration of colonialism inflicted a political, economic, and social trauma on indigenous Bolivians, a trauma that fractured people's historical memory and consciousness, relegating Aymara history to the underground. "From this moment [of conquest]," Mamani writes in a booklet on the methods the THOA used in its research, "our historical memory was destined to survive clandestinely and to manifest itself in myths and oral traditions." Oral history provided a way to weave together the indigenous histories fractured and displaced by colonialism and neocolonialism, and to rescue indigenous history, and therefore identity, from imminent disappearance. "If we do not care to know our own history and to recuperate our own historical destiny, very soon the aymaras, quichwas, urus, guaranís will be converted into museum artifacts," Mamani writes.[5]

The THOA's publications were widely distributed to rural areas and had a direct political and social impact. In the early years, member-investigators used their research to create short and inexpensively produced works for distribution in rural communities. Themes included histories of indigenous rebels of the early twentieth century, women's avenues of resistance in indigenous movements, the history of the ayllu, a collection of important dates in Bolivian history on resistance and oppression, popular indigenous traditions, and children's stories set in rural Aymara communities.

The THOA also organized radio programs and public discussions that brought debates on indigenous culture and politics out of the university and into the wider public, in La Paz and rural highland communities. Beyond its publications and radio shows, the THOA organized groundbreaking cultural events in university spaces where, for the first time, academic debaters spoke publicly and intentionally in Aymara and, instead of wine, shared coca leaves in the communal act of *acullicu*, the ritual "chewing" of coca. THOA publications were available in Spanish but, most notably, were also published in Aymara and Quechua, a move that was rare at the time for history publications.[6]

The THOA's work was ubiquitous in the communities in which it worked. In 1993, rural community members reported to external investigator Virginia Ayllon that THOA publications were accessible, useful, and widely read.[7] The impact of the THOA's work is easy to measure. Traces of its research and historical production can be found across the Bolivian political and intellectual landscape today. From its recovery of the life and actions of Santos Marka T'ula to the pathbreaking publication on ayllu history and reconstruction that served the CONAMAQ so well in later years, the THOA, more than any other historical research organization in the country at the time, made lasting contributions to the indigenous cause in Bolivia.

The THOA emerged from a period in which indigenous organizations challenged the state's racist and assimilationist policies. Such a shift was reflected in the country's universities, where Aymara students and committed professors promoted discussions and research methods to elevate indigenous history and culture. The creation of the THOA began in the halls of one of the country's most important public universities, the UMSA. Located in the very center of downtown La Paz, on the city's main street, the UMSA has long been a site of student protests and organizing. In the early 1980s, a new generation of indigenous students and professors sought to promote and research indigenous histories of Bolivia.

The THOA was a generational expression of the influx of indigenous students from rural parts of the country into the university system. These heirs of the educational reforms of the 1952 National Revolution found allies among indigenous university professors. The seeds of the THOA were planted in the classrooms where indigenous issues were newly included in the curricula and openly discussed. Indigenous professors and students addressed what they saw as the ongoing colonization of Bolivia and found indigenous histories that existed on the margins of society, in the oral testimonies and archival fragments of this past that remained.

SHIFTS IN ACADEMIA AND THE STREETS

The cover of the 1986 THOA publication *Mujer y resistencia comunaria: Historia y memoria*. This work includes testimonies from Quechua and Aymara women on their participation in indigenous uprisings. Courtesy of the Andean Oral History Workshop.

The THOA challenged the dominant intellectual currents in the university with its emphasis on indigenous histories and world-views. Just as Bolivian governments and elite intellectuals in previous decades had subjugated or erased indigenous culture and identity from depictions and discussions of the country's historical narrative and social landscape, many professors' dominant Marxist analyses in university classrooms of the 1980s sidelined the lived experiences and dynamic culture that indigenous students carried with them to the university. UMSA sociology professor, activist, and THOA cofounder Silvia Rivera remarks that questions of neocolonialism and indigeneity were pushed aside in the university by a Marxist approach that considered everything in narrow class terms. Rivera contextualizes the university and political setting in which the THOA was created: "We [the THOA] were in a context in which we left the dictatorship, the university went back to having its autonomy, but still I saw a very strong, let's say Marxist, hegemony."[8] This analysis perceived as "primitive" the communities from which many indigenous students came. Rivera elaborates on the implications of this trend in the university and in Bolivian society at large: "Theory and social investigation served to cover up new paternalistic and colonial practices facing the ethnic question, [and] the leftist elites, with their roots in Western creole culture, had a strictly instrumental vision of the ethnic demands: they were useful only as long as they would not autonomize the popular mobilization controlled by the Left."[9]

In the early 1980s, groups of women, youth, and, most importantly here, indigenous Andeans contested this view. At a time when indigenous issues were not widely discussed in the classroom, an influx of Aymara students brought other perspectives to the mix. Their views were oriented by their roots in rural Bolivia and the memory of their communities and ancestors.[10] Such indigenous histories and shared experiences converged in UMSA classrooms, leading to the creation of the THOA.

Rivera explains that as they worked for self-determination and rights, indigenous movements also reclaimed their "right to generate their own ideological and political systematizations, displacing the role of intermediaries assumed by the intellectuals and social scientists of diverse disciplines."[11] Such political mobilizations demanded a rethinking of anthropological methods and research approaches practiced by academics regarding indigenous people and culture. This shift, Rivera writes, came "thanks to the fact that Indian mobilizations and organizations assumed a growing and critical control in the face of the researchers' and leftist politicians' attempts at instrumentalization [of their movements]."[12]

The THOA fused the demands, ideologies, and organizational strategies of the new indigenous movements with a historical research approach that placed the power of investigation into the hands of the indigenous subjects themselves. Rivera writes, "Obviously, the emphasis on history is central to all these movements. The past acquires new life in being the central foundation of cultural and political Indian identity, and a source of radical criticism to the successive forms of oppression that *q'ara* [Western] society exercises on the Indian. It is in this context that the oral history projects of the THOA emerge, as an attempt to put the Indian movements' demands for historic recuperation into practice."[13] The THOA's work contributed to the shifts in historical consciousness, both within and outside of the academy, that were taking place thanks to a new generation of indigenous leaders.

THE URBAN-RURAL CONNECTION

In the late 1970s and early 1980s, Silvia Rivera's work at the UMSA put her in touch with a new generation of young Aymara students hailing from rural areas and urban migrant communities. They became allies in the project to rebuild indigenous politics and scholarship.[14] Like the growth of Katarismo, newly established political parties, and campesino unions, the THOA was one of many initiatives and organizations that emerged from the growing ties between the countryside and the city. As THOA member and historian Esteban Ticona writes, "What enriches the debate and the proposals is the mutual relationship between those who arrived from the country and [those with] greater insertion in the city. If this exchange is missing, those from the countryside tend to be too pragmatic and immediatist, and those from the city, too theoretical."[15] The intellectual combination of these two worlds fused in the THOA, embodied directly in the young indigenous migrants who made up its core, resulting in a potent combination of life experiences and politics that fed the organization's work and vision.

The group of students who joined the THOA had a shared history. Most had grown up in the countryside and migrated to the city to work, study, or live with their families. According to a number of THOA members, participation in the founding and the early years of the organization reflected their experiences in the countryside, their debates in secondary school, the racism they faced in the city, and their drive to explore their own identities and histories as indigenous people.

Felipe Santos, an eloquent longtime member of the THOA who remains active in the organization to this day, was part of the generation of students who migrated from the countryside in the 1970s. The Bolívar secondary school he attended in La Paz had a large number of indigenous students, and there he formed bonds with other Aymara and Quechua youth. This new flow of indigenous students into the secondary schools and universities was a direct result of the expanded access to education enabled by the National Revolution. Santos said that the political and ideological direction he developed in his youth was emboldened by a reflection among his peers about their rural roots, the dictatorships, and the gains and pitfalls of the National Revolution.[16]

Such discussions paved the way for what would become the THOA. Santos recalls that he and his classmates were already discussing indigenous politics, history, and liberation in high school. Later, in the university, he and his friends carried on these debates in the Julián Apaza University Movement (MUJA), the same group that had influenced leaders such as Raimundo Tambo and Genaro Flores. Santos also studied with Fausto Reinaga, as did many of his contemporaries.[17]

These young indigenous activists felt a need to return to their past, to their historical and cultural roots, to the ayllu. "So we said, 'We have to go back to reclaim, to investigate what is actually our reality,'" Santos explains.[18] These students found willing and eager allies in university professors Silvia Rivera and Tomás Huanca. Huanca, a cofounder of the THOA alongside Rivera, was involved early on with this group of Aymara students at the university and had lived until he was twenty in a small community near Lake Titicaca. He worked as a rural teacher until going to the UMSA to study sociology under Rivera's guidance.[19] With support from Rivera and Huanca, discussions deepened among a new generation of activist-scholars at the UMSA, and the collective process of moving toward what would become the THOA was put into motion.

The philosophy of the THOA was directly oriented by the lived experiences of recent migrants to the city. "We came from the communities," early THOA member Filomena Nina told me in the THOA offices. Nina had become a member of the THOA as an interview transcriber and still worked at the organization decades later while also teaching Aymara classes. Though soft-spoken, she was matter-of-fact about the profound racism that she and other indigenous students faced in the early 1980s: "When we arrived in the city from communities, we suffered discrimination just because of our language, just because of our appearance."[20] Early THOA members like Nina were drawn to the organization as a haven from the marginalization they felt as indigenous students and recent migrants to the city.[21]

Indigenous students felt acute discrimination in the halls of the university. Early THOA member Marcelo Fernández Osco, speaking to me in downtown La Paz at one of the municipal traditional medical centers he now directs (in addition to his work as an indigenous law professor), arrived in La Paz from the shores of Lake Titicaca to study sociology. "That process of getting the bachelor's degree was tremendously chaotic because first, I mean, you could not speak [Aymara] . . . in that moment, I'm talking about the late seventies and early eighties. The university did not allow you to say that you were Indian, that I am Aymara. Speaking Aymara was almost a crime."[22]

The odds were stacked against students' early initiatives to reflect on and study indigenous culture and history. Students had to officially change their indigenous surnames to Spanish names in order to enter the university. But in the early 1980s, Nina recalled, students began to refuse to change their names. They expressed a growing sentiment among indigenous students at the UMSA that, as Nina explains, "We can't go on this way, right? We are also part of this nation, so we have all the liberty of, well, expressing ourselves."[23] Early THOA members such as Nina, Fernández, and Santos collaborated with Rivera and Huanca to confront the structural racism within the academy.

Bolivia was changing, and so too was the university. Rivera's classes, the debates she helped foster, and her relationships with Aymara students were all critical points of convergence where the rising indigenous politics of Bolivia found fertile ground. The UMSA, a home for this nexus, created the first department of sociology in its halls during the 1970s, but it was not until the 1980s that an anthropology department was founded.[24] Students' and teachers' efforts to build new avenues to explore indigenous culture, history, and politics came together and grew during this period, paving the way to the independent entity that was the THOA.

CHANGE FROM INSIDE THE UNIVERSITY

THOA cofounder and sociologist Silvia Rivera Cusicanqui works in the urban gardens of the self-managed Colectivx Ch'ixi in La Paz in October 2014. Photographer: Benjamin Dangl.

Many THOA members recall the classrooms and discussions at the UMSA as spaces that led to the THOA's creation. Some of the early debates came out of Rivera's course in ideological superstructure. Longtime THOA member Lucila Criales, who holds a leadership role producing publications for the organization, recalls that Marxism was the hegemonic theory in the classroom at the time. "They talked about [Lenin's] *Imperialism, the Highest Stage of Capitalism*, all the history of the Russian Revolution, the famous seventeenth of October, [Marx's] 'Eighteenth of Brumaire,' and the Asian modes of production." One teacher told them, "'The primitive peoples enter in the Asian mode of production.' And to us, it wasn't convincing," Criales says. This Marxist view of the past and political change did not fit with her experience in the world as an indigenous person.[25] She was not alone; many students who felt such worldviews silenced and disparaged the experience and histories of indigenous societies found their way into the THOA.

The predominance of Marxist thought in UMSA classrooms was a consequence of the fact that a number of the faculty were trained in European and Latin American social science institutions where Marxism reigned. Historian René Arze, a student at the UMSA during this period, explains, "It was an era very much influenced by the Cuban revolution, when everyone talked in orthodox Marxian terms of the 'proletariat,' the 'national bourgeoisie,' and the 'theories of labor surplus,' while those interested in, say, the Chaco's indigenous peoples were still seen as a bunch of weirdos, totally out of touch with mainstream intellectual and political thinking."[26] Dependency theories of André Gunder Frank and Fernando Henrique Cardoso were embraced enthusiastically by many in the university seeking to understand the roots of poverty, the lack of development in Bolivia within a global economic context, and how Western nations profited from Bolivia's underdevelopment. Yet the longtime scholar of Bolivia Kevin Healy writes, "While useful corrective lenses, in some respects, neither the Marxist nor the dependency paradigm gave any importance to the positive role of indigenous culture. Frank went so far as to say that the Indians 'lacked culture.'"[27] Students grasping for answers about their own indigenous identity and culture rejected these ideologies and sought alternative approaches.

Such tensions and debates deeply marked the early THOA members. Marcelo Fernández, for example, says he and his friends read

Marx and Lenin as young radicals, but that these authors did not help them understand their reality as indigenous people or build alternatives to neocolonialism. They read the classics, he explains, "but it turned out that this reading, in instrumental terms and conceptual terms, did not make sense when we were analyzing our reality; that was the great deficiency. We said, 'Something [else] is happening.' It was like having a machete that doesn't cut."[28] This sentiment pushed many young indigenous activists and thinkers to explore their own histories and projects for social change.

The efforts among indigenous students at the UMSA to build intellectual alternatives percolated up and assisted in crucial changes to the university curriculum. The sociology faculty and a handful of historians in the UMSA began to incorporate indigenous issues and culture into their research methods and political discussions. Rivera was a key trailblazer during this period. Healy writes, "The daughter of a prominent medical doctor, Rivera was unusual in having a second surname that was indigenous. Cusicanqui revealed bloodlines of Aymara hereditary chieftains (*caciques*) from the La Paz–based aristocracy active during the colonial period."[29] Rivera conducted fieldwork in the Pacajes Province where Katarismo flourished, and studied anthropology in Peru in an MA program with noted Bolivian scholar Jorge Dandler. She was working at the UMSA when members of the 1980 García Meza military regime in Bolivia confiscated her personal library and pushed her into exile in Mexico, where she wrote the classic and influential book *Oppressed but not Defeated*, which provides a broad overview of indigenous movement struggles in twentieth-century Bolivia. She returned to Bolivia in 1982 and cofounded the THOA shortly after.[30]

The tumultuous era had a direct influence on Rivera's thinking about memory and oral history. As she recalls:

I started with Oral History because they stole all of my documents. When the García Meza dictatorship sacked my library with all my documents, which were "subversive," in so much as they were thought of as documentation of politics in that moment, in the 80s, but . . . well, they were very ancient questions. But the fact that they stole them from me and they left me with only my memory reminded me very much of what I had seen and heard. From there it was very impressed upon me that they can steal everything from you, but not your memory.[31]

Rivera's thinking about the power of memory and oral history shaped debates in her classroom and was received enthusiastically by a new generation of students at the UMSA. Early THOA member Lucila Criales recalls finding something different in Rivera's class than in the classes of other professors: "Silvia started [the class] with her speech about oral history, of learning the history of the Indians." When inquiring about what indigenous people in Bolivia did during different periods of history, however, the class ran into a silence. The archives, the books, and the libraries barely contained any histories from the point of view of indigenous people. It was then, says Criales, that they chose to take another direction: oral history. The students and professors of the THOA sought to populate that silence by interviewing elders in indigenous communities, leaders of past revolts and forgotten rebellions, and those who had heard stories passed down from generation to generation about indigenous struggles.[32]

"WHO ARE WE?" THE THOA AS AN AVENUE FOR SELF-REFLECTION AND DECOLONIZATION

The THOA offered an avenue of self-reflection and self-investigation for many members. For Filomena Nina, it was a profoundly personal experience to address and discuss the fundamental question: Who are we? It was pivotal for her to know that "our ancestors had struggled, but that this was not even recognized by [the official] history." The THOA sought to uncover these histories. "So, in this sense, I think that yes, history contributes a lot, because if we did not know, we would not have had a trajectory, we would not know who we are, because we have to have all this to fortify ourselves as well as our identity."[33] THOA members were passionate about their work because it fed their own sense of dignity, of belonging within the social struggle.

The activities of the THOA were unprecedented in Bolivia. Indeed, historical research in the universities at the time was dominated by people working in politics and law who ignored the role of indigenous people in Bolivia's history.[34] Mary Money, Bolivian historian and former director of the La Paz Historical Archives, explains that the THOA opened up a new focus and direction for Bolivian history. "Before, history [consisted of] administrative acts, or memorizing battles where they eulogized the figure of the elite classes that governed the country," Money said. "These Aymara intellectuals turned to oral history, which consists of visiting the countryside, interviewing the live actors who had participated in the indigenous emancipation movements . . . retaking the course of their history in rejection of that history of the European and North American elite that was transmitted in the universities."[35]

The dominant narratives about Bolivian history in secondary school textbooks relegated indigenous heroes and their rebellions to the margins. Carlos Mamani was deeply involved in the ayllu reconstruction efforts in the 1990s and helped produce many of the THOA's influential works. Mamani critiqued mainstream Bolivian versions of history in which the revolts of Túpac Katari were mentioned as a mere footnote to the War of Independence from Spain and the Republican era.[36]

In this literature, according to Mamani, the precolonial period is simplified, Katari's struggle is painted as simply a precursor to independence, and the National Revolution of 1952 is portrayed as a glorious turning point for the country. He explains, "In the whole Republican period, our people, in spite of our weight as making up the majority of the population, were practically erased from the map."[37] The THOA members had to find a way to "return to ourselves," says Marcelo Fernández. "It's not because we have read Lenin or Marx, nor because we've read Western historians," he explains. "It was when we returned to our own history [that we asked,] 'Who was Túpac Katari? Who was Julián Apaza? Who was Bartolina Sisa?'" The THOA "flipped history over" and found that these leaders "were important builders of the country. But in the historiography absolutely nothing is said about that history."[38]

THOA members began by piecing together the few historical sources available. "What we needed to make was also the reconstitution of a minimum bibliography," Fernández says. They read Reinaga, books from the United States on Black Power, Frantz Fanon, oral histories from the Franco period in Spain. "This literature . . . has given us the conceptual *background* to understand or analyze the reality, in addition to the oral memory of the elders, because the oral memory of the elders was also like talking with a philosopher or with a historian."[39]

It was the drive to confront the silences surrounding indigenous history that led students like Fernández to dig deeper, to look down other avenues for answers, for hidden histories. He explains, "As students, we said, 'What is happening? Why isn't Bolivian [indigenous] history being debated in university classrooms? What has happened? We don't have heroes? We don't have forefathers? We don't have proto-martyrs? There's no history, no civilization?' So at the root of that entire process . . . in reality is a racism that is still alive and practiced in the university, and we decided to research ourselves, and the Andean Oral History Workshop comes from there."[40]

DECOLONIZING HISTORICAL RESEARCH METHODS

The THOA's methodology was bound up in the organization's political and intellectual commitments, which aimed to decolonize research and historical production. The THOA members' closeness to the communities and cultures they were researching helped their work immensely. Their horizontal research methods aided the recovery of communal memory and knowledge. The THOA's efforts to piece fragments of memory and historical traces together into a whole helped fill in silences and reweave the narrative fabric of indigenous resistance.

THOA members were not strangers waltzing into an indigenous community from afar; they were considered part of the same community, albeit part of the wider Aymara diaspora triggered by migration to cities. When THOA members conducted their interviews, they approached their work from a space of intimate understanding: they spoke the same language and many had lived in rural communities when they were younger. "The fact of being indigenous, indigenous researchers, made us part of the same community," Felipe Santos explains.[41] For many THOA researchers, the experience of gathering testimonies was like an extended family reunion.

Don Lúcas Miranda, son of the cacique Toribio Miranda, conducts an Andean ceremony during a gathering of indigenous elders in 1990. The meeting was organized by the THOA to collect oral histories on the struggle of the caciques apoderados. Courtesy of the Andean Oral History Workshop.

The THOA's work was a process of mutual reflection and collective remembering; the line between the researchers and the researched was blurred. Members were investigating themselves, their own identities and pasts. "It was a kind of self-reflection, and we shared this self-reflection with the communities," Santos explains. There was no lack of trust. "We woke up together in the communities conversing, debating."[42] The activist-researchers and community members were getting to know their ancestral history, culture, and worldview, but also getting to know themselves.[43]

Many of the THOA participants, or their immediate family members, had lived in the rural regions the group worked in. Carlos

Mamani, for example, lived into his teenage years in a highland community in which local resistance had prevented the arrival of the hacienda. This personal experience, as well as his firsthand knowledge of the culture and traditions of his community, assisted in his research in the region where he grew up.[44]

The fact that the THOA members spoke Aymara offered another bridge. Speaking an indigenous language was a requirement for early THOA members. These were the languages of trust and confidence in the communities. Marcelo Fernández reflected on language's essential role in their early work: "When we speak in Aymara, when we *acullicamos* [chew coca], when we talk in the evenings, a deep history arises, and it is a deep history that comes from long ago."[45] Researchers would not have been able to access the same stories, the same meaning and sentiment, without speaking the languages of the communities.

Just as the language provided an inroad, sharing coca—a leaf used widely throughout the Andes for medicinal and spiritual purposes—during conversations helped ground the discussions in the rituals and the cultural foundations of the community. "Coca is an element in making a dialogue," Nina explains. "It is a way of saying, 'Let's chat.' It's not necessarily *saying*, but rather *showing*, and giving coca, so that already has another significance, which is to say, we already know the symbolic language of the communities."[46] When THOA members conducted their research, they typically brought coca with them for just this purpose.

The THOA audio files from the early 1980s bring their methodologies in the communities to light. In various recordings, where Aymara is predominantly spoken, one can hear the rustle of participants grabbing at piles of coca leaves and chewing the leaf during the interviews. In other THOA recordings, snippets of rural daily life are present in the sound of chickens clucking, birds singing, or the wind whipping over the microphone during an outdoor conversation.[47] Hours and hours of such recorded interviews and conversations in rural communities formed the core of the THOA's historical productions.

The THOA deployed various techniques to help elders recall the past with precision and fill in incomplete historical accounts. In the case of interviewees who had traveled extensively during the period under investigation, as was the case for some of the scribes of caciques apoderados, THOA members took interviewees to visit places related to their past in order to help them recall significant events with more detail.[48] The THOA also sought out extended interviews with people who were not necessarily tied to historical events important to the community but were superb narrators or had a deep knowledge of local history and culture. Through repeated interviews, such people provided a wider view of history. These life histories, Carlos Mamani explains, helped "enrich our vision of what the common cultural rules are and the individual variants are in a society like ours."[49]

The researchers and those who provided testimonies shared much of the same culture and lived experience, identified with each other, and spoke the same language, providing the foundation for a participatory and horizontal production of history. This process decentered the typical power of the researcher and focused on a genuine collaboration that the THOA members say decolonized their methodology. This style of research was evident in the ways the interviews were organized. In Rivera's reflections on the THOA's early work, she describes how the interviewees themselves decided on the research approach and topics, how the interviews would be formatted and conducted, how the transcriptions would be returned, evaluated, and discussed by the community, and how the final product would be used.[50]

The THOA researchers were not, in a top-down manner, instituting the elements of participation and production in the research process, thus reproducing Western research methods that oppressed indigenous peoples, Rivera explains. The THOA's approach, she writes, was "a *collective exercise of disalienation*, as much for the researcher as for the interlocutor." This active and collaborative participation on the part of "investigated communities and movements [aimed] toward the disalienation and decolonization of history."[51] In such a process, the interviewee is not considered an "object of study," but rather a participant in a collective reflection.[52] Through such collaborations in interviews and discussion, Rivera explains, "one will discover the complexity and richness of the ways of thinking and visions of history that the actors themselves generate in their lived experience."[53]

The THOA's interviews were not solely about collecting facts, but were often investigations into the past's role in the transformation of society. Such an approach enabled rich discussions, for example, about the persistence of colonialism in contemporary times. "This allows us to reflect on the present in light of the past: to ask ourselves, for example, if we are living the same reality, or if some change has been produced," Mamani writes. "In this way, in some communities, collectively or individually, we have generated a reflection about the permanence of the colonial situation as a system of domination of our peoples, and this reflection has enriched the consciousness-raising of the syndical, communal and other organizations."[54]

The ideal of such research methods guided the THOA's work at each stage of the organization's historical production. From the collection of testimonies to the shaping of the narrative and the piecing together of fragmented histories, this nonhierarchical relationship was an essential part of the THOA's work to rebuild an indigenous people's history of Bolivia.

GROUP INTERVIEWS

Group interviews were a central way to gather testimonies from indigenous community members. When interviewing community elders, the THOA developed the discussion as a group conversation; many of their recordings reflect this technique, in which a discussion is guided not so much by the THOA researcher as by the interviewees themselves. Such an approach is on display in a THOA book, *Jiliri-naksan arsüwipa: "Testimonios de nuestros mayores,"* produced and compiled by Carlos Mamani and Tomás Huanca from interviews with contemporaries of T'ula and other early twentieth-century caciques apoderados.[55] The group interview process that went into this work helped interviewees reflect as a community, complement one another's views, and fill in gaps in historical memory. When a group of elders from various communities shared their stories for this work, their combined memory produced a richer, more complete version of the past than could be drawn from any single narrative. As more community members spoke and shared stories, they generated and experienced a collective memory, where the shared historical knowledge of the community was brought into sharper focus.

The cover of the 1991 THOA publication *Jilirinaksan arsüwipa: "Testimonios de nuestros mayores."* This book includes oral histories from various group interviews the THOA conducted with indigenous elders (pictured in the group photo on the cover) on the caciques apoderados. Courtesy of the Andean Oral History Workshop.

Jilirinaksan arsüwipa documents how THOA researchers gathered
testimonies from the first meeting of a group of elders who shed light
on the caciques apoderados movement. The meeting took place in La
Paz during the first week of September 1988.[56] As Huanca, the editor
of the book, explains, the testimonies were gathered by the THOA to
fill in the silences in the archival record regarding the caciques apoderados network. The elderly men interviewed included Don Leandro
Condori Chura, the main *escribano* (scribe) of cacique Santos Marka
T'ula, and another scribe of the caciques apoderados, Don Plácido
Jacinto, as well as children and grandchildren of the caciques themselves. In the text, Huanca explains that, after searching in vain in the
archives for more material on the caciques apoderados movement,
he and others in the THOA realized they needed to go to these men,
the living archives of their memory, as they were "the most direct
custodians of the thought and knowledge" of the caciques apoderados, particularly T'ula.[57]

Open discussions and collective reflections were central to the
group interview, which was conducted over the course of various
days. The THOA invited the *mayores* (elders) themselves to decide
how to proceed with the testimony. As a group, participants elected presidents and secretaries to guide the discussion, and chose the
order in which the interviewees—ten in all, from various communities—would speak. "Between them they chose three moderators to
run the meeting. . . . After a brief discussion (between those chosen),
they came to an agreement about how to move the meeting forward,"
Huanca writes.[58]

The interviewees decided that each man (no women were interviewed in this case) would speak about his experiences and knowledge, then they would talk about the themes of land titles, school,
education, and religion, one after the other, as a way to clarify and
deepen the history of the caciques apoderados movement. Toward
the end of the encounter, they decided to additionally talk about
the contemporary "difficulty and the importance" of these issues
in the communities.[59] The text of *Jilirinaksan arsüwipa* itself reflects
the democratic nature of the interviews. After the discussion plan
is established, the book includes a selection from the testimonies.
There are two columns on each page, one in Aymara on the left and

the other in Spanish on the right. There are also photographs of each of the speakers at the gatherings, helping to bring the conversation to life on the page.

Throughout the histories shared by these men are regular comments from the speakers on the order and organization of their reflections. This was a process of constant deliberation and decision-making in which the people giving testimony were in complete control, without interference or direction from Huanca. The elected president of the conversation, Don Andrés Jach'aqullu, leads the discussion at the start by introducing the meeting and stating that each participant will explain his story. "He gave the word to each one of the guests, in such a way that each of them would explain their knowledge about life, the fight and thought about the *comunarios* and *caciques*," Huanca explains.[60] After Lúcas Miranda relates the story of his father's claims to land in the Chuquisaca Department and the promises made to his community by various presidents, Juan Condori follows, beginning his account of labor exploitation on an hacienda with, "That's good, brothers, I will also take a turn to speak."[61] Such a process of reflection is repeated by the men throughout the conversations. While the discussions proceed according to the logic established by the speakers, the elder with the most knowledge—in this case, T'ula's scribe Condori—often dominates the conversation.

The narratives are rich with emotion as the men relate tales of oppression, injustice, and struggle. As Juan Condori explains, on the hacienda, indigenous people were treated "like dogs. Because of this, for us there was only injustice." As the discussions go forward, the colonial and Republican period blend into one another, and the past bleeds into the present; the dates and facts are less important to these speakers than the sentiment behind the memories, the conviction that colonization never stopped. "Brothers, once more we reflect together," Jach'aqullu, the elected president of the discussion, summarizes. "We continue suffering for the last 500 years, in spite of the fact that we are the legitimate owners [of this land]."[62] Such a group interview process was typical of the THOA and sheds light on the methods it established. Rather than ignoring or sidelining the community's strength in favor of a single narrative, the THOA's approach brought collective memories to the center of the stage.

UNITING FRACTURED HISTORIES

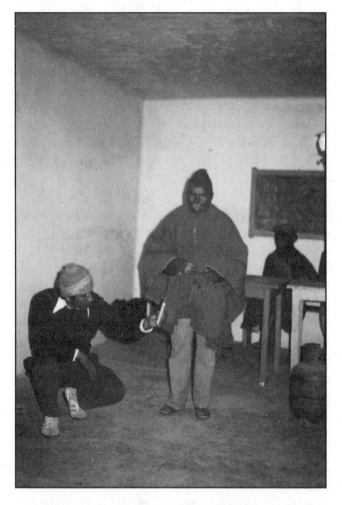

A radio theater performance on Santos Marka T'ula involving
members of the THOA and the Radio Teatro Patacamaya in Ch´oxña,
Gualberto Villarroel Province, in 1988. Courtesy of the Andean Oral
History Workshop.

As in the case of the Santos Marka T'ula project, using oral testimonies helped the THOA uncover histories and memories that were not
accounted for in the country's archives. The THOA picked out the

traces of written evidence in land titles and newspaper articles from the National Archive in Sucre and the departmental archive in La Paz, and wove them together with oral histories to produce a more cohesive whole out of the scattered fragments. As silences and gaps were filled, individual testimonies and collective memories all fed into the THOA's reconstruction of the past.

This process often required extensive travel. The search for documents took THOA members to archives in La Paz, Sucre, and Potosí, but they often came up empty-handed. They began to search for the communities of the historical figures they were researching, such as Santos Marka T'ula and Eduardo Nina Qhispi. Carlos Mamani explains in a 2015 interview, "We knew where [T'ula's] community was, so we went to his community and we talked with the sons and daughters of his people, we even had the good luck of speaking with some [participants in the movement], such as [T'ula's scribe] Leandro Condori Chura, who was still fairly strong at that time. He was the one who had learned to write on a typewriter and so wrote everything that the caciques apoderados asked him to."[63] By speaking with people such as Condori, the THOA was able to expand its base of knowledge, dates, and events, which guided both its archival research and its additional interviews with living witnesses and descendants.

Following the trail of certain rebel leaders led THOA researchers to crisscross the country's unpaved roads, going into archives in La Paz for information on land struggles and out to the highland countryside to chase leads. In an undated recording with Leandro Condori, almost certainly from the early 1980s, the interviewer tries to get more information from the caciques' scribe about the location of certain letters and documents, when they were produced, and what government office they may have been directed to, so the THOA could find them in the archives.[64]

At the same time, when gathering testimonies, "individual memory was found to be fractured," Felipe Santos writes in a 2008 article about the group's work. The THOA strove to make up for these gaps by collecting a wide array of testimonies. The older generations were dying, however, and so the researchers also had to rely on the "family memory"—the recollections and stories from leaders' relatives. It was through this process that the prominence of collective memory in indigenous communities emerged for the THOA researchers. "After a half-decade of investigation," Santos continues, "we realized that the construction of memory in the indigenous sphere is collective; the permanent confrontation of the individual memory with the communal one brought new life to its transition to the new generations."[65]

A THOA book published in 1991 on the highland community of Taraqu exhibits how such historical fragments, archived documents, individual firsthand narratives, and collective and secondhand narratives were pieced together by the organization. In his book *Taraqu 1866–1935: Masacre, guerra y "Renovación" en la biografía de Eduardo L. Nina Qhispi*, Carlos Mamani grapples with the relationship between the individual history of indigenous leader and intellectual Eduardo L. Nina Qhispi and the history of Qhispi's community. Originally, Mamani had planned to write a biography of Qhispi, but scarce archival records on the figure forced him to ask the question: "In what documents could we investigate the life of an Indian? From the beginning, the only thing we had was the date of his birth and that of his death." He sought to fill these silences by looking to the history of Qhispi's wider community. This research approach, Mamani writes, "allows us to recognize the history of the person in the history of the *ayllu*, of the *marka* [ayllu network], and of the other Indians of the republic and, in this way, address the other face of Creole history, so carefully hidden by traditional historiography."[66]

Mamani conducted oral histories on Qhispi's life only to find that, in order to write about him, he had to also write about Qhispi's ayllu and neighboring ayllus.[67] Bolivia scholar Marcia Stephenson writes, "By decentering the individual subject, Mamani Condori was able to uncover an alternative history that criollo official histories had ignored or dismissed as irrelevant."[68] Mamani explains that his initial attempts to write a standard biography of Qhispi were based on a Western tradition of holding up leaders as protagonists of history. "We tried to individualize the leader and separate him from the community, in an eagerness to equate the thinking heads and the noted men of indigenous history with the pantheon of heroes and great men of the creole historiography," he explains. Yet as he moved forward with the research and writing, Qhispi's biography came to make up only one chapter of the book.[69]

The resulting publication, *Taraqu 1866-1935*, is largely a history of the ayllu of Ch'iwu. Mamani writes, "We realized that the history of aggressions and resistances through which this collectivity travelled was not an isolated case, and its necessary model was the *marka* of Taraqu, [in which Ch'iwu] was one of . . . eight component ayllus." The research process Mamani went through reflects the experience of many THOA members as they conducted their work. Mamani writes, "Our methodology of investigation was then the result of a process of searches and estimates, through which we understood—returning to an old communal wisdom—that the history of an individual is no more than a thread in the fabric of the collective history."[70]

Reflecting the ethics of the THOA, Mamani shared his work with the Taraqu community and used the publication to spur further discussions, political organizing, and historical reflection. Shortly after the publication of *Taraqu 1866-1935*, a weekend seminar based on the book was organized by the THOA and the Taraqu Agrarian Center. The seminar was called "La lucha anticolonial de los comunarios de Taraqu" (The Anticolonial Struggle of the Community Members of Taraqu); it aimed to "return" the book to the community and to reflect on indigenous people's history "without paternalistic criollo-mestizo mediation."[71] The return of the publication to the community was part of the THOA's commitment to using its work to support and stand alongside the country's rising indigenous movement.

While indigenous movements were struggling in the streets and barricades for political power and rights, the THOA was fighting intellectual battles to put indigenous people on the historical map of the country. THOA members used oral history techniques to recover the silenced and fragmented past of indigenous people, and produced histories for political action in an era of indigenous resurgence. In their efforts to decolonize historical research and history, they inspired and oriented historical awareness around Bolivia's indigenous culture and histories.

CHAPTER FIVE

RECOVERING SANTOS MARKA T'ULA

The Caciques Apoderados Movement

Santos Marka T'ula's son, Gregorio Barco Guarachi, in El Alto on March 25, 2015. Photographer: Benjamin Dangl.

Rain poured from the sky as we climbed into a bus from La Paz to El Alto. I was riding with Alejandro Marka, Santos Marka T'ula's

great grandson, and he was bringing me up to Senkata, a neighborhood in El Alto where his uncle Gregorio Barco lived with relatives
after moving from his rural home. Barco was T'ula's ninety-six-year-
old son. I was astounded to hear that Barco was still alive and living
in the city. "We have to go see him now," Marka told me. "He is sick
and could die at any moment."[1]

After a series of buses and taxis brought us to Barco's neighborhood, we walked down dirt roads with gutters brimming with
water; the streets were beginning to flood. Finally, Marka entered a
courtyard that was home to a snarling dog and opened up a creak-
ing metal door into a single adobe room. The rain pounded on an
exposed metal corrugated roof, and a cold wind blew through cracks
in the walls. Santos Marka T'ula's last living child was resting on a bed
beneath a pile of blankets in the room.

Marka gently woke up his uncle, who was wearing two hats for
warmth and bore a small, white beard on his chin. He spoke only
Aymara and was almost entirely deaf and blind. Marka yelled so that
he could be understood by Barco, who greeted his nephew warmly.
We shared food and coca with the elderly man while explaining the
nature of our visit.

In spite of his age and illness, Barco's memory of his father was
strong. He told us he was proud to be T'ula's son and thought a lot
about his father's struggle in his old age. Indeed, Barco explained that
he had tried to carry on his father's fight and share histories of T'ula's
resistance. But he faced repression and marginalization from an early
age; the same landowner class that tried to stop his father's organizing efforts clamped down on the young Barco.

As a youth, Barco said wealthy landowners in his region would
ask him, "Why are you speaking so much about T'ula and in favor of
T'ula? You are creating a false history."[2] They told him to work his
land quietly and not cause any trouble. "If you go to school to learn
how to read and write, we will punish you," they said. While Barco
watched others in his community go to school, he did not go "because
authorities told me that if I went to school they would take out my
eyes and cut out my tongue."[3] Barco explained that nearly a century
after T'ula began his fight, his family was still struggling to maintain
ownership of their land. He told me, "We have suffered since the

time that the Spanish arrived."[4] The efforts to silence Barco and prevent him from following in his father's footsteps were part of a larger attempt to erase the history and legacy of Santos Marka T'ula.

At the turn of the twentieth century, a renewed expansion of the hacienda in Bolivia led to the breakup of indigenous-owned land. In response, a network of caciques apoderados rose up to resist this land grab and to defend besieged indigenous communities from abuse. These leaders were empowered by late-nineteenth-century laws allowing them to legally represent their communities in court, as well as to use colonial land titles in defense of their territories. Caciques apoderados were appointed by their communities and sought out such titles as a tool in their struggle. They coordinated their efforts and strategies and shared lawyers, the titles they recovered, and scribes in what would become a national network of nearly one hundred leaders, representing some four hundred communities across the departments of the eastern high plains of Bolivia. One of the most prominent leaders of the caciques apoderados was Santos Marka T'ula, a figure whose life story was recovered by the THOA in the early 1980s, largely through the collection of oral histories.

According to the THOA, the story of T'ula was unknown in the early 1980s outside of a few rural communities in the Bolivian highlands. Once the research organization heard of the cacique apoderado struggle, however, they gathered fragmented archival evidence and disparate stories on T'ula from his living descendants, collaborators, neighbors, and contemporaries to produce a history of the leader. Some eleven members of the THOA were involved in this research process, which included visits to a number of rural communities to conduct interviews and make trips to the national archives in Sucre. The result was a small booklet on T'ula's life originally published in 1984 and titled *El indio Santos Marka T'ula: Cacique principal de los ayllus de Qallapa y apoderado general de las comunidades originarias de la republica.*[5] The initial booklet was accessible, affordable, and widely distributed to rural Aymara communities, where it was used in numerous primary schools. The THOA also turned their work on T'ula into a widely popular *radionovela* (serial radio program) that was broadcast in Aymara by radio stations nationwide in the mid-1980s. The work of the THOA helped spur discussions about indigenous

people's movements in Bolivia and the role of oral history in historical consciousness.

The story of T'ula provides an interesting case study on the political uses of history in Bolivian indigenous movements. What is particularly fascinating are the unique ways in which the THOA discovered,
researched, and distributed this history. In the first place, the THOA's
methodology, focused on oral testimonies, enabled the group to
explore the largely unknown history of T'ula and the caciques apoderados. Its collective research techniques, which pooled efforts, archival
resources, and testimonies, strengthened the group's capacity to create such a rich historical document. The THOA researchers' embrace
of the mythical accounts of T'ula's story also helped them uncover
elements and meanings present in oral versions of this history that
were completely absent in the archival record. Finally, the researchers' emphasis on reciprocity, returning the booklet and radionovela to
the communities they worked with and collectively reflecting on the
history with community members, contributed fundamentally to the
popularity and impact of their history of T'ula.

THE RISE OF THE CACIQUES APODERADOS

Santos Marka T'ula (middle row, center, with hat) and T'ul'a's scribe
Leandro Condori Chura (right of T'ula, wearing dark suit) at a gathering
of caciques in La Paz, circa 1925. Courtesy of the Andean Oral History
Workshop.

A brief look at the historical circumstances and rise of the caciques apoderados helps to understand the world in which T'ula lived and fought. A renewed grab for indigenous land at the turn of the twentieth century, triggered in part by the growth of the national railroad network, besieged indigenous communities facing hacienda expansion. The caciques apoderados, chosen by their communities to fight the land grab through bureaucratic means, developed a network to legally resist incursions onto indigenous land and to champion communities' rights and demands in government and in court. The caciques apoderados themselves drew from two laws passed in the late nineteenth century. The 1874 Disentailment Law enabled indigenous leaders to be legally recognized as mediators between the government and the communities they represented, hence the term *caciques apoderados*.[6] The Law of November 23, 1883 stipulated that land titles acquired by indigenous people during the colonial period could be used as proof of legal ownership. The goal of the caciques apoderados was to locate and use such titles for proving ownership in their defense of indigenous land.[7]

At the time, a small class of Spanish-speaking elites maintained political and economic power at the expense of the indigenous majority. Fifty-one percent of the Bolivian population was indigenous in 1900, 73 percent lived in rural areas, and the Spanish language was spoken by a minority.[8] The implications of such a social divide for indigenous land ownership were stark. Complicating matters, Liberal party leaders prioritized completing a rail system connecting Bolivia to Chile and its Pacific ports. From 1905 to 1915, rail construction raised the accessibility, and therefore prices, of land in rural areas in the departments of La Paz and Oruro where the hacienda had not yet reached, contributing to increased elite interest in acquiring indigenous-owned land.[9] Overall, from 1900 to 1930, a boom in hacienda agriculture placed a disastrous stranglehold on indigenous land. In 1880, indigenous communities still held half the land in Bolivia, but by 1930, just a third of the land was in their hands. This contributed to a disintegration of many rural communities and led displaced indigenous people to migrate to urban areas.[10]

The caciques apoderados fought against this elite land grab and developed the highest level of national coordination among indigenous movements of their time, with leaders based throughout the departments of La Paz (where activity was widespread), Oruro, Cochabamba, Potosí, and Chuquisaca. The network petitioned the government for land ownership, education, and rights in what was a well-coordinated movement.[11] The struggle against land expropriation was fierce; in many cases, particularly in northern Potosí, communities physically prevented government authorities from entering indigenous-controlled regions to survey land or hand out individual titles.[12]

While the 1874 Disentailment Law broke up communal indigenous landholdings and divided them into private parcels to be sold off, it also allowed indigenous community leaders (caciques) to gain government recognition as legal representatives (apoderados) of their community to negotiate with the government in land disputes.[13] The Law of November 23, 1883 allowed colonial era land titles to be used to verify ownership of land.[14] This law established the legitimacy and legal power of colonial property titles from the sixteenth century, certified by colonial officials, which identified land indigenous people had purchased or acquired through the *mita*, a system of forced labor during the colonial period.[15] For the indigenous communities seeking to defend their right to land in the late nineteenth and early twentieth century, the first step was to find the colonial titles that named colonial caciques as owners. In some cases, this required travel to archives in colonial administrative centers as far away as Lima and Buenos Aires. The descendants of the cacique listed in the title then had to be found to confirm them as the rightful owners of the land. Finally, the descendants had to be named apoderados by the community so that they could defend their rights in court.[16]

The passage of the 1883 law recognizing colonial land titles produced an "exegesis of the archival documents," Silvia Rivera explains. The caciques traveled widely to gather these titles over decades. "And based on these titles, four hundred markas—we are speaking of the marka, the federation of ayllus—reorganized themselves, and they recuperate[d], let's say, the memory of their territory," she says.[17] The testimonies that the THOA gathered described instances in which the four-hundred-year-old documents were used as tools of resistance in the twentieth century. Rivera recalls one such occasion in which the Bolivian government, in 1918, took the papers of a cacique from Pacajes. The documents were from the sixteenth century and demonstrated, Rivera explains, that the communities had "already gone to the mita, that they had paid tribute, that, for this reason, they had no reason for their lands to be usurped. And that was subversive. So, this seemed key to us, right? To see how history, it is used in the present, in this present of the 1920s."[18] Caciques apoderados in many communities at the turn of the century made similar claims based on hereditary lines and developed a wide network of leaders.[19]

During this period of heightened activity from roughly 1910 to 1935, the network of caciques apoderados spread across the country. In 1913, ninety-six caciques apoderados were based in four departments, with forty-six in La Paz, twenty in Oruro, fourteen in Potosí, and sixteen in Cochabamba.[20] As the political capital, La Paz was a center of activity, the point of encounter where many caciques apoderados met to discuss common needs and strategies and to coordinate shared legal defense.[21] The title of *apoderado*, legally recognized by the state and justice system, enabled leaders to access various levels of judicial, legislative, and executive power. With the support of lawyers, scribes, and receptive politicians, the caciques apoderados navigated labyrinthine bureaucracies in their defense and advocacy of the communities they represented.[22]

Their efforts focused on restoring land ownership to communities whose land had been taken by hacienda owners but also encompassed a wider array of demands including an end to obligatory military service, the establishment of rural schools for indigenous students, and indigenous leadership in local government.[23] Caciques apoderados also denounced abuses by hacienda owners, including labor exploitation, physical abuse, and land and livestock theft.[24] The very legitimacy of the caciques apoderados, in the eyes of the communities they represented, depended on demonstrating clear gains. Such victories often included winning the approval for rural schools, retrieving land titles, and gaining government land surveys, which benefited indigenous communities' claims to ownership.[25]

The caciques apoderados at this time enjoyed varied political support—depending on the region—from leftists, workers' unions, and politicians. Most notably, the Republican president Bautista

Saavedra was an occasional ally, even while violently repressing and criminalizing other indigenous rebellions and leaders.[26] Such Republican support for the caciques' cause was part of a political strategy to undermine Liberal politicians who were involved in dispossession of indigenous land at the time. In some cases, Republicans built alliances with caciques where high-profile Liberals owned land. Indeed, two of the biggest buyers of land in the early twentieth-century land grab were Liberal presidents José Manuel Pando (1899–1904) and Ismael Montes (1913–1917). Saavedra, in 1916 and 1917, before becoming president, gave legal advice to T'ula on land issues and criminal charges, and in 1919 sponsored legislation that defended indigenous people from fraudulent acquisition of their land.[27]

When Saavedra won power in 1920, expectations were high. He advocated for a certain level of legislative protection for indigenous communities and approved cacique requests for schools. However, he also sought to make indigenous people obedient and productive subjects through industrial labor and the military, and to segregate them from creole society through a 1925 decree that barred indigenous people from walking on sidewalks and entering the governmental plaza in La Paz.[28] It was out of this conflictive era that T'ula rose as an indigenous leader. To recover T'ula's story and that of the wider cacique apoderado network, the THOA used a toolbox of unique research approaches.

THE THOA'S RECOVERY OF T'ULA'S HISTORY

In the 1980s, many indigenous groups and campesino unions in Bolivia were reviving and celebrating histories of anticolonial struggles. But little beyond the revolt of indigenous leader Zárate Willka was known about indigenous movements active around the turn of the twentieth century.[29] The THOA set out to complement the histories of Willka by producing a history of T'ula and the wider cacique apoderado movement.

THOA members first gathered every trace of information they could find on the leader's life, as well as that of other participants in the wider cacique apoderado network of the era. The archival and oral history work was conducted, Rivera explains, according to the "technique of an *olla común* [shared pot]," in which all researchers contributed their efforts and research into one collective set of files. They began meeting to "generate the lines of investigation, above all looking for the descendants of the caciques apoderados."[30] Some THOA members went to the Gualberto Villarroel Province, where T'ula was from, and looked for contemporaries of the leader, people who had stories about his struggle. Meanwhile, other THOA members searched for documents in the prefect documentary collection at the La Paz Archives, the library at the UMSA, and newspaper archives to find reports from the late nineteenth and early twentieth century.[31] Everything went into the "shared pot" files on the caciques apoderados.

The cover of the booklet on T'ula's life, originally published by the THOA in 1984. Courtesy of the Andean Oral History Workshop.

THOA member Felipe Santos elaborates on the process of the shared pot: "The construction of knowledge in the THOA was and is communal. . . . [A]ll reflection is shared collectively, through it each one feeds their own reflection, giving place to the system of *aynnoqu* (themes of work). On this understanding, the operative and logistical work of the THOA applies the 'Shared pot' [theory] which consists of the support of the individual for the central project. This is to say, through the strengthening of the central topic, the subthemes of the work are generated, in this way the member and the collectivity cooperate among themselves reciprocally."[32]

Collectively working in this way, the THOA set out to organize meetings among elderly people from the Gualberto Villarroel Province to gather stories and connect the historical dots. Rivera explains that through such meetings, "these fragmented memories started to connect."[33] The THOA discovered a wider, coordinated indigenous movement. Up until that point, Rivera recalls, the official historical account portrayed such rebellions as "explosions of irrational violence, which [were organized] with no program, no proposal."[34]

But the THOA found that the caciques apoderados—ignored by most historical accounts of the era, according to the THOA—were a very sophisticated network of indigenous leaders who utilized a variety of legal and political tools in peaceful defense of their communities. Rivera speaks of how this discovery highlighted the ways in which "the official version of history always shows when the indigenous rise up in a violent way, but never shows the peaceful struggle, the legal struggle."[35] The THOA's research approach helped its members, Rivera notes, to reinterpret supposedly spontaneous rebellions "as the culminating point of a process of subterranean ideological accumulation that emerges cyclically to the 'surface' to express the continuity and autonomy of Indian society."[36] The story of T'ula provided fertile ground for the THOA to apply such historical practices and analyses.

In their approach to researching and producing histories around the caciques apoderados, the THOA tapped into what its members saw as a vein of continuous indigenous historical memory that spanned centuries. "THOA members began with a working hypothesis positing that despite the ongoing history of colonialism and

repression, an autonomous indigenous historical memory and sub-
jectivity persisted throughout the nineteenth and early twentieth
centuries," scholar Marcia Stephenson writes.[37] Such a theory echoed
the role of "long memory" in indigenous resistance, as developed
by Rivera. Similarly, historian Brooke Larson writes on indigenous
movements and memory in the Andes: "In moments of political crisis
and rupture, local indigenous peoples might tap into those long-term
historical memories, or they might conjure Inca or Andean utopias,
as armament in local struggles for land and justice."[38] The THOA
explored such memory and used it as a historical source.

The THOA found that subterranean histories of resistance persisted among indigenous communities and were revived by the search
for information about the caciques apoderados. "The search for colonial titles permitted in this way the opening of a horizon of collective
memory that legitimized the legal and violent actions and bestowed
an ethical sense of restitution of justice to the struggle of the *comunarios*," Rivera writes.[39] Katari's struggle similarly inspired and oriented
the caciques apoderados' efforts, according to T'ula's scribe Leandro Condori Chura. In a book of his testimony, Condori recalls that
the caciques he wrote for would say, "Tupaj Katari had risen against
the Spanish, considering that the Spanish had wanted to finish off
the Indians at any cost; that's why Tupaj Katari had risen against the
Spanish, to defend himself and that's why the Spanish had killed him,"
they said. "That's why we have to fight."[40]

The caciques apoderados of the era not only recovered Katari's
history and connection to their struggle but also tried to literally recover a part of Katari's quartered body. In an interview Rivera
conducted with Julián Tanqara, the grandchild of a cacique apoderado, Tanqara describes how the caciques involved in the struggle in
Pacajes searched a hill near Caquiaviri for Katari's buried arm.[41]

Once the shared pot was full, the THOA's explicit goal was to
produce a history of T'ula for the people. The THOA created the
T'ula booklet in 1984 in a very readable form, ready for broad distribution in rural areas. It is a short booklet, at fifty-five pages, and
includes drawings on every other page to accompany the narrative,
bringing dominant themes and characters to life. For example, illustrations depict an angry judge sentencing a humble indigenous man.

Other drawings depict T'ula's long, tiring journeys, meetings of caciques apoderados, and everyday scenes of farming and llama herding.[42]

While archival sources and documentation are regularly cited, much of the text consists of block quotes in both Aymara and Spanish of testimonies from T'ula's contemporaries or community and family members. Though the focus is on T'ula, his life is contextualized both within his community as well as in the wider span of Andean history, from brief summaries of precolonial civilizations and the suffering under colonialism and the Republican state to descriptions of indigenous resistance in the twentieth century through the 1930s Chaco War. T'ula's life is the vehicle of the narrative, positioned as a crucial step in a much longer journey toward justice.

SANTOS MARKA T'ULA: STRUGGLE AND MYTH

Santos Marka T'ula was born in approximately 1879 in the community of Ilata, in what is today the Gualberto Villarroel Province. According to THOA members, he was known as a quiet man who never raised his voice.[43] During his political organizing work, T'ula spent months and months waiting and demanding attention at the doors of lawyers and in judicial and political offices. He walked a lot, quietly, carrying his papers, THOA member Lucila Criales explained in a 2008 film on T'ula's life.[44] His scribe, Leandro Condori Chura recalls that he was kind, "calm and humble." T'ula dressed as other indigenous men of the highlands did, in "thick woolen pants and a lead-colored poncho," and he used a ch'uspa bag that held coca leaves.[45] He was remembered fondly by those who knew him closely.[46]

As an indigenous youth, T'ula did not have access to school and, as a result, was illiterate. Despite this, T'ula knew all of his documents and land titles by heart and could recite them.[47] "Santos Marka T'ula's only school was experience," the THOA booklet states. He was a man marked from a young age by the oppression his community faced in attacks on their land and rights.[48] He was very likely a young adult participant in the Willka uprising of 1899.[49] Later, as a leader organizing the wider cacique apoderado network and pressuring officials on behalf of the communities he represented, he lived a life of constant travel, persecution, and flight. Though he was regularly jailed, he maintained close relationships with the communities he fought for until the end of his life.[50]

T'ula's involvement in the caciques apoderados network can be traced back to 1914, when, after a railroad line arrived in T'ula's region, a hacienda owner encroached on ayllu land in Ilata. In response, local indigenous member Martín Vásquez traveled to Lima in search of colonial land titles that could establish the community's right to its land.[51] In Lima, he found a title from his home area that went back to an old line of caciques from the Marka T'ula family.[52] The title was in the name of Juan Marca Tola, who served the community as a cacique roughly between 1578 and 1580.[53] After Vásquez made the contemporary Santos Marka T'ula aware of this connection, T'ula was named a cacique apoderado by his community. Vásquez was jailed shortly afterward for his subversive activities, and T'ula carried on the struggle. T'ula's parents, facing repression for their own fight to defend land, had switched their family name to Barco. "But Santos," the THOA writes, "in entering into the struggle, had decided to take up again the original surname of his ancestors." The THOA's research methods, particularly the gathering of testimonies from elders, helped them piece together this history. Indeed, many of the details about Vásquez's role in the struggle are known to the public only because of THOA interviews with Vásquez's nephew, Celestino Vásquez.[54]

Almost immediately upon assuming leadership of the community, T'ula worked to recover land titles that had been seized from Vásquez by authorities. A document from 1914 in the La Paz Prefect Archive mentions T'ula's request for the sixteenth-century titles. During his search for and recovery of the titles, he and other leaders built up and strengthened a network of caciques apoderados largely through meetings held in La Paz, where they pressured elected officials and advocated for their communities in court.[55]

Beyond uncovering the little-known history of T'ula and the caciques apoderados, the THOA also used mythical elements from interviewees' stories on T'ula as a guide to the deeper meanings of the history. Such mythical versions of T'ula's struggle were not represented in archives and written sources, and had only been passed down through oral history. Using oral history was therefore an important avenue to explore this vein of indigenous historical consciousness. "For us," writes the THOA's Carlos Mamani, "the dichotomy between myth and history is very relative, because we recognize the value of the myth as a category of historical thought in our communities."[56] In the case of T'ula, the attention to myth as part of the historical narrative uncovered versions of events that took on extraordinary tones. Mamani writes, "None of this would have been possible without the resource of oral history, and without the intent to replant the history from our own perspective."[57]

Rivera writes that in the case of indigenous histories, myth operates as an "interpretive mechanism" that helps to "understand the form in which Indian societies think and interpret their historical experience." Mythical history, she continues, "puts us back to long time, to slow rhythms and relatively immutable conceptualizations, where what is important is not so much 'what happened,' but rather why it happened and who was right in the events: which is to say, the worthiness of the events in terms of the justice of a cause."[58]

In many of the oral accounts the THOA gathered on T'ula's life and struggle, his activities and character were described in mythical terms. His relatives and contemporaries recalled that T'ula would speak with animals and plants and that, on his journeys, T'ula often asked them for protection. In a documentary about the leader, THOA member Felipe Santos states that T'ula "spoke with nature and the spirits, and when leaving his house, he always spoke in a manner to request protection, to ask for clarity in knowledge for the legal fight."[59] This is one way that communities explained his ability to sustain such long journeys and endless harassment: he drew from the spiritual world for aid in surmounting political and legal hurdles.

To protect him on his journeys and during his work on behalf of the communities, the THOA writes that T'ula "turned to the guardian spirits of the Indian communities, asking them to protect the documents in their laborious progression through the chambers of the creole legal system. In return, the documents had to be purified in order to protect their bearers from any evil forces which they might harbor."[60] One testimony recalls this process: "Whenever anyone arrived at the house, the first thing that they would do was to make offerings for the documents, and if they failed to do this someone would fall ill," the interviewee recalled. Once T'ula left with the purified documents, "we did not see [him] for years."[61]

Incredible stories followed T'ula wherever he went. Many remember him as much for his political efforts as for his invincibility. His son, Gregorio Barco Guarachi, told me of the various circumstances in which T'ula defied threats on his life. Barco recalled how soldiers once tried to burn T'ula alive after arresting him. "But Santos was not affected by the fire, so the soldiers doubted themselves. They said, 'What do you have so that you do not burn?'" Barco said that his father somehow resisted fire: only parts of his body were burned. Because of this, the soldiers sought to drown him in a nearby river. "But they were unsuccessful there, too, because the river was very cold and frozen; they could not drown him," Barco explained. "Then suddenly, a change in the wind, the wind blew, so they had to go elsewhere." In Barco's version of events, T'ula was able to summon protection from his alliance with the natural world.[62]

Another of T'ula's sons recalls that authorities "carried him to a lake, and they watched him from a distance with a telescope. They threw big stones at him, enough to destroy him. They also pierced him on all sides with spears cut in the jungle. They still kept watching him with their telescope, saying: 'This is no mortal. This is he who grieves for all people, for the poor throughout the world. One part of him [the left side] is the moon, the other [the right side] is the sun. He is like God, we should keep our distance.' That is how my father escaped."[63] Such descriptions of T'ula's mythical powers provide an explanation of how of the leader survived persecution by the authorities.

T'ula's long journey of struggle, suffering, and imprisonment came to end in 1939 when he became ill, was captured, and died shortly thereafter in La Paz on November 13. The cacique's son related that after his death, "they cut Santos Marka T'ula open. They saw his heart; they put it in a dish, and it blossomed. . . . My father saw his heart blossoming. Many people still remember it." T'ula's last words, as recounted by his son, echoed the popular version of Katari's promise before his own death: "'You can kill me, but I shall have a thousand thousand descendants.'"[64]

THE PROMOTION OF T'ULA'S HISTORY

Recording the Tuturani radionovela in the THOA recording studio
in 1991, with Valentina Jacha Collo (center, at the microphone),
Maria Eugenia Choque (left), and Nicanor Huanta and Lucia
Quispe (back). Courtesy of the Andean Oral History Workshop.

THOA members worked concertedly to promote their booklet on T'ula's life, returning to the communities where they gathered testimonies on T'ula to share the history. In addition to the booklet, the THOA produced an immensely popular Aymara radio program titled *El indio Santos Marka T'ula* (the same title as the booklet) that was broadcast throughout the country. The wide reach of the publication and radio program not only generated more awareness about T'ula but also helped spur discussions about the role of oral history and memory in indigenous communities and the need for greater understanding of such little-known histories of indigenous resistance in the Andes.

One of the THOA's most notable promotional events of its work on T'ula took place on the forty-fifth anniversary of his death. On November 13, 1984, indigenous community members from dozens of ayllus gathered to celebrate the memory and legacy of T'ula in Ch'uxña of Ilata Baja, the community of T'ula's birth. The large crowd, including T'ula's relatives and contemporaries, members of the CSUTCB, and representatives from some forty communities in the region, demonstrated the rich meaning of the gathering, which was marked by the distribution of the THOA's booklet.[65]

"It was not just an act of remembrance," THOA member Esteban Ticona recalls, "but the beginning of the strengthening of the historical identity of the original people of the Andes and the spreading of struggle through hundreds of originario ayllus and ex-haciendas, which, together in the movement of the caciques apoderados, were protagonists of the indigenous resistance in the face of expanding hacienda and state aggression. [T'ula's caciques apoderados movement] was the most important indigenous mobilization in the first fifty years of the twentieth century."[66] THOA members handed the T'ula history booklet to the crowd. Ticona, who worked on the publication, explains, "This act helped to awaken the ethnic conscience of the new leaders and indigenous comunarios [community members] of the 1980s."[67]

Various descendants, family members, and contemporaries of T'ula were present at the event. T'ula's son, Gregorio Barco, gave a speech in Aymara:

Esteemed Mallkus [community leaders], I appreciate your company, I appreciate you very much. What is the motive for this
enormous concentration of people? We gather the experiences
of our grandfathers and our own thought, for this we are meeting here, brothers. . . . There are many things I do not understand
because I am illiterate, this is how I was raised because my father
was persecuted. Brothers that are present here, my father spoke
of many things and I would like to speak to you about them. My
father said, "My son will defend our rights, if he does not, then my
grandson will, and if he does not then someone from the community will. And if this person from the community of the nine ayllus
does not do it, then others will arrive from other distant markas,
because our rights are recognized," he said. Thank you. Today this
is being achieved.[68]

The THOA's principles were reflected in its involvement in the
commemoration and in its distribution of the booklet in the community where its protagonists were based. Ticona notes, "It was
something entirely atypical at that time, that an investigation was
presented in a community." The custom was to present the results of
academic research only in an urban university setting.[69] Thanks to the
THOA's distribution and radio program efforts, the booklet on T'ula
was read widely in indigenous communities and used as an educational tool in rural schools.[70]

THOA members also recall the sometimes intense and emotional impact the diffusion of T'ula's history had in rural communities. As
a part of the MNR's policies, indigenous histories and culture had
been dismissed by state unionization efforts and attempts to erase
indigenous identity and encourage assimilation to creole culture.
The T'ula publication fought this tendency and promoted indigenous politics and histories in rural areas. Rivera speaks of one community's strong reaction to the 1984 presentation of the booklet in
Ch'uxña. At the event, the elders accused the younger generation,
their children, those who had embraced the MNR's syndicalism, of
silencing the community's history of struggle. But it was the grandchildren, Rivera recalls, a new generation, who had made this history visible again.[71] Therefore, following the event surrounding the

presentation of the booklet on T'ula, emotions were running high, as Rivera explains:

> So it produced a stampede of the people, just like that, everyone to the tomb of Santos Marka T'ula, to a forgotten cemetery, all swept by the wind, a tomb without a name, and the children, Celestina Barco and Gregorio Barco, there, standing on the tomb, made a kind of restitution of dignity of the struggle, accusing the [MNR] syndicalism of having wanted to erase them from the map, right? And this drove the people, let's say, to question the syndical system, above all, for its clientelist dependency with the political parties, and to search for their own autonomy, their own philosophy of organization, and their own authorities.[72]

The THOA went beyond the written page and onto the radio airwaves by producing a ninety-episode radionovela on T'ula's life. It was broadcast in Aymara three times across Bolivia. According to scholar Kevin Healy, "The Santos Marka T'ula story climbed to the top of the popularity charts of rural radio programming in the altiplano towns and hamlets."[73] The radio program ran throughout the week and on Saturdays, and the THOA organized on-air discussions to engage with Aymara listeners about their own memories, community histories, and reflections on T'ula's life. In some cases, people called in with corrections to the story or with more documents to share with the THOA.[74] The THOA is still well known today for this radionovela work in the 1980s. As the THOA's Marcelo Fernández explained, "If you go to a community and say to a campesino, 'Did you ever hear the radionovela of Santos Marka T'ula?' Ah yes."[75]

In the creation of the radionovela, the THOA was participating in what was already a relatively established Aymara tradition on the radio. In the 1970s, the social justice–oriented Center for the Study and Promotion of the Peasantry (CIPCA) produced an Aymara-language history of the life of Túpac Katari. Under the Banzer dictatorship, for example, the use of Aymara on the airwaves camouflaged the political nature of the program content from the predominantly Spanish-speaking centers of political power. In addition, the meta-phorical messages of apparently simple stories could hide deeper political meanings. In the case of *The Stories of Achachila*, a show broadcast under Banzer's regime, animals acted out moments in the lives of campesinos. The veneer of the program hid a critique of Banzer's regime. For example, a lion in the stories represented Banzer, dogs symbolized the military, and the campesinos were portrayed as sheep, controlled by the more powerful animals.[76]

The THOA's decision to produce a radionovela on T'ula came in part from Carlos Mamani's own experience with the radionovelas produced by the CIPCA in the 1970s, particularly the series on Katari. He recalls that the written histories on Katari were not well known, "but the radionovela had an impact . . . it was important for me." Mamani also had a younger brother who was proud of being involved in the production of the Katari radionovela . "And so for me, this really served me personally as an example, in order to support the production of radionovelas with historical documentation."[77] As part of their work on the program, the THOA members collaborated with Florentino and Inocencia Cáceres, who had been involved previously in Aymara radionovela production, most notably with the CIPCA's work on Katari.[78] Radio provided the THOA with a clear avenue for wide distribution. The show played on various radio stations, including a number of smaller community stations, but most notably on the popular Radio San Gabriel, an evangelical station reaching across the country that had, since 1955, been broadcasting a mixture of religious and indigenous-centered programming in Aymara.[79]

The THOA wanted to return the T'ula story to the communities, and the radio program was an ideal format to do so, Mamani recalls.[80] The THOA's decision to broadcast a show based on T'ula also grew out of THOA members' commitment to returning their completed histories to the communities in which they had conducted research. Rather than just publish the material without sharing it with the communities—as was the custom with most academic work, according to the THOA members—they wanted to return the final product in an act of reciprocity.

As part of this exchange, Mamani recalls, the THOA worked in the ayllu of Jiscaco Llana, near Lake Titicaca, where it produced shows every Saturday. The THOA invited members of local ayllus to go on the air and speak about what they knew of the caciques apoderados' history. Many people arrived to share their stories. Soon, Mamani recalls, "they began to bring in documents, to fill in the information more, and memory was becoming more complete."[81] In response to the radio program, the THOA offices in La Paz were visited regularly by people from rural Aymara communities who shared documents on their family's or community's land struggle in the event the organization could use them for further historical research.[82]

The radionovela also had the effect of helping people embrace their Aymara identity instead of wanting "to be someone else," as THOA member Filomena Nina puts it.[83] In sharing a largely unknown history of indigenous resistance, the THOA was honoring and vindicating indigenous culture and political power. The THOA's Marcelo Fernández explains, "In reality, the THOA has been structured to counter what's unsaid in the academy, or rather, to argue that another society exists, another culture that has knowledge, that has struggles, that has its contributions."[84] This other culture, other society, came together around the THOA's work and continued producing its own historical awareness and narratives about indigenous resistance. The radio program, through the collective reflections it generated, "wasn't a simple act of recollection," Esteban Ticona and Xavier Albó write, "but rather the beginning of a process of revalorization of the historic identity and diffusion of the struggle of hundreds of indigenous and ex-hacienda communities."[85] For this reason, the THOA members believe the T'ula radionovela had an even wider impact than the text itself.[86]

The radionovela was educational, but it also brought the wider Aymara-speaking communities together to listen to, reflect on, and discuss T'ula's history and its relevance to contemporary times. At the end of each radio show, THOA member Felipe Santos explains, the THOA announcer asked listeners for their reactions and invited T'ula contemporaries into the studio, bringing people from various generations into discussions about history and memory. Community leaders would often cry when listening to the program. "The radionovelas had a huge impact," Santos says. Through the process of reflection, "history would come to life."[87]

The booklet and radio program reverberated throughout the country and put T'ula on the political map. In subsequent decades, it was common to hear T'ula's name evoked at political and indigenous movement gatherings alongside those of Katari and Willka, as evidenced by audio recordings and textual archives of speeches, as well as references made by contemporary indigenous and campesino leaders. For example, many indigenous activists and students attended one of the THOA's presentations of their booklet in the mid-1980s. According to an audio recording of the event, Zenovio Alavi Patzi, an indigenous leader from T'ula's province, told the crowd that T'ula was a symbol of the struggle against neocolonialism. "To remember Santos Marka T'ula signifies teaching ourselves, and making the [political] project ourselves, so that we manage ourselves, and we decide what to do," he told the crowd, before folk music rose in the wake of his speech. "For this reason, we already have the example of Santos Marka T'ula: what's left is to follow his path and in his footsteps."[88]

In its work on T'ula, the THOA put its trailblazing theories and methodologies to use with impressive results. THOA researchers uncovered a silenced history of resistance in Bolivia and, using oral history and their perception of enduring collective memory in indigenous communities, were able to piece together the fragments of T'ula's story. They popularized the rebel leader in accessible formats and distributed their histories widely throughout rural Bolivia. Thanks to the THOA's work, T'ula's history lived on for generations. The research organization's efforts would take on new political significance in the 1990s with its participation in the movement to reconstruct a national network of ayllus, one legacy of T'ula's struggle.

CHAPTER SIX

THE ENDURING AYLLUS

Aymara mothers gather in an ayllu meeting in Ilata in 1985. They are ritually sharing and chewing coca leaves, which are spread out in the center of the group, as a part of coming to a resolution for the meeting. Courtesy of the Andean Oral History Workshop.

Ayllu members and leaders from around the country gathered in La Paz for a national meeting in April 2014. Among them was Tomás Saqueli Huaranca, a founder of the Consejo Nacional de Ayllus y Markas de Qullasuyu (National Council of Ayllus and Markas of Qullasuyu, CONAMAQ), a national network of ayllus. He showed me notebooks in which he kept track of the history of his ayllu and the wider ayllu movement. Pages upon pages were filled with notes from countless meetings, marches, and communities. The struggle was kept alive on the page and in Saqueli's memory. "When the Spanish arrived, they took all of our power, and even took control of our culture and language," he told me, linking the contemporary ayllu movement to centuries of resistance. "But we feel proud to say, damn, since the conquest, our parents and all of us, Túpac Katari, Túpac Amaru, Bartolina Sisa . . . and others have been the defenders of our historic indigenous cause."[1] Saqueli was participating in an ayllu struggle that had gone on for hundreds of years and had entered a period of resurgence at the end of the twentieth century.

In the 1990s, indigenous people in Bolivia developed a movement to reconstitute ayllus, a form of community organization in the Andes dating back to before the Incan empire and surviving to this day. Within the movement, ayllu advocates, through historical reflection and research, sought to recover and strengthen the history of the ayllus and their traditions of governance, rotational leadership, and consensus-based decision-making. They were encouraged in the 1990s by political openings and new legislation that guaranteed indigenous rights, autonomy, and territory. This work culminated in the 1997 founding of the CONAMAQ.

Ayllu reconstitution efforts recovered and strengthened ayllu history and political organization in a neoliberal era, and indigenous grassroots historical research by ayllu proponents and the THOA successfully aided ayllu reconstitution. The ayllu movement and the historical consciousness it supported fed into a larger series of uprisings by workers, indigenous peoples, and other sectors of society that overturned imposed structures of neoliberalism in Bolivia in the early 2000s.

THE LONG HISTORY OF THE AYLLU

"We live in ancestral and millennial territories. We have been here since before the [conquest]," explains contemporary CONAMAQ leader Nilda Rojas, a young mother from Potosí, in a 2014 interview. "The struggle comes from our grandfathers, from our grandmothers; they always fought, and have given their lives to defend the territory where we live."[2] This sentiment speaks to the power of historical consciousness in the struggle articulated through the creation and platform of the CONAMAQ. A look to the long history of the ayllu illustrates why its political capital is based partly on its antiquity.[3]

Ayllus were the basis of the preconquest Andean world through which many rural community members organized their land, labor, and social relations. Ayllu members sustained themselves as farmers in precolonial society by spreading their networks over various ecological zones in "vertical archipelagos" to diversify production in areas of extreme geography and climate.[4] Organized through real and fictive kinship ties, these communities spanned from the highlands, where livestock grazed, to the fertile and warmer lowlands, where agricultural production was more robust and varied.[5] The network of dispersed households maintained crops and livestock that communities shared and exchanged for the common good of all ayllu members.[6] The agricultural production of the ayllu itself was based on communal labor and shared resources. Members were bound together through traditions of reciprocity and mutual obligations. Ayllu authorities, whose legitimacy depended on the well-being of the ayllu, managed the social organization of the communities and upheld norms to protect the livelihood of everyone who shared in the community's labor. Leaders organized communal projects, celebrations, and the production, distribution, and storage of agricultural goods.[7] The ethic of mutual aid within the ayllu guided cooperation between communities in shared work projects building bridges, irrigation systems, and farming terraces. The term *ayni*, which in Aymara and Quechua is the root word for measured reciprocity, speaks to this tradition of pooling labor and resources. For example, the Quechua adage *aynillmanta llamkakuni* means "to work the same for another, as him for me."[8]

Under Incan rule, subjugated ayllus were required to pay tribute and work on behalf of the empire in return for protection, infrastructure, and supplies during periods of drought and famine. This tribute in the form of labor and goods never drew from the fundamental labor and agricultural production needed for subsistence; this was essentially a surplus. However, in the colonial period, the demands placed on ayllus by the Spanish increased exponentially, sapping the communities' ability to survive.[9] Following the Spanish conquest of the Andes, colonial authorities sought to extract constant and arduous mining labor and a stream of goods as costly payments to the crown from ayllus, but they kept the ayllu system intact and under indigenous management. The legitimacy of ayllu leaders was respected by Spanish authorities; in return, the leaders coordinated the Spanish exploitation of labor and goods much as they had done under Incan domination.[10] However, unlike the Incan empire, the colonial state provided little in return besides the ayllu members' tenuous right to work their own land.[11]

Soon, the Spanish wanted even more control over indigenous labor, and the makeup of ayllus went through a profound transformation under the Viceroy Francisco Toledo Reforms of 1572 to 1576. The Toledo Reforms aimed to extract indigenous labor in mining and agricultural production more effectively. To do this, Toledo took the clusters of small ayllus spanning various ecological zones and regrouped them into larger centralized towns. Such centralization made it easier for Spanish authorities to standardize the collection of taxes, to evangelize, and to extract labor. This reorganization became pervasive throughout much of the Andes.[12] In addition to the taxing labor demands, Toledo's reforms weakened ayllu self-sufficiency by curtailing their territorial expanse over ecological zones, thus diminishing their economic and agricultural capacity.[13] However, Toledo's goal was not to destroy the ayllu and their system of operation entirely. The Spanish reformer understood that if the indigenous subjects were to produce agricultural products, sustain themselves as laborers, and pay tribute, they would have to rely to a certain extent on their own traditions and institutions.[14]

Many ayllus, because of their isolation and the limited reach of the colonial state, remained intact for hundreds of years, both in their vertical territorial presence and in the organization of their members and leadership.[15] By the late colonial period, for example, six ayllus in Chayanta, in the department of Potosí, were still remarkably dynamic. Research by scholar Tristan Platt found that the enduring traditions and self-sufficiency of the ayllu had been preserved through communities' dependence on dispersed agricultural production spanning the mountains and valleys of their region. Much like former ayllus, these communities crossed various ecological zones, producing, for example, potatoes in the highlands and corn in the valleys. Members' shared labor was coordinated on the basis of traditions of reciprocity between communities and individuals.[16]

In 1982, Platt found that ayllus in northern Potosí crossed three geographic levels, including herding areas in high altitudes of forty-two hundred meters or more, *puna* (high Andean plateau) agriculture at thirty-five hundred meters and up, and valley agriculture at two thousand to thirty-five hundred meters. The higher altitudes were dedicated to herding and to potato, quinoa, and wheat production. The midrange included the production of additional fruits and corn, while the valleys produced sugar cane, chili peppers, squash, and corn. Ayllu members maintained small parcels, often far from one another, across these zones. Such dispersion helped prevent extreme weather from destroying all crops at once. In addition, the mutual aid and the sharing of crops and labor between ayllu members meant that farmers did not have to maintain a constant presence in each zone in order to enjoy a diversity of crops. Some members could produce chili peppers, corn, and squash in the valleys while other ayllu members focused on llama grazing in the highlands, contributing to the overall self-sufficiency of the wider community. Fertilizer from grazing animals on the highlands was used for fields in the puna, and oxen in the valleys were brought up to sow seeds and transport harvested goods. The sharing of ayllu labor among families based in different tiers also corresponded to such vertical agriculture: because the agricultural calendar varied in each zone, with the puna sowing and harvesting taking place months before that in the valley, laborers could work in alternating zones throughout the year.[17]

Such agricultural models helped ayllus survive in marginal regions of the country. After independence, the Bolivian government allowed the remaining ayllu communities to remain intact for much of the first half of the nineteenth century in order to guarantee crucial indigenous tax revenue to the state. Ayllus faced a renewed assault, however, with the late nineteenth-century Disentailment Law, which aimed to break up indigenous communal lands into individual plots to aid the spread of the lucrative hacienda model of agricultural production. Around the turn of twentieth century, hacienda land-holdings in Bolivia doubled, and ayllu members subsumed by the hacienda were forced into brutal conditions of servitude that were not abolished until the 1953 Agrarian Reform. However, ayllu community resistance movements, such as that of the caciques apoderados, as well as the fact that the hacienda did not reach all parts of rural Bolivia, kept a certain number of ayllus and their territories intact in the first half of the twentieth century.[18]

The roots and structure of the ayllu persisted through the National Revolution and the CSUTCB unionization efforts.[19] "In spite of the presence of the campesino union, the ayllu continued expressing itself by means of symbolic representation, territorial unity through [land] titles, and the structure of organization and authority that lay beneath the syndical form," explain María Eugenia Choque and Carlos Mamani, THOA members who were actively involved in ayllu reconstitution efforts.[20] For example, rotational leadership, a hallmark characteristic of the ayllu, was often maintained within the union structure, and the ayllu authority was often also the union leader. When the MNR sought to replace ayllus with unions, the large *marka* (a network of ayllus) of Machaqa, for example, was broken into seventy-two unions by the MNR government. However, many ayllus maintained their structure under the union label and operated clandestinely in the communities.[21] The union never completely replaced the ayllu authorities in Jesús de Machaca, according to extensive research by Xavier Albó. By the 1970s, the community's union and ayllu leadership were fused together.[22]

In his travels and work through the THOA in the ayllu reconstitution efforts in the 1990s, Carlos Mamani recalls hearing complaints regarding union leadership from residents of the Ingavi Province, outside of La Paz, who approached him and the THOA for assistance in recovering the community's ayllu structures. Leaders from Ingavi arrived one day in La Paz and told Mamani,

> "Look, it turns out that the priests are owners of our lands, they
> build where they want . . . and the cement factory that poisons and
> exploits us any way they want, because this is the Ingavi Province
> and it turns out that the union does not have a response to that,

no response. You have started talking about rights, you have mentioned to us the International Labor Organization Convention
169 [which the Bolivian government had signed onto to pledge its
respect for indigenous rights and territory] and so what we want is
to return to how it was before, we don't want the union, because
we are not campesinos, we are *originarios.*" This was like a shock
for me personally, because all the education that I received was a
developmentalist education in which if the country had to change,
well, we had to accept social change and stop being Indians then,
and we had to modernize ourselves and the key to success was to
be found in modernization.[23]

The THOA found other instances of allyu organization in
northern Potosí, which lacked a union presence and where *jilaqatas*
and *mallkus* (indigenous community leaders) were still the respected
authorities.[24] In many cases, the names and roles of the positions of
authority had remained the same over centuries. Research conducted
by the THOA in the 1980s on the organization of a group of ayllus
in the centuries-old Chayanta marka, in the department of Potosí,
demonstrated how complex governance structures had remained
intact over time. Chayanta's political structure, which had eight
ayllus, included nine *segundas mayores*—a name based on a colonial
term for leaders who, in that region in precolonial times, were called
mallkus or *kurakas.* These leaders, who were elected on a rotational
basis, handled issues across the Chayanta territory regarding land
use, spiritual rites, and communities' relationships with the Bolivian
central government. Below this position was the *jilanqu*, a leader who
dealt with internal familial and land conflicts at the ayllu level and
handled issues relating to crop cultivation and communal labor. The
alcalde comunal dealt with similar issues at a more localized level, and
autoridades auxilares assisted with ceremonies and rituals as well as
agricultural tasks, depending on the time of the year. This overarching structure was held in place in part by rotational leadership, which
prevented abuses of power, and decision-making through consensus,
which allowed the community to hold leaders' power in check. Both
practices helped maintain a flexible political structure that could
adapt to changing circumstances and community needs.[25]

In a THOA pamphlet on the structure of ayllus in the Ingavi Province, the authors describe how a patchwork of ayllu networks endured across Bolivia:

> Today there are only the ayllus divided into communities left, some conserving their ancestral names, but there are also ayllus and communities with strange names, and many ayllus have converted themselves in pieces, others are at the point of disappearing, and, finally, various ones are in the hands of new owners. Huge Catholic temples, constructed with the blood and sweat of our ancestors, are witnesses of ideological subjection, for example: San Andrés and Jesús de Machaca Santiago de Guaqui, Santa Rosa de Taraqu, San Agustín de Viacha, and chapels in all the communities that were a tremendous economic, personal, and obligatory burden.[26]

Though many ayllus were diminished and weakened, the reconstitution efforts sought to turn back this tide. Just as rural communities responded to the MNR's agrarian reform by embracing rural unions, ayllu reconstitution efforts in the 1990s responded to political, legislative, and international openings that made it politically opportune to strengthen the ayllu.[27]

POLITICAL OPENINGS

The ayllu reconstitution efforts took place during a period of neoliberal rule, leaving indigenous activists with an unusual set of political allies in power: politicians who promoted policies aiding ayllus and empowering marginalized sectors of society while privatizing services and natural resources and dismantling workers' rights. In 1993, the MNR's Gonzalo Sánchez de Lozada became president of Bolivia. He was part of a new generation of right-wing politicians in the country and a graduate of the University of Chicago, the home of Milton Friedman, the father of neoliberal economic policy. Sánchez de Lozada enacted neoliberal policies in the country through reforms oriented around the decentralization of political power. In order to win more of the indigenous rural vote, the MNR ran indigenous intellectual and politician Víctor Hugo Cárdenas as their vice-presidential candidate under Sánchez de Lozada. Cárdenas helped the Sánchez de Lozada administration develop policies related to indigenous communities, but he also helped legitimize a neoliberal regime that would later sell off the country's infrastructure and natural resource riches, and disempower the same indigenous communities that celebrated his election.[28]

In 1991, during the administration of President Jaime Paz Zamora, which preceded Sánchez de Lozada's first presidency, Bolivia became one of many countries to ratify the Labour Organization Convention 169 (ILO 169), an agreement that bound nations to recognize and uphold the collective rights of indigenous people's cultures, languages, identities, local governing institutions, labor, and territories.[29] The Sánchez de Lozada administration developed a package of policies and legislation to ensure such rights were protected. The Bolivian constitution was amended by the Sánchez de Lozada government in 1994 to declare Bolivia a "free, independent, sovereign" nation that was also—and this was unprecedented in Bolivian history—"multiethnic and pluricultural." A hallmark of the Sánchez de Lozada administration was the passage of the Law of Popular Participation (LPP), which gave more political and economic power to municipalities, creating 311 new municipal governments where before there had only been a few dozen. Through the LPP and the 1996 Land Reform, indigenous communities were granted legal standing, upholding their right to land, communal property, and traditional practices and customs.[30]

An objective of the LPP was to bring indigenous communities into the governing and political sphere of the country. The LPP worked toward this goal by distributing federal government funding directly to local, municipal governments, extending new fiscal power to the peripheries of the country. The LPP also created new frameworks for local organizational participation in politics through what it referred to as organizaciónes territoriales de base (Grassroots Territorial Organizations, OTBs). Under the new legislation, OTBs were defined as community structures such as ayllus (though, notably, OTBs could not include rural unions allied with the CSUTCB) that could now work closely with the newly empowered municipalities. In addition, tierras comunitarias de origen (original communal lands,

TCOs), established by a new land reform law, encouraged rural people to identify as members of an indigenous community. Specifically, the legislation defined TCOs as spaces where indigenous people lived and relied on traditional social, economic, and cultural organization to survive.[31] This led to soul-searching in some regions where residents had to choose between organizing themselves into unions or ayllus. "Given these new political, economic, and cultural benefits," Andean scholar José Antonio Lucero writes, "many communities that previously identified as peasant communities (in line with the 1953 agrarian laws) now opted for re-constituting themselves as ayllus."[32]

The TCO concept was seen by CONAMAQ member Vicente Flores as "an instrument to recover the original lands of indigenous peoples; it is [a] reencounter with cultures, uses and customs; it is reparation for five hundred years of injustice and oppression; it is synonymous with life and development."[33] Besides offering the benefits of funding and legal status, TCOs, following the framework of ILO 169, emphasized the importance of indigenous territories. This was significant for indigenous communities in Bolivia interested in protecting their natural resources, preventing pollution of their land, and utilizing communally managed territory rather than depending on individually owned plots of land.[34] TCO status enabled ayllus to define their territories beyond the borders of a municipality or department, spread as a mosaic across ecological zones, just as the ayllus had done historically. The status also reflected ILO 169 in that it established that community resources needed to be distributed and used by the community according to traditional uses and customs, such as the collective ownership of land and the required ayllu communal labor and service. Finally, TCOs enshrined the right of prior consultation, which mandates that an outside entity has to consult with the community before it can exploit resources or land within the ayllu's domain.[35]

The CSUTCB protested the laws because they strategically excluded and deincentivized indigenous participation within campesino unions. CSUTCB leaders claimed that the government, through such legislation, sought to sideline leftist unions while encouraging indigenous organizations aligned with the state.[36] Proponents of ayllu reconstruction filled some of the political void left by the fall of the Soviet Union, the rise of debilitating internal divisions in the

CSUTCB, and the closure and privatization of many mines in Bolivia, which devastated the Bolivian Workers' Central (COB). Sánchez de Lozada's policies opened up spaces for indigenous organizations that did not contest the neoliberal direction of the government outright. However, leaders like Evo Morales of the coca farmers' union and Felipe Quispe of the CSUTCB refused to embrace Sánchez de Lozada's projects because of their neoliberal nature, emphasis on privatization of public services and natural resources, and anti-union approach. The policies divided the movements, which various scholars argue may have been the government's intent.[37]

At the same time, pro-ayllu indigenous activists used new laws provided by the government to rebuild their ayllus. As mallku Don Marcelo explained about the LPP, "The law grabbed us, and we grabbed the law."[38] Because of international and national support for indigenous communities, the 1990s were an opportune moment for strengthening ayllus in Bolivia. The legal openings provided by the 1996 Land Reform and the ILO 169, and direct financial aid provided to communities by decentralized federal funding, coincided with a collective desire in many rural areas to rebuild past governing structures, rescue traditions and customs from obscurity, and gain new rights recognized by the government.[39]

RECONSTITUTION OF THE AYLLUS

The 1990s movement to reconstitute ayllus can be traced back to earlier efforts in the 1980s. Ayllu federations were formed by indigenous communities in the 1980s in Oruro and Potosí as a way to survive a major drought and harmful economic reforms. These efforts toward self-sufficiency led to the creation of the Federación de Ayllus del Sur de Oruro in 1987, and the Federación de Ayllus del Norte de Potosí in 1988.[40] The 1988 reconstitution of the ayllus of Quillakas Asanaki, which span the departments of Potosí and Oruro and are part of the Federación de Ayllus del Sur de Oruro, involved authorities walking the boundaries of their territory, from ayllu to ayllu, to "make visible their own territorial structures defined within the Quillakas Asanaki 'nation,'" sociologist Pablo Mamani explains. The strengthening of these ayllus involved meetings between local leaders where they discussed the history of the ayllus, and a gathering in 1989 in the town of Quillacas to celebrate and mark the reconstitution with a parade, cheers, and wiphalas. In some cases, the structures of the ayllus in this region were still intact. For example, ayllu leader Eusebio Pizarro said, "In the community of Pampa Aullagas . . . we do not use the word reconstitution. Why? Because historically my community has remained in the same [ayllu] form that was left to us by our ancestors."[41]

A ceremony and general assembly during the foundation of the CONAMAQ in Challapata in 1997. Courtesy of the Andean Oral History Workshop.

Cancio Rojas, an indigenous leader from northern Potosí, was involved in the reconstitution efforts starting in 1992. In 2015, when he himself was the leader of the CONAMAQ, he reflected on the importance of the reconstitution work in the 1990s, a process to which he had "given nearly all of his life." For him, the reconstruction of the ayllus was critical to the survival of indigenous communities because "the indigenous authorities, the structure of the ayllu, signified having our own power, territorial control, self-governance, free determination, [and] to do the same with our cultural identity, because this was negated for centuries in this country."[42]

THOA members observing this transformation considered using the phrase "to return to the ayllu" to describe the process, but discarded it because they felt that it referred too specifically to a return to the past. They decided that the term "reconstitution" was more appropriate. As Carlos Mamani recalls, "If we said *we are working on the reconstitution*, it was specifically because the organizing indigenous structures had been begrudgingly handed over by the process of colonization that did not end with independence, but rather is still in place, right? So we said that the reconstitution is precisely to return, to put together all the pieces and strengthen them."[43] But more than simply describing the process of ayllu reconstitution, the THOA promoted the ayllu during this period with its production of historical narratives and informational support for reconstitution efforts.

The booklets and radio programs produced by THOA members on the caciques apoderados and T'ula helped generate debates about ayllu history and traditions.[44] THOA member Filomena Nina recalls that, following THOA radio broadcasts, people often called or visited the THOA offices with questions, looking for documents and information on land ownership, the boundaries of landholdings, historical information regarding how the land was worked and held communally within the ayllu, and which families were part of a given community throughout its history.[45] According to scholar Marcia Stephenson, ayllu members raised such questions because the reconstitution of ayllu required a reconstitution of indigenous history, culture, and traditions.[46] The THOA helped ayllu members find and organize their land titles and spread awareness about ayllus, their traditions, histories, and rights. THOA members also offered legal assistance to help communities gain Original Communal Land (TCO) status and worked to strengthen their organizational capacity.[47]

Many people in rural indigenous communities approached the THOA seeking help regarding the legal use of their land titles to claim land and gain federal recognition for their ayllu. People arrived to the THOA offices in La Paz and said, "Just as you say that Santos Marka T'ula, Nina Quispi, and all these people were successful in the defense of the lands of the ayllu, with the backing of the titles obtained from the Crown of Spain, well, OK, here we have [titles], now what we want is for you to help us."[48] The documentary evidence illustrated the extent to which ayllu members had labored and paid to maintain titles to their land. A 1646 colonial document referenced by the THOA from the ayllu network of the Marka Sora, for example, explained that ayllu members had gone to the mita in Potosí, paid their taxes, and thus gained titles to their land from the Crown in Toledo, maintaining their territory "from the Inca until today."[49]

The shared history of this defense of ayllu territory was also preserved orally by ayllu members. In the ayllus, CONAMAQ activist and advisor Elizabeth López explains, community members often "tell you about how the cacique so-and-so had traveled so many days, to such-and-such a place, with so much money to buy the territory. So those are the elements of owning. Once they have done this, what is left in the imagination is that it is *our* territory; they did not buy the ground, they bought the territory."[50]

Ayllu members also turned to other historical sources to recover the history of their communities. In the town of Umala, in the Aroma Province, for example, the revitalization of ayllus involved the community reading and discussing its colonial land titles and boundary surveys from the eighteenth and nineteenth centuries.[51] Yura indigenous people in Potosí drew from scholar Roger Rasnake's dissertation on the Yura community; the dissertation had been translated from English to Spanish and published as a book in Bolivia. Yura leaders used the research to gain legal recognition for the historic boundaries of their ayllu, which leaders said had been encroached upon for centuries.[52] Similarly, Sora indigenous people used a reference to Sora as a "pre-Incan" nation from the 1582 *Memorial de Charcas* to prove their status as a *suyu*, a large territory of ayllus, and cited it in their case for recognition and inclusion in the CONAMAQ network.[53]

On January 16, 1993, in Desaguadero, a town bordering Peru next to Lake Titicaca, approximately seven hundred people from around the Ingavi Province gathered to discuss how they could strengthen their ayllus, culture, language, and regional networks.[54] It was no random coincidence that this meeting of ayllu leaders took place in Ingavi. The province is home to Jesús de Machaca, where the ayllu system of leadership had survived intact in spite of the unionization of the rural community. Indigenous authorities at the meeting decided to focus on recuperating the ayllu as a form of government and to reject the campesino union more forcefully.[55] They formed a commission of sixteen people, two per canton, to study ayllu governance, customs, and traditions. Their goal was to produce a document that could aid ayllu reconstitution efforts nationally.[56] In the months following this historic meeting, ayllu authorities, dressed in their traditional clothing, regularly traveled to La Paz to represent their communities in meetings with government and NGO officials. Ayllu leaders often converged together in the capital city on such trips, became better acquainted with each other, and began forming a national network of ayllus.[57]

The network of leaders and researchers from the Desaguadero meeting published the results of their study in April 1993 in their Estructura Orgánica document, which outlines the organization and traditions of the ayllus of Ingavi. The document was approved by the ayllu network of the region, then presented and distributed as a text published by the THOA to be used and adapted by other ayllus depending on their needs and traditions.[58] According to Stephenson, "Disseminated widely by THOA, this booklet has served as a useful guide for other communities wanting to strengthen their traditions and reconstitute customary forms of governance."[59] The publication was read and used by other largely Aymara highland communities in northern La Paz, Loayza Province, Inquisivi, Omasuyus, Los Andes, and beyond.[60]

The Estructura Orgánica of the Ingavi Province outlines important elements for the organization of the ayllus in this region. It describes, for example, that the goals of the ayllus are to defend their territory, language, natural resources, and culture, as well as Tiwanaku (located within the province). They pledge to work for the economic development of the region and the extension of services such as improved roads, electricity, and water irrigation. The positions of leadership are described as well. According to the Estructura Orgánica, leaders can seek positions of authority only if they have leadership experience, do not have union or political ties, and are honest and responsible to the community. The *mallku provincial* is described as the highest position of leadership and involves convoking other leaders for general meetings, resolving conflicts, and working for the well-being of the province. Other positions include the *yapu kamani*, who oversees agricultural and livestock issues; the *yati kamani*, who focuses on education and children's health; and the *chaski kamani*, who is dedicated to communicating with the wider community regarding ayllu news, events, and decisions. Ayllu rules in the document outline possible infractions committed by leaders, such as corruption, not following through on promised projects, and not participating in organizational marches. The punishments range from fines to removal from leadership positions.[61]

The need to formally coordinate between ayllus and articulate a common agenda deepened throughout the mid-1990s. Ayllu members wanted to build a stronger national network to enable communities to more effectively assist each other and pressure elected officials. They wanted to build an organization that could mobilize members for resources, rights to self-governance, and services. Out of this desire, and following many coordinating meetings among ayllu leaders and eight smaller ayllu and indigenous regional networks, ayllus from across the country founded the CONAMAQ, a national ayllu organization, in Challapata on March 22, 1997.[62]

Through the CONAMAQ, ayllu members advocated for increased rights, services, governmental support, and protection of their autonomy and self-governing structures.[63] The objectives and goals of the CONAMAQ spoke of its historical mandate and connection to past indigenous struggles for land, rights, and sovereignty.[64] "The objective of the CONAMAQ is to recuperate our mother organization as it was before, before the Spanish," Fidel Condori of the Qara Qara nationality of Chuquisaca and Potosí, and a mallku leader from 2012 to 2013, explains. "The CONAMAQ has to recuperate its ancestral territoriality."[65]

GOVERNING TRADITIONS IN THE CONAMAQ

The governing structures and traditions within the CONAMAQ communities demonstrate how individual ayllus have maintained their historical roots in the administration of communal politics, meetings, labor, and votes within the network. The CONAMAQ is organized from the smallest local level, in the ayllu, to the largest territorial body of ayllus, the suyu. The network includes primarily Aymara and Quechua communities in the departments of La Paz, Oruro, Cochabamba, Potosí, and Chuquisaca. At the local level, each ayllu has its own representatives, and each region has its own unique structures, traditions, and forms of governance. The structure of the CONAMAQ itself reflects the ayllu and suyu governing systems with its rotational leadership, term limits, and consensus-based decision-making.[66] This dispersal of authority helps prevent the monopolization and abuse of power by leaders.[67]

A meeting among members of various ayllus from the Omasuyus Province on the sacred hill of Paxchiri for a ritual to honor Mother Earth on August 1, 1994. Courtesy of the Andean Oral History Workshop.

Organizational structures vary across the communities of the CONAMAQ's broad network, given that the ayllus, suyus, and markas in each department often have distinct characteristics. In the case of Suyu Jach'a Carangas, the elected *máximas autoridades originarias* (maximum indigenous authorities) serve two years, and the longest term for authorities of the ayllus is one year. Other communities, like the Jatun Killakas Azanajaqi suyu, establish different leadership positions to handle relations with international entities, manage the development of the suyu, and replace the maximum leader during absences. In the Consejo de Ayllus Originarios de Potosí, ayllus maintain different names for authorities and systems of organization in distinct communities within the ayllu network. For example, the organizational structure of Talina includes *autoridades ancestrales* (ancestral authorities) and the correlating terms and types of office, as well as authorities "imposed in the colonial period" such as the *segunda mayor*, involved with communal work, and the *tesoro*, which originates in the union structure and is involved with administrating communal funds. Other systems are based entirely on ancestral forms of governance and titles, such as *curacas* and *jilaqatas*. All have the same legitimacy within the CONAMAQ.[68]

Regardless of the technicalities of the leadership role or its historical roots, the rotational aspect of leadership at each level of the CONAMAQ is critical to the network's functioning and balance of power, from the local ayllu to the wider suyu. Longtime CONAMAQ advisor Elizabeth López explains that the rotation of traditional leadership positions within the ayllu obliges authorities to care for and respect ayllu members and their territory: "Why is there turn-taking? First, it is the sense of authority, as they call it, the 'sense of service.' So, more than service, it is like the obligation that you have to assume and the responsibility of your suyu. So, more than being at service, you become like a father, a mother, and you have the real obligation of solving the problems of the territory."[69]

According to former CONAMAQ leader Renán Paco Granier, the nature of the organization dictates that one may become a leader only after serving the community from the ground up in a variety of positions—in schools or water management, for example—obtaining more responsibilities the higher one climbs in new positions. Within this cycle, Paco explains, reaching higher positions of authority requires great effort and sacrifice, involving an "enormous trajectory of bureaucratic work."[70] Through such traditional systems of hierarchy, leaders thus gain authority and command respect through hard work and by gaining the support of colleagues, other leaders, and the community base. An ayllu leader's tenure then, according to López, becomes part of the way that the community records and remembers its own history and events. "Because if you talk with the people," she explains, "in the historical memory of the people, they are going to say to you, 'There was a flood when such-and-such authority was there, and such-and-such happened.' So the physical, climactic phenomena [is related by community members to] the authorities who have come and gone."[71]

Ayllu practices carried on in the CONAMAQ network are built to ensure transparency and direct ties with the grassroots level of the community. *Tantachawis*, or assemblies, are convoked by the CONA-MAQ to bring together representatives from the national network of ayllus. At this "parliament of the ayllus," as Pablo Mamani describes it, members discuss pressing political and social issues of the day, confer about the needs of their communities, and come to decisions through a process of consensus.[72] In local ayllu meetings, CONAMAQ leader Gregorio Choque explains, the leadership must decide what to prioritize and how to help and guide the community. Meeting participants might discuss, for example, the production in the agricultural community, the economic well-being of the ayllu, how to better support indigenous languages, or ways to help a neighbor who is ill.[73] In a consultation process called *muyu*, ayllu authorities such as *mallkus* and *jilaqatas* make rounds to each house in the community to see how people are behaving, producing, and interacting—to see that all is in order—and issue penalties and suggestions accordingly. For example, a leader may inquire at one household if the family is dedicating sufficient time to farming or livestock care, if they have enough food in the house, if the weaving is going well, and if the children are completing their chores. Within the muyu process, leaders also receive feedback from the community about what is needed.[74]

THE GATHERING STORM

The 1990s offered new openings for indigenous communities, but it was also an era of privatization and attacks on workers' rights that would shake the country to its core, resulting in an economic crisis and a series of uprisings that fundamentally reshaped Bolivian politics. The national railroad, electricity, airline, telecommunications, oil, and gas businesses were privatized by the government between 1995 and 1997.[75] The government's assault on workers, its privatization efforts, its embrace of International Monetary Fund (IMF) and World Bank policies, and its violent crackdown on the *cocalero* (coca growers) movement paved the way for massive revolts in the early 2000s. These protests at the turn of the century were against the privatization of natural resources, human rights violations resulting from the US-led war on drugs, IMF-backed austerity measures, and government repression against indigenous protesters. In the 1990s Sánchez de Lozada, like other neoliberal leaders of the time, touted his policies as a way to lift people out of poverty and give marginalized sectors of the country a political voice. Yet the effect on the majority of the population was devastating as the poverty rate soared and protests filled the streets of Bolivia.[76]

Sánchez de Lozada's policies were examples of "neoliberal multiculturalism," a political philosophy that granted a minimum of cultural rights to indigenous people while expanding neoliberal reforms in the economy and in governance. This model, according to anthropologist Charles Hale, provides a way for neoliberal states to "'manage' multiculturalism while removing its radical or threatening edge."[77] Neoliberal multiculturalism was an effort to appease marginalized sectors of society who were calling for reform.

In Bolivia in the 1990s, the Sánchez de Lozada administration's reforms did indeed grant indigenous communities new rights and spaces to articulate demands and strengthen traditional structures of ayllu organization. At the same time, the government undermined unions, privatized national industries and services, and removed safety nets for poor communities. Anthropologist Nancy Postero writes that, under the Bolivian neoliberal model, "civil society organizations were encouraged to engage in decisions over small development projects at the local level, with limited or shared funding," rather than to protest large resource extraction plans or contest neoliberalism and economic policy head-on.[78] This led to the government integrating some demands from indigenous sectors, in order to placate them, while moving ahead with structural changes to the economy.

In this sense, Sánchez de Lozada's policies sought to create what Silvia Rivera has labeled the "permitted Indian," a domesticated subject whose voice is elevated through multicultural policies, but only if that voice does not contest the government's neoliberal agenda.[79] However, Bolivia's wide and diverse indigenous movement did not, in fact, succumb to the strict parameters of neoliberal multiculturalism or of the "permitted Indian." Various social movements—including the cocalero movement, members of the MAS, the neighborhood councils of El Alto, and the ayllus in the CONAMAQ—used the openings for political leverage. They also, as Postero points out, used neoliberalism's language of participation, multiculturalism, and promise of rights to demand deeper, structural reforms, pushing beyond the contradictions imposed by the "permitted Indian" paradigm. Postero argues that the protests of the 2000s emerged in Bolivia because of the failure of neoliberal reforms that "often reinforced the structures of exclusion that keep Indians poor and powerless."[80] In this sense, the government's application of neoliberal multiculturalism had the unintended result of mobilizing movements that contested neoliberalism from the late 1990s into the early 2000s.

Even as newly reconstituted ayllus gained recognition under the LPP, indigenous communities continued to remind the central government that new reforms were only the latest in five centuries of broken promises, and they threatened to use their reclaimed organizational power. In 1994, shortly before the passage of the LPP, President Sánchez de Lozada traveled to Jesús de Machaca, a site of historic indigenous resistance and ayllu organization, to promote his new legislation. Upon the president's arrival, Saturnino Tola, the *jach'a mallku* of Jesús de Machaca, gave a speech. Tola's words evoked the power of the past in his community and pointed toward the insurrections to come:

> For more than 500 years, we, the campesinos of Bolivia, have seen ourselves submitted to a series of injustices, which translates to the imposition of a foreign culture, in the plundering of our lands, in the death of our dearest children, trying to destroy our traditions and our own history, trying to convert us into compulsory citizens in our own lands. They have never allowed us to remember our

heroes. . . . [W]e have always had to make homage to our martyrs clandestinely. . . . What we are hoping for today is that all the offers that they make us be fulfilled fully, because we are tired of receiving promises that they never fulfill. If not, as campesino authorities we will find ourselves obligated to take the means that the case demands, because we cannot wait anymore. . . . Mr. President, you have in your hands the staff of power of the country, on the other hand, we have the whip to make sure everything you promise us is fulfilled.[81]

Nearly a decade later, in 2003, Sánchez de Lozada was dramatically ousted from his second term in office by popular protests.

The revolts of the 2000s point to anything but a population of neoliberal subjects standing idle while their natural resources and services were sold off. Instead, indigenous communities and wider social and labor movements across Bolivia challenged the neoliberal model with an array of uprisings, protest tactics, and grassroots pressure that overturned water privatization efforts, IMF structural adjustments, and foreign corporate exploitation of gas reserves. Among the many social forces that contributed to this cycle of popular resistance to neoliberalism were Bolivia's enduring ayllus.

CONCLUSION

"Looking Back, We Will Move Forward"[1]

A portrait of Túpac Katari on display at the ruins of Tiwanaku during Evo Morales's ceremonial inauguration on January 22, 2015. This portrait is made out of corn husks, beans, carrots, and potatoes. Photographer: Benjamin Dangl.

Road blockades led by Aymara activists strangled La Paz during protests in 2000 and 2003. These revolts rejected neoliberal policies, toppled presidents, and ushered in a new era in Bolivian politics. The barricades in La Paz and the Bolivian highlands harkened back to indigenous rebel Túpac Katari's 1781 siege of the city. Bolivian

activist and sociologist Marxa Chávez said that when people at the
road blockades and protests evoked Katari, they were recovering not
just "empty words" but "an idea of collective power," a living memory
put to practice in the streets. "It was truly a rebel memory, a recollection that you, yourself, were performing through the assemblies,
through the meetings, through the control that you demanded of
your leaders."[2]

The indigenous people's histories explored here were not trans-
formative on their own; they were made powerful by people who acti-
vated them in the streets, gave them meaning at the barricades, and
wielded them as a tool to change their world. This book has demonstrated that the production and mobilization of indigenous people's
histories of resistance by activists and intellectuals was a critical tool
used in indigenous struggles from 1970 to 2000 and beyond. Such
uses of the past oriented and empowered indigenous movements,
strengthened alternative models of governance and land reform, and
helped activists develop an indigenous vision for the transformation
of Bolivian politics and society.

In the shadow of the National Revolution, Kataristas lifted
up indigenous history and identity in a struggle for rights, political
power, and dignity. Challenging the assimilationist policies of the
National Revolution and the repressive dictatorships that followed,
Kataristas held up the wiphala, preconquest Andean utopias, and the
historic models of Katari, Sisa, Willka, Marka T'ula, and others as
banners for an indigenous resurgence. This intellectual and historical
labor was articulated most visibly in the CSUTCB, founded in 1979.
This independent campesino union used Katari's strategy of laying
siege to La Paz through road blockades to force governments to meet
the union's demands for political power, land, services, and self-determination. Both Kataristas and the CSUTCB indigenized civil
society and politics during this period. They elevated and popularized
indigenous historical consciousness and the awareness of centuries of
resistance in Bolivia. Kataristas and CSUTCB members opened up
new discursive and political spaces to imagine and work toward indigenous liberation in a neoliberal era.

The THOA was created in these spaces largely by Aymara professors and students in La Paz in 1983. The THOA gathered oral

histories from elders in rural Aymara communities in the Bolivian highlands to piece together little-known histories of indigenous resistance. They filled in the silences in the archives and official accounts of Bolivian history by drawing from a wellspring of oral traditions in rural areas. Their collaborative research methods and horizontal relationships with interviewees helped them produce groundbreaking histories, which were widely distributed as pamphlets and radio programs. One of the THOA's most influential projects was a history of the early twentieth-century cacique apoderado Santos Marka T'ula. Their work on T'ula brought together dozens of interviews with contemporaries and relatives of T'ula, and resulted in a popular booklet and nationally broadcasted radio program. The THOA's work on T'ula and other indigenous people's histories of rebellion promoted indigenous pride and spurred people to action.

The THOA was also instrumental in the 1990s movement to reconstitute the ayllu, a centuries-old form of local communal governance, decision-making, and agricultural production in the Andes. Ayllu advocates in this era conducted their own historical research and reflections to recover the histories and traditions of their ayllus. They utilized political openings to gain rights, autonomy, and political power. In this process, indigenous activists revitalized and strengthened ayllu governance, labor organization, and traditions. The grassroots historical investigations and discussions conducted by ayllu members culminated in the 1997 founding of the CONAMAQ, a national ayllu network that contributed to the defeat of neoliberal government policies in Bolivia through a wave of protests in the early 2000s.

Over the decades, the indigenous movements of Bolivia grew from a force that was undermined by the MNR and subsequent dictatorships to a political power that overthrew political tyrants, rejected corporate globalization, and reshaped the socioeconomic landscape of the nation. These groups were at the forefront of the country's uprisings at the turn of the century, paved the way for the election of Morales in 2005, and continue to play a pivotal role in the development of alternatives to neocolonialism and capitalism in Bolivia.

The road to Evo Morales's election was a long and tumultuous one, forged in coca fields and street rebellions. Morales is a former coca grower and union leader who rose up from the grassroots as an activist fighting against the US militarization of the tropical coca-growing region of the Chapare in the central part of the country. (Although it is a key ingredient in cocaine, the coca leaf is used legally for medicinal and cultural purposes in Bolivia.) Morales and other coca farmers saw the US-led drug war in the country as an attempt to undermine radical political movements, such as the coca unions Morales led. He became an early figurehead and dissident congressman in the MAS political party, which grew in part out of the coca unions and ran a nearly successful presidential bid by Morales against neoliberal president Sánchez de Lozada in 2002.

The MAS has always defined itself as a political instrument of the social movements from which it emerged. During the early 2000s, Bolivia saw numerous uprisings.[3] In the 2000 Cochabamba Water War, the people of that city rose up against the privatization of their water by Bechtel, a multinational corporation. After weeks of protests, the company was kicked out of the city, and the water went back into public hands. In February 2003, police, students, public workers, and regular citizens across the country led an insurrection against an IMF-backed plan to cut wages and increase income taxes on a poverty-stricken population. The revolt forced the government and IMF to surrender to movement demands and to rescind the public wage and tax policies, ushering in a new period of unity and solidarity between movements as civil dissatisfaction gathered heat, reaching a boiling point during what came to be called the Gas War.

The Gas War, which took place in September and October 2003, was a national uprising that emerged among diverse sectors of society against a plan to sell Bolivian natural gas via Chile to the United States for eighteen cents per thousand cubic feet, only to be resold in the United States for approximately four dollars per thousand cubic feet. In a move that was all too familiar to citizens in a country famous for its cheap raw materials, the right-wing Sánchez de Lozada government worked with private companies to design a plan in which Chilean and US businesses would benefit more from Bolivia's natural wealth than Bolivian citizens themselves would. Bolivians from across class and ethnic lines united in nationwide protests, strikes, and road blockades against the exportation plan.

They demanded that the gas be nationalized and industrialized in Bolivia so that the profits from the industry could go to government development projects and social programs. Neighborhood councils in the city of El Alto, many with ex-miners as members, banded together to block roads in their city. The height of the Gas War recalled Katari's siege as it involved thousands of El Alto residents, organized largely through neighborhood councils, blocking off La Paz from the rest of the country and finally facing down the military. The government's crackdown intensified as state forces in helicopters above shot the civilians below, leaving over sixty people dead. The repression pushed movements in the city into a fury that emboldened their resistance. By mid-October, the people successfully ousted Sánchez de Lozada and rejected the gas exportation plan, pointing the way toward nationalization.

Such protests and others promoting land reform and demanding a new, progressive constitution opened up new spaces for radical alternatives to the neocolonial state, putting Bolivian sovereignty and a full rejection of the neoliberal model at the center of the country's politics. The MAS and Morales emerged from this period of discontent as the most adept at channeling the energy and demands of the grassroots while navigating the country's national political landscape—one dominated at the time by right-wing political parties.

In 2005, Morales won the presidential election, largely thanks to the political space and popular hope inspired by social movement victories in the previous five years. Because he was the first indigenous president of Bolivia, his election was seen as a watershed moment in a nation where the majority was poor and indigenous. That Morales could be elected on a socialist, anti-imperialist platform after roughly twenty years of neoliberalism was historic. Perhaps even more significant was that, in a nation rife with racism and neocolonialism, an indigenous man from a humble background could take up residence in the presidential palace.[4]

Shortly after assuming office, Morales moved quickly to institutionalize many of the social movement victories that had been won in the streets. He nationalized sectors of Bolivia's rich gas industry, convened an assembly to rewrite the country's constitution, and followed through on many of his campaign pledges to alleviate poverty and empower the poor and indigenous people living on the margins of society. His election notably took place at a time in Latin America when other progressive presidents were in power; from Argentina to Venezuela, Morales was not alone in asserting national sovereignty and rejecting imperialism.[5]

The economic changes in the country point to some of the reasons Morales was so popular throughout much of his time in office. Bolivia's GDP rose steadily from 2009 to 2013, contributing to what the UN called the highest rate of poverty reduction in the region, with a 32.2 percent drop between 2000 and 2012. The rates of employment and pay went up, buoyed by a 20 percent minimum wage increase. Much of this economic success can be tied to the government placing many industries and businesses—from mines to telephone companies—under state control, thus generating funds for the MAS government's popular social programs, including projects seeking to lift mothers, children, and the elderly out of poverty. Thanks to a successful literacy program, UNESCO has declared the country free of illiteracy. Much of the funding created by nationalization also pays for infrastructure and highway development, as only 10 percent of the country's roads are paved.[6]

The MAS political project has not been without its pitfalls.[7] Some of the same indigenous and rural communities that the Morales government seeks to support with its social programs and politics have been displaced by extractive industries. Fields of GMO soy, accompanied by toxic pesticides, are expanding across rural areas in the eastern part of the country with the government's support. Abortion is still largely illegal in Bolivia, and rates of domestic abuse against women and femicide have been on the rise. Major corruption scandals have beset the MAS and its movement allies, including the CSUTCB and the Bartolina Sisa movement. Morales is pushing forward with a controversial nuclear power plant to be built near earthquake-prone La Paz, and the MAS plans to build a highway through the Isiboro-Sécure Indigenous Territory and National Park (TIPNIS), a move which has sparked protests. The contradictions inherent in the Morales administration's decision to deepen extractivist projects in mining, gas, and mega-dams while simultaneously cheerleading Mother Earth will impact the nation and its indigenous movements for decades to come.[8]

When I sat down in Cochabamba, Bolivia, in 2003 for an early morning interview with Evo Morales, then a coca farmer leader and congressman, he was drinking fresh-squeezed orange juice and ignoring the constant ringing of the landline phone at his union's office. Just a few weeks before our meeting, a nationwide social movement demanded that Bolivia's natural gas reserves be put under state control. How the wealth underground could benefit the poor majority aboveground was on everybody's mind. As far as his political ambitions were concerned, Morales wanted natural resources to "construct a political instrument of liberation and unity for Latin America."[9] He was widely considered a popular contender for the presidency and was clear that the indigenous politics he sought to mobilize as a leader were tied to a vision of Bolivia recovering its natural wealth for national development. "We, the indigenous people, after five hundred years of resistance, are retaking power," he said. "This retaking of power is oriented towards the recovery of our own riches, our own natural resources."[10] Two years later he was elected president.

Fast-forward to March 2014. It was a sunny Saturday morning in downtown La Paz, and street vendors were putting up their stalls for the day alongside a rock band that was organizing a small concert in a pedestrian walkway. I was meeting with Mama Nilda Rojas, a leader of CONAMAQ. Rojas, along with her colleagues and family, had been persecuted by the Morales government in part for her activism against mining and other extractive industries. "The indigenous territories are in resistance," she said, "because the open veins of Latin America are still bleeding, still covering the earth with blood. This blood is being taken away by all the extractive industries."[11] While Morales saw the wealth underground as a tool for liberation, Rojas saw the president as someone who was pressing forward with extractive industries without concern for the environmental destruction and displacement of rural indigenous communities they left in their wake. "This government has given a false discourse on an international level, defending Pachamama, defending Mother Earth," Rojas explained, while the reality in Bolivia is quite a different story: "Mother Earth is tired."[12]

Critiques of the MAS and Morales are rampant among Bolivia's dissident indigenous movements and thinkers. "I had so much hope at the moment when Evo Morales came into the government," Silvia Rivera explained.[13] "But he has come to crave centralized power, which has become a part of Bolivia's dominant culture since the 1952 revolution. The idea that Bolivia is a weak state and needs to be a strong state—this is such a recurrent idea, and it is becoming the self-suicide of revolution. Because the revolution is *what the people do*—and what the people do is *decentralized.*" She continued, "I would say that the strength of Bolivia is not the state but the people."[14]

While Bolivia's diverse social and indigenous movements wield power from the streets, the MAS and Morales have successfully maintained and deepened their influence in part by mobilizing indigenous and working-class identity as an extension of party politics. The coca leaf is often used by the MAS in political campaigning as a symbol both of indigenous history and of the fight against US imperialism. Similarly, the government's championing of indigenous culture more broadly, and its connecting that culture to a nationalist project of liberation and development, resonates with many voters who felt they had been manipulated by previous political leaders who, rather than seeking to decolonize and refound the nation on the basis of its indigenous roots, instead wanted to turn Bolivia into a mirror image of the West.

Many of the same histories, discourses of indigenous resistance, and symbols of revolt produced and promoted from below by indigenous movements over the period examined here are now celebrated as part of official state policy and rhetoric under Morales. The administration has made the wiphala part of the official national flag, granted new rights and power to indigenous communities, named a satellite after Katari, and published new editions of the works of Fausto Reinaga and other formerly dissident thinkers and historians.[15] Some of these government approaches have popularized images of Katari more as a distinguished head of state—to suit Morales's position—than as a rebel leader. Katari has been portrayed in a number of ways throughout Bolivian history: during the MNR revolutionary period he was sometimes depicted in paintings holding a gun, and the Kataristas saw him as a defiant, chain-breaking symbol of their struggle. During its first months in office, the MAS government chose another version that represented Katari as a stately leader, not a revolutionary. This version of Katari was requested in 2005 by former president Carlos Mesa, not Morales. In the portrait, scholars Vincent Nicolas and Pablo Quisbert explain, "Katari is no longer represented as a rebel, but as a dignitary of the State, dressed in a kind of jacket and a modern shirt, covered in an elegant poncho adorned with textile figures, and grasping a special staff of authority, a symbol of his power."[16] Though produced before Morales's election, this image was taken up by his administration and widely distributed to tie Morales to Katari. "The Evo-Katari affiliation," Nicolas and Quisbert write, "has been supported very much in this iconography, and is placed as a kind of backdrop to Morales himself."[17]

Such political uses of the past and historical symbols can be traced to the government's Vice Ministry of Decolonization, which was created in 2009 and works with other sectors of government to promote, for example, indigenous language education, gender parity in government, indigenous forms of justice, antiracism initiatives, indigenous autonomy, and the strengthening of indigenous traditions, symbols, and histories.[18] One of the people involved in such decolonization efforts in the vice ministry was Elisa Vega Sillo, a former leader in the Bartolina Sisa movement and a member of the Kallawaya indigenous nation. She spoke of the process of decolonizing indigenous history in Bolivia. "We try and recover an anticolonial vision above all," she said, focusing on how indigenous people, over centuries of resistance, "rebelled to get rid of oppression, the slavery in the haciendas, the taking over of land, of our wealth in Cerro Rico in Potosí, our trees, our knowledge—they rebelled against all of this. But in the official history, the colonial history, they tell us that the bad ones were the indigenous people, and that they deserved what they got." She explained, "We recuperate our own history, a history of how we were in constant rebellion and how they were never able to subdue us."[19]

As a part of these efforts, government-led rituals now take place every November 14 to mark the death of Túpac Katari. Yet, sociologist Pablo Mamani asks, why remember Katari only every November 14, as though he is dead? "We must put this kind of ritual behind us to enter a more everyday rituality," he explains. Mamani sees no need to remember Katari just one day a year, because "Túpac Katari has returned and is among us, and we, ourselves, are the thousands of men and women that we have in these territories, and we are on our feet, walking."[20]

ACKNOWLEDGMENTS

The journey of this project from rough outline to book has spanned many years, street protests, days in the archives, flights across the equator, late-night conversations, early-morning bus rides, shared beers, bags of coca leaves, and friendships. Over the time of this book's production, some family and friends have said goodbye while others have just arrived. Like the centuries of Andean rebellions that shape today's movements and memories, each person I have relied on and shared this journey with has made a mark on these pages.

The many afternoons and evenings I spent at the offices of the Andean Oral History Workshop in La Paz, Bolivia, were among the most rewarding and memorable experiences of this research project. I particularly appreciated the time and stories shared by current and former THOA members Felipe Santos Quispe, Filomena Nina, Rodolfo Quisbert, Carlos Mamani, and Marcelo Fernández Osco. Thanks also to members of the Katarista and Indianista movements, CSUTCB, Bartolina Sisa movement, and CONAMAQ who opened their doors and histories to me. Without the crucial guidance and insight provided by the writings of Silvia Rivera Cusicanqui, Javier Hurtado, Xavier Albó, Esteban Ticona, Carlos Mamani, Pablo Mamani, and the THOA, this book would not have been possible.

During the course of this research, I learned the most from the people I was able to interview in Bolivia, including Juanita Ancieta Orellana, José Oscar Ávila, Gregorio Barco Guarachi, Isabel Elena Burgos, Oscar Calisaya, Félix Cárdenas Aguilar, Marco Antonio Castro, Beatriz Chambilla Mamani, Marxa Chávez, Roberto Choque Canqui, Jorge Choque Salomé, Gregorio Choque, Gonzalo Colque, Cristóbal Condorena, Fidel Condori, Paulino Cruz Canaviri, Marcelo Fernández Osco, Joel Guarachi Morales, Humberto Guarayo, Agustín Gutiérrez, Máximo Freddy Huarachi Paco, Alberto Huata Manza, Alejandro Ilaquita Marka, Constantino Lima, Elizabeth López, Carlos Mamani, Pablo Mamani, Filomena Nina, Isabel Ortega, Renán Paco Granier, Justino Peralta, Anselma Perlacios, Pedro Portugal, Rodolfo Quisbert, Ismael Quispe Ticona, Zenón Quispe,

Apolinar Quito Mamani, Hilda Reinaga, Cancio Rojas, Nilda Rojas, Felipe Santos Quispe, Tomás Saqueli Huaranca, Juan Carlos Valencia Zentero, Elisa Vega Sillo, and Vique Villalobos. Gracias a todos y todas.

Thanks to my friends in Bolivia for their camaraderie while I researched this book: Marielle Cauthin, Ida Peñaranda, Oscar Vega, David Dougherty, William Wroblewski, Jorge Derpic, Sarah Shariahri, Tanya Kerssen, Gabriel Zeballos, Marcela Olivera, Sarah Hines, Rosseline Ugarte, Reyna Ayala, Linda Farthing, Kathryn Ledebur, Jorge Ocsa, and the late Abraham Bojorquez.

Thanks to the many people and institutions that made this project feasible. Lola Paredes at the Biblioteca Fundación Xavier Albó in La Paz was a constant source of advice, contacts, and resources. Thanks to Alejandra Tineo and Carolina Ricaldoni for their interview transcription work. I am grateful to April Howard for her help translating many of the quotes here from Spanish to English and for copyediting the book. Thanks to Bear Guerra for the cover photo, and thanks to journalist William Wroblewski, Rodolfo Quisbert of the THOA, and Vladimir Salazar of the Archivo del Museo Nacional de Etnografía y Folklore for helping me find and use the photos included in this book. Additional thanks to William for use of the photo of Fausto Reinaga's office. Thanks to scholars Carmen Soliz, Bret Gustafson, Linda Farthing, Jason Tockman, and Sinclair Thomson for helpful advice in early stages of this project; to Okezi Otovo, my MA advisor at the University of Vermont, for her encouragement; and to the late Chinua Achebe, who was an important mentor during my undergrad years at Bard College.

Thanks to the wonderful archivists and librarians at the Museo Nacional de Etnografía y Folklore, Archivo y Biblioteca Nacionales de Bolivia, Biblioteca Fundación Xavier Albó, Archivo Histórico de la Asamblea Legislativa Plurinacional, Biblioteca Pública Municipal de La Paz, Biblioteca y Archivo Arturo Costa de la Torre, and Archivo Histórico de La Paz.

Before I turned this work into a book, it was a doctoral dissertation I completed at the History Department at McGill University in Montreal, Canada. I am very thankful to everyone in the department for their guidance and for the generous financial support from McGill

University, including the Richard H. Tomlinson Doctoral Fellowship, Friends of McGill Fellowship, and Graduate Excellence Awards, all of which enabled this work and my participation in the doctoral program. Mitali Das at McGill's History Department helped my years in the program go smoothly, Eamon Duffy of the McGill Library helped with citation guidance, and Nancy Piñeiro and Julie Scheveneels provided helpful translation assistance for the project.

I deeply appreciate the support, expertise, and time of the McGill history professors who helped shape this project. My advisor, Daviken Studnicki-Gizbert, provided crucial guidance. His enthusiasm for the project, careful feedback on many drafts, and encouragement to dig deeper in my research constantly elevated the quality of this work. Conversations over the years with Catherine LeGrand always helped me make my writing more precise and enabled me to understand my work within the wider Latin American historiography. Jon Soske's course on oral history was a crucial first step in the development of this work, and his thought-provoking feedback enriched this entire process for me. Overall, these professors helped strengthen not just my research and writing but also, most importantly, my thinking. Thanks also to the additional members of my thesis defense committee, Professors Kris Onishi, Jeremy Tai, Allan Downey, and Cynthia Milton, and to Marc Becker for his review of this work.

As I worked on transforming the thesis into a book, I was happy to reunite with my friends at AK Press to make this publishing project a reality. It has been a joy to work with Zach Blue and Charles Weigl and everyone at AK again on what is our third book together. I am grateful for their belief in this project and their enthusiasm to bring it into the world.

I was unable to incorporate all of the suggestions and advice I received on this project, and I alone bear the responsibility of any shortcomings or mistakes in this book.

My family and friends have been wonderful allies throughout these years of work. Thanks, as always, to my rock star of a mother, Suzanne Summers, my grandmother and original cheerleader, Betty Summers, and my brothers Nick and Jim Dangl. During the writing of this book, I have been very happy to welcome Paul Elkan into the family. Thanks also to Tom, Meg, and Eli Howard, our great community in Vermont, everyone at *Toward Freedom*, and my friends in Burlington and Montreal. My grandfather, Linden Summers Jr., and father, Jon Dangl, would have loved to see this process come to fruition. I am sorry they did not live to see it, but their spirit has been with me each step of the way.

Finally, thanks to my wife, April Howard. I would not have been able to complete this without the belief she has in me. Her optimism, brilliance, humor, and support helped carry me through this journey. Our son, Leon, was born just as this project was taking shape, and our daughter, Eulalia, was born as it was wrapping up. They have filled us with love and wonder each day since. It has been the joy of my life to walk into the future alongside April, Leon, and Eulalia. This book is dedicated to them.

NOTES

Introduction: The Five Hundred Year Rebellion

1. Ministerio de Comunicación, Estado Plurinacional de Bolivia, "Ceremonia ancestral de posesión de mando, Tiwanaku—La Paz," *Somos Sur*, January 21, 2015.

2. Ismael Quispe Ticona, interview with the author, Tiwanaku, Bolivia, January 22, 2015. Also see Benjamin Dangl, "The Power of the Spectacle: Evo Morales' Inauguration in Tiwanaku, Bolivia," *Toward Freedom*, January 29, 2015, https://towardfreedom.org/archives/americas/the-power-of-the-spectacle-evo-morales-inauguration-in-tiwanaku-bolivia/.

3. Elizabeth López, interview with the author, La Paz, Bolivia, October 16, 2014.

4. Yuri F. Tórrez and Claudia Arce C., *Construcción simbólica del estado plurinacional de Bolivia: Imaginarios políticos, discursos, rituales y celebraciones* (La Paz: PIEB, 2014), 122–23. Also see Vincent Nicolas and Pablo Quisbert, *Pachakuti: El retorno de la nación* (La Paz: PIEB, 2014); Nancy Postero, "Andean Utopias in Evo Morales's Bolivia," *Latin American and Caribbean Ethnic Studies* 2, no. 1 (2007): 1–28; and Nicole Fabricant, "Symbols in Motion: Katari as Traveling Image in Landless Movement Politics in Bolivia," *Latin American and Caribbean Ethnic Studies* 7, no. 1 (2012): 1–29.

5. Sergio Serulnikov, *Revolution in the Andes: The Age of Túpac Amaru* (Durham, NC: Duke University Press, 2013), 116–17. Also see Steve Stern, ed., *Resistance, Rebellion, and Consciousness in the Andean Peasant World: 18th to 20th Centuries* (Madison: University of Wisconsin Press, 1987).

6. Sinclair Thomson, *We Alone Will Rule: Native Andean Politics in the Age of Insurgency* (Madison: University of Wisconsin Press, 2002), 184. For this quote, Thomson cites Archivo Nacional de Bolivia, EC 1788 [1788] No. 29, fol. IIV.

7. Ibid., 10. For this quote, Thomson cites Archivo General de Indias, Buenos Aires 319, "Cuaderno No. 4," fols. 60v, 77.

8. Serulnikov, *Revolution in the Andes*, 115–16.

9. María Eugenia del Valle de Siles, *Historia de la rebelión de Tupac Catari* (La Paz: Plural Editores, 2011), 179. For accounts of the siege, also see Ward Stavig and Ella Schmidt, eds. and trans., *The Tupac Amaru and Catarista Rebellions: An Anthology of Sources* (Indianapolis: Hackett, 2008), 227–37.

10. Thomson, *We Alone Will Rule*, 209–10.

11. Serulnikov, *Revolution in the Andes*, 130–31, 127–28. Also see Nicholas A. Robins, *Native Insurgencies and the Genocidal Impulse in the Americas* (Bloomington: Indiana University Press, 2005), 49–50.

12. Sinclair Thomson, "Moments of Redemption: Decolonization as Reconstitution of the Body of Katari," *Rasanblaj Caribeño* 12, no. 1 (2015); Thomson, *We Alone Will Rule*, 19, 208; Stavig and Schmidt, *Tupac Amaru and Catarista Rebellions*, 241–42; Lyman L. Johnson, ed., *Death, Dismemberment, and Memory: Body Politics in Latin America* (Albuquerque: University of New Mexico Press, 2004).

13. Though this is the widely accepted phrase attributed to Katari, there is no historical evidence proving he said it. However, Farthing and Kohl point

out that such reconstructed stories "neatly tie into powerful collective memories that promise the cyclical return of indigenous power and the sense of obligation to ancestors." Linda Farthing and Benjamin Kohl, "Mobilizing Memory: Bolivia's Enduring Social Movements," *Social Movement Studies* 12, no. 4 (2013): 368.

14.   Raquel Gutiérrez Aguilar, *Rhythms of the Pachakuti: Indigenous Uprising and State Power in Bolivia* (Durham: Duke University Press, 2014).

15.   Marxa Chávez, interview with the author, La Paz, Bolivia, February 19, 2015.

16.   Ibid. As Hylton and Thomson explain in their work on this topic, "Insurrectional indigenous culture had inspired itself in the memory of previous uprisings and has nourished itself from the practical experience accumulated by those who had participated in past processes of struggle." Forrest Hylton and Sinclair Thomson, "Ya es otro tiempo el presente: Cuatro momentos de insurgencia indígena," in *Ya es otro tiempo el presente: Cuatro momentos de insurgencia indígena*, Forrest Hylton, Felix Patzi, Sergio Serulnikov, and Sinclair Thomson (La Paz: Muela del Diablo Editores, 2005), 8. On how such accumulations of experience feed into rebellions, see Adolfo Gilly, "Historias desde adentro: La tenaz persistencia de los tiempos," in Hylton et al., *Ya es otro tiempo el presente*, 22; and Luis Tapia, "Bolivia: Ciclos y estructuras de rebelión," in *Bolivia: Memoria, insurgencia y movimientos sociales*, ed. Maristella Svampa and Pablo Stefanoni (Buenos Aires: El Colectivo, CLACSO, 2007), 176, 185. Also see Felipe Quispe Huanca, *Tupak Katari Vive y Vuelve . . . Carajo* (La Paz: Ediciones Pachakuti, 2007).

17.   For more on the uprisings of the 2000s and the rise and presidency of Evo Morales, see Benjamin Dangl, *The Price of Fire: Resource Wars and Social Movements in Bolivia* (Oakland: AK Press, 2007); and Dangl, *Dancing with Dynamite: Social Movements and States in Latin America* (Oakland: AK Press, 2010).

18.   Peter Winn, *Americas: The Changing Face of Latin America and the Caribbean* (Berkeley: University of California Press, 2006), 39–85; Sinclair Thomson et al., eds., *The Bolivia Reader: History, Culture, Politics* (Durham: Duke University Press, 2018), 45–70; and Roxanne Dunbar-Ortiz, *An Indigenous Peoples' History of the United States* (Boston: Beacon Press, 2014).

19.   Edward W. Said, *Culture and Imperialism* (New York: Vintage Books, 1994), 8. Said cites Harry Magdoff, *Imperialism: From the Colonial Age to the Present* (New York: Monthly Review Press, 1987), 29, 35.

20.   Vijay Prashad, *The Darker Nations: A People's History of the Third World* (New York: New Press, 2007); Prashad, *The Poorer Nations: A Possible History of the Global South* (New York: Verso, 2012); Dane Kennedy, *Decolonization: A Very Short Introduction* (New York: Oxford University Press, 2016); and Todd Shepard, *Voices of Decolonization: A Brief History with Documents* (Boston: Bedford/St. Martin's, 2015).

21.   Frantz Fanon, *The Wretched of the Earth* (New York: Grove Press, 1963), 235.

22.   Ibid., 238. Also see Peter Hudis, *Frantz Fanon: Philosopher of the Barricades* (London: Pluto Press, 2015).

23.   Carlos Mamani Condori, "The Path of Decolonization," in *New World of Indigenous Resistance: Noam Chomsky and Voices from North, South, and Central America*, eds. Lois Meyer and Benjamín Maldonado Alvarado (San Francisco: City Lights Books, 2010), 285.

24.   Rigoberta Menchu, *I, Rigoberta Menchu: An Indian Woman in Guatemala* (New York: Verso, 2010); Heather Gies, "The New Colonization: UN Expert Urges Guatemala to End Structural Racism against Indigenous People," *Toward Freedom*, June 5, 2018, https://towardfreedom.org/archives/americas/the-new-colonization-un-expert-urges-guatemala-to-end-structural-racism-against-

indigenous-people/. For more on memory, political history, and justice in Guatemala, see Kirsten Weld, *Paper Cadavers: The Archives of Dictatorship in Guatemala* (Durham: Duke University Press, 2014).

25.   Rosa Isolde Reuque Paillalef, *When a Flower Is Reborn: The Life and Times of a Mapuche Feminist* (Durham: Duke University Press, 2002); Raúl Zibechi, "The Mapuche People's New Forms of Struggle," *NACLA Report on the Americas*, March 13, 2008, https://nacla.org/news/mapuche-people %E2%80%99s-new-forms-struggle.

26.   Wendy Wolford, *This Land Is Ours Now: Social Mobilization and the Meaning of Land in Brazil* (Durham: Duke University Press, 2010); Wyre Davies, "Brazil's Indigenous Leaders Risk Their Lives Fighting for Survival," *BBC News*, June 20, 2016, https://www.bbc.com/news/world-latin-america-36573075.

27.   Pablo Mamani Ramírez, *Geopolíticas Indígenas* (El Alto: Centro Andino de Estudios Estratégicos, 2005), 61.

28.   Javier Sanjinés C., "The Nation, an Imagined Community?" in *Globalization and the Decolonial Option*, eds. Walter D. Mignolo and Arturo Escobar (London: Routledge, 2010), 152–53.

29.   Ibid.

30.   Pamela Jacquelin-Andersen, *The Indigenous World: 2018* (Copenhagen: International Work Group for Indigenous Affairs, 2018), 175.

31.   Javier Sanjinés C., *Mestizaje Upside-Down: Aesthetic Politics in Modern Bolivia* (Pittsburgh: University of Pittsburgh Press, 2004), 187.

32.   Aníbal Quijano, "Coloniality and Modernity/Rationality," in Mignolo and Escobar, *Globalization and the Decolonial Option*, 24.

33.   Mamani, "Path of Decolonization," 286.

34.   Kennedy, *Decolonization*, 3.

35.   Rebecca Earle, *The Return of the Native: Indians and Myth-Making in Spanish America, 1810–1930* (Durham: Duke University Press, 2007), 100–102.

36.   Serulnikov, *Revolution in the Andes*, 136–37.

37.   Carlos Montenegro, *Nacionalismo y coloniaje* (La Paz: Librería Editorial "Juventud," 2003; first published 1944).

38.   Sinclair Thomson, "Revolutionary Memory in Bolivia: Anticolonial and National Projects from 1781 to 1952," in *Proclaiming Revolution: Bolivia in Comparative Perspective*, eds. Merilee S. Grindle and Pilar Domingo (London: Institute for Latin American Studies, 2003), 125–26. Also see Donna Yates, "Pre-Conquest Utopia and How a 'Republic' Becomes 'Plurinational': The Bolivian State in the 21st Century" (paper presented at the 110th Annual Meeting of the American Anthropological Association, Montreal, 2011); and Postero, "Andean Utopias."

39.   Fanon, *Wretched of the Earth*, 148.

40.   Linda Tuhiwai Smith, *Decolonizing Methodologies: Research and Indigenous Peoples* (London: Zed Books, 2012), 36. In *The Politics of Memory*, Joanne Rappaport looks at the Páez indigenous community in Colombia and their use, manipulation, and interpretation of their own history to suit the political and social needs of the time. For Nasa indigenous intellectuals, Rappaport writes, "chains of transmission of historical knowledge are only important insofar as they help their recipients to elicit powerful images of the past, images which move people to action." Joanne Rappaport, *The Politics of Memory: Native Historical Interpretation in the Colombian Andes* (Durham: Duke University Press, 1998), 23. Also see Joanne Rappaport, *Intercultural Utopias: Public Intellectuals, Cultural Experimentation, and Ethnic Pluralism in Colombia* (Durham: Duke University Press, 2005).

41.   Smith, *Decolonizing Methodologies*, 203–4.

42. Also see Farthing and Kohl, "Mobilizing Memory," 364. For more resources on the rise, philosophy, methods, development, production, and impact of the THOA, see Silvia Rivera Cusicanqui, "El potencial epistemológico y teórico de la historia oral: De la lógica instrumental a la descolonización de la historia," *Voces recobradas: Revista de historia oral* 8, no. 21 (2006): 12–22; Marcia Stephenson, "Forging an Indigenous Counterpublic Sphere: The Taller de Historia Oral Andina in Bolivia," *Latin American Research Review* 37, no. 2 (2002): 99–118; and Felipe Santos Quispe, "Una mirada autocrítica a la historia del THOA: 1980 al 1997," in *XXI Reunión Anual de Etnología I* (La Paz: Museo Nacional de Etnografía y Folklore, 2008): 153–70.

43. Nathan Wachtel, "Introduction," *History and Anthropology* 2, no. 2 (1986): 208.

44. Paul Thompson, "The Voice of the Past: Oral History," in *The Oral History Reader*, eds. Robert Perks and Alistair Thomson (London: Routledge, 2006), 28.

45. Alessandro Portelli, "What Makes Oral History Different," in Perks and Thomson, *Oral History Reader*, 36–37.

46. Myth was particularly relevant in the THOA's work on cacique apoderado Santos Marka T'ula: Taller de Historia Oral Andina, *El indio Santos Marka T'ula: Cacique principal de los ayllus de Qallapa y apoderado general de las comunidades originarias de la republica* (La Paz: Ediciones del THOA, 1988). While the THOA operated in a similar vein to other oral history groups throughout the world over this time, interviews with THOA members point to the extent to which the impetus, theory, and methods of their group were quite specific to Bolivia and the Andes. For further work on oral history, see Ciraj Rassool, "Power, Knowledge and the Politics of Public Pasts," *African Studies* 69, no. 1 (2010): 79–101; Bill Schwarz, "History on the Move: Reflections on History Workshop," *Radical History Review* 57 (1993): 203–20; Popular Memory Group, "Popular Memory: Theory, Politics, Method," in *Making Histories: Studies in History-Writing and Politics*, eds. Richard Johnson et al. (London: Hutchinson, 1982), 206–20; Michael Frisch, "Commentary: Sharing Authority: Oral History and the Collaborative Process," *The Oral History Review* 30, no. 1 (2003): 111–13; Urvashi Butalia, *The Other Side of Silence: Voices from the Partition of India* (Durham: Duke University Press, 2000); Alessandro Portelli, *The Order Has Been Carried Out: History, Memory, and Meaning of a Nazi Massacre in Rome* (London: Palgrave Macmillan, 2007); Portelli, "The Peculiarities of Oral History," *History Workshop*, 12, no. 1 (1981): 96–107; Ronald Fraser, "Politics as Daily Life: Oral History and the Spanish Civil War," *New Left Review* 75 (2012): 61–67; and Daniel James, *Doña Maria's Story: Life History, Memory and Political Identity* (Durham: Duke University Press, 2000).

47. Fundación Para la Investigación Estratégica en Bolivia, *THOA: Taller de Historia Oral Andina*, YouTube video, 15:02, posted by AribibiTV, September 17, 2010, https://www.youtube.com/watch?v=P5iGTO0TjQM.

48. On this topic, also see Florencia Mallon, *Courage Tastes of Blood: The Mapuche Community of Nicolás Ailío and the Chilean State, 1906-2001* (Durham: Duke University Press, 2005); and Kay B. Warren, *Indigenous Movements and the Critics: Pan-Maya Activism in Guatemala* (Princeton: Princeton University Press, 1998).

49. Steven Palmer, "Carlos Fonseca and the Construction of Sandinismo in Nicaragua," *Latin American Research Review* 23, no. 1 (1988): 94–96.

50. Suzana Sawyer, *Crude Chronicles: Indigenous Politics, Multinational Oil, and Neoliberalism in Ecuador* (Durham: Duke University Press, 2004), 115.

51. Fernando Garcés, "Quechua Knowledge and Writings," in *Decolonizing Native Histories: Collaboration, Knowledge, and Language in the Americas*, ed. Florencia E. Mallon (Durham: Duke University Press, 2012), 89–90.

52. See Thomas Benjamin, "The Time of Reconquest: History, the Maya Revival, and the Zapatista Rebellion in Chiapas," *American Historical Review* 105, no. 2 (2000): 417–50; and Robert S. Jansen, "Resurrection and Appropriation: Reputational Trajectories, Memory Work, and the Political Use of Historical Figures," *American Journal of Sociology* 112, no. 4 (2007): 953–1007.

53. Comandancia General del EZLN, "Primera Declaración de la Selva Lacandona," *Enlace Zapatista*, January 1, 1994, http://enlacezapatista.ezln .org.mx/1994/01/01/primera-declaracion-de-la-selva-lacandona/. Also see Jeff Conant, *A Poetics of Resistance: The Revolutionary Public Relations of the Zapatista Insurgency* (Oakland: AK Press, 2010).

54. Howard Zinn, *A Power Governments Cannot Suppress* (San Francisco: City Lights, 2006), 11.

55. Ibid., 11–12.

56. Álvaro García Linera, Marxa Chávez León, and Patricia Costas Monje, *Sociología de los movimientos sociales en Bolivia: Estructuras de movilización, repertorios culturales y acción política* (La Paz: Plural Editores, 2008), 22.

57. Ibid., 199.

58. Ibid., 200.

59. Pablo Mamani Ramírez, *El rugir de las multitudes: La fuerza de los levantamientos indígenas en Bolivia/Qullasuyu*, 2nd ed. (La Paz: La Mirada Salvaje/Willka, 2010), 23–24. The use of symbols to define and mobilize social movements is explored in Sidney Tarrow, *Power in Movement: Social Movements and Contentious Politics* (Cambridge: Cambridge University Press, 1998), 106, 122.

60. For more on such uses of the past, see Farthing and Kohl, "Mobilizing Memory"; José Antonio Lucero, *Struggles of Voice: The Politics of Indigenous Representation in the Andes* (Pittsburgh: University of Pittsburgh Press, 2008); Hylton and Thomson, "Ya es otro tiempo el presente"; Tapia, "Bolivia: Ciclos y estructuras de rebelión"; and Andrew Canessa, "The Past Is Not Another Country: Exploring Indigenous Histories in Bolivia," *History and Anthropology* 19, no. 4 (2008): 355. Regarding the ayllu reconstitution efforts, see Kevin Healy, *Llamas, Weavings, and Organic Chocolate: Multicultural Grassroots Development in the Andes and Amazon of Bolivia* (Notre Dame: University of Notre Dame Press, 2001); Pablo Mamani Ramírez, "Reconstitución y cartografía del poder del ayllu: Experiencia organizativa y lucha del movimiento de los ayllus en Qullasuyu/Bolivia," in *Sistematización de experiencias de movimientos indígenas en Bolivia,* eds. Pelagio Pati Paco, Pablo Mamani, and Norah Quispe (La Paz: UMSA, 2009), 75–149; María Eugenia Choque and Carlos Mamani Condori, "Reconstitución del *ayllu* y derechos de los pueblos indígenas: El movimiento indio en los Andes de Bolivia" in *Los Andes desde los Andes,* ed. Esteban Ticona Alejo (La Paz: Ediciones Yachaywasi, 2003), 147–70; Lucero, *Struggles of Voice*; Donna Lee Van Cott, *The Friendly Liquidation of the Past: The Politics of Diversity in Latin America* (Pittsburgh: University of Pittsburgh Press, 2000); Benjamin Kohl and Linda C. Farthing, *Impasse in Bolivia: Neoliberal Hegemony and Popular Resistance* (London: Zed Books, 2006); Forrest Hylton and Sinclair Thomson, *Revolutionary Horizons: Past and Present in Bolivian Politics* (New York: Verso, 2007); and Deborah Yashar, *Contesting Citizenship in Latin America: The Rise of Indigenous Movements and the Postliberal Challenge* (Cambridge: Cambridge University Press, 2005).

61. The idea of a return to a preconquest utopia was, and still is, particularly strong in the Andean context because of the embrace of a cyclical view of time. The conception of time as cyclical is based in part on the logic of the Aymara language, which, Bolivia scholars Linda Farthing and Benjamin Kohl write, "has no grammatical demarcation that distinguishes the present from the simple past, a characteristic that keeps the past discursively alive. As a result, multiple historical periods

operate simultaneously, and the present articulates the past to the future." The past is considered to be ahead because it is already known and is therefore visible to the speaker. "The unknown future is behind—out of sight. This suggests that returning to a known past is a means of moving forward, which in Aymara is expressed through the concept of *nayrapacha*—literally 'eyes in time/space.'" Farthing and Kohl, "Mobilizing Memory," 365. In their discussion of cyclical time, the authors cite Ignacio Apaza Apaza, *Estructura metafórica del tiempo en el idioma aymara* (La Paz: Instituto de Estudios Bolivianos, 2008). Also see Sanjinés, *Mestizaje Upside-Down*, 5. Carlos Mamani discusses the Aymara phrase "Qhiparu nayraru uñtas sartañani" (Looking back, we will move forward) in Carlos Mamani Condori, *Los aymaras frente a la historia: Dos ensayos metodológicos* (Chukiyawu–La Paz: Ediciones Aruwiyiri/ THOA, 1992), 14.

    62.   Similarly, in anthropologist James Scott's work on peasant resistance, he found that "a person may dream of a revenge or a millennial kingdom of justice that may never occur. On the other hand, as circumstances change, it may become possible to act on those dreams." James Scott, *Weapons of the Weak: Everyday Forms of Peasant Resistance* (New Haven: Yale University Press, 1985), 38. Thomson and Hylton also explore the ways in which "re-remembering and re-animating Andean history incites dream visions of a different, better future; visions that inspire collective action." Hylton and Thomson, *Revolutionary Horizons*, 30.

    63.   Alberto Flores Galindo, *In Search of an Inca: Identity and Utopia in the Andes* (Cambridge: Cambridge University Press, 2010), 27.

    64.   Ibid., 247. Quijano explains that the model of Tawantinsuyo could be destroyed, yet with parts of it persisting, rearticulated, through other power structures over time. Aníbal Quijano, "Coloniality of Power, Eurocentrism, and Social Classification," in *Coloniality at Large: Latin America and the Postcolonial Debate*, eds. Mabel Moraña, Enriqué Dussel, and Carlos A. Jáuregui (Durham: Duke University Press, 2008), 202.

Chapter One: Katari's Return

    1.   Álvaro García Linera, "Indianismo y marxismo: El desencuentro de dos razones revolucionarias," in Svampa and Stefanoni, *Bolivia: Memoria, insurgencia*, 155.

    2.   The following interviews helped me understand the events, impact, and aftermath of the National Revolution: Pedro Portugal, interview with the author, La Paz, Bolivia, March 31, 2014, and October 14, 2014; Gonzalo Colque, interview with the author, La Paz, Bolivia, January 27, 2015; and Constantino Lima, interview with the author, La Paz, Bolivia, October 14, 2015.

    3.   Herbert S. Klein, *A Concise History of Bolivia* (Cambridge: Cambridge University Press, 2003), 206–8. For a comprehensive overview of the rural rebellions and indigenous movements that led up to the National Revolution, see Laura Gotkowitz, *A Revolution for Our Rights: Indigenous Struggles for Land and Justice in Bolivia, 1880–1952*. An extensive scholarly work on the National Revolution and its aftermath is Robert Matthew Gilder, "Indomestizo Modernism: National Development and Indigenous Integration in Postrevolutionary Bolivia, 1952–1964" (PhD diss., University of Texas at Austin, 2012).

    4.   James Dunkerley, *Rebellion in the Veins: Political Struggle in Bolivia, 1952–1982* (New York: Verso, 1984), 38–40. Also see Mario Murillo, *La bala no mata sino el destino: Una crónica de la insurrección popular de 1952 en Bolivia* (La Paz: Plural Editores, 2012).

5. Ibid., 41–42.

6. Ibid., 72–73.

7. Silvia Rivera Cusicanqui, *"Oprimidos pero no vencidos": Luchas del campesinado aymara y quechwa, 1900–1980* (La Paz: Aruwiyiri, Editorial del Taller de Historia Oral Andina, 2003), 104–6.

8. Kohl and Farthing, *Impasse in Bolivia*, 63.

9. Xavier Albó, "From MNRistas to Kataristas to Katari," in Stern, *Resistance, Rebellion, and Consciousness*, 387.

10. Xavier Albó, "The 'Long Memory' of Ethnicity in Bolivia and Some Temporary Oscillations," in *Unresolved Tensions: Bolivia Past and Present*, eds. John Crabtree and Laurence Whitehead (Pittsburgh: University of Pittsburgh Press, 2008), 21.

11. For example, the 1967 military attack on mining families at the Catavi-Siglo mines and the 1974 killing of campesino protesters outside the city of Cochabamba.

12. Healy, *Llamas, Weavings, and Organic Chocolate*, 14.

13. Ibid.

14. Roberto Choque Canqui, *El indigenismo y los movimientos indígenas en Bolivia* (La Paz: Instituto Internacional de Integración del Convenio Andrés Bello, 2014), 231.

15. Félix Patzi Paco, *Insurgencia y sumisión: Movimientos sociales e indígenas, 1983-2007* (La Paz: Ediciones DRIVA, 2007), 33–34.

16. Albó, "From MNRistas to Kataristas," 383–84.

17. Choque, *El indigenismo y los movimientos indígenas*, 238–39.

18. Healy, *Llamas, Weavings, and Organic Chocolate*, 15.

19. Brooke Larson, "Capturing Indian Bodies, Hearths and Minds: The Gendered Politics of Rural School Reform in Bolivia, 1920s–1940s," in *Natives Making Nation: Gender, Indigeneity and the State in the Andes*, ed. Andrew Canessa (Tucson: University of Arizona Press, 2005), 32–59; and Larson, "Forging the Unlettered Indian: The Pedagogy of Race in the Bolivian Andes," in *Histories of Race and Racism: The Andes and Mesoamerica from Colonial Times to the Present*, ed. Laura Gotkowitz (Durham: Duke University Press, 2011), 134–56.

20. Larson, "Forging the Unlettered Indian."

21. Larson, "Capturing Indian Bodies," 35.

22. Herbert Klein, *Bolivia: The Evolution of a Multiethnic Society* (New York: Oxford University Press, 1982), 264.

23. Aurolyn Luykx, *The Citizen Factory: Schooling and Cultural Production in Bolivia* (Albany: State University of New York Press, 1999), 47–48. Also see Andrew Canessa, "Reproducing Racism: Schooling and Race in Highland Bolivia," *Race Ethnicity and Education* 7, no. 2 (2004): 185–204; and Bret Gustafson, *New Languages of the State: Indigenous Resurgence and the Politics of Knowledge in Bolivia* (Durham: Duke University Press, 2009).

24. Manuel E. Contreras, "A Comparative Perspective of Education Reforms in Bolivia: 1950-2000," in Grindle and Domingo, *Proclaiming Revolution*, 260–63.

25. Klein, *Concise History of Bolivia*, 222–25.

26. Hervé Do Alto, "Cuando el nacionalismo se pone el poncho," in Svampa and Stefanoni, *Bolivia: Memoria, insurgencia*, 27.

27. Albó, "From MNRistas to Kataristas," 385–88; Hylton and Thomson, *Revolutionary Horizons*, 83–84.

28. Rivera, *"Oprimidos pero no vencidos,"* 145.

29. Javier Hurtado, *El Katarismo* (La Paz: Instituto de Historia Social Boliviana, 1986). 25. Other campesino organizations in the departments of Santa Cruz,

Beni, and Cochabamba were developed by campesinos as alternatives to the state-led unions and PMC, and they protested large-scale, commercial agriculture and the competition that small producers faced within the national market. A wide array of small federations and groups emerged out of these concerns in the eastern part of the country in the late 1960s and were organized under one umbrella in February 1971 as the National Confederation of Rural [Campesino] Settlers of Bolivia (CNCB), also linked to the COB. However, the position of these defiant groups remained in the minority, as the rural masses still largely embraced the PMC. See Rivera, *"Oprimidos pero no vencidos,"* 148–49.

30. Albó, "From MNRistas to Kataristas," 388.
31. Hurtado, *El Katarismo*, 41–42.
32. Klein, *Concise History of Bolivia*, 226–28.
33. Ibid.
34. Healy, *Llamas, Weavings, and Organic Chocolate*, 70. Also see Nicolas and Quisbert, *Pachakuti*, 41.
35. Esteban Ticona Alejo, *CSUTCB: Trayectoria y desafíos* (La Paz: Centro de Documentacion e Información, 1996), 14.
36. Rivera, *"Oprimidos pero no vencidos,"* 181.
37. Do Alto, "Cuando el nacionalismo se pone el poncho," 29.
38. Rivera, *"Oprimidos pero no vencidos,"* 150.
39. Ibid., 153.
40. Albó, "From MNRistas to Kataristas," 393.
41. Rivera, *"Oprimidos pero no vencidos,"* 153.
42. Silvia Rivera Cusicanqui, "Aymara Past, Aymara Future," *NACLA Report on the Americas* 5, no. 3 (1991): 19.
43. Rivera, *"Oprimidos pero no vencidos,"* 179, 180. Rivera's work is a key text on indigenous movements in the twentieth century with rich detail on this postrevolutionary period in Bolivia.
44. Esteban Ticona Alejo, *Organización y liderazgo aymara: La experiencia indígena en la política boliviana, 1979–1996* (La Paz: Plural Editores, 2000), 81.
45. Ticona, *CSUTCB*, 14.
46. Hylton and Thomson, *Revolutionary Horizons*, 87. For more information on Indianismo, see Diego Pacheco, *El indianismo y los indios contemporáneos en Bolivia* (La Paz: HISBOL/Musef, 1992); and Luciano Tapia, *Ukhamawa Jakawisaxa (Así es nuestra vida): Autobiografía de un aymara* (La Paz: HISBOL, 1995).
47. Verushka Alvizuri, *La construcción de la aymaridad: Una historia de la etnicidad en Bolivia (1952–2006)* (Santa Cruz: Editorial El País, 2009), 107–8.
48. The information regarding sales is based on the author's observations over a fifteen-year period up to the point of this writing, during which Reinaga's books continued to sell widely among book street vendors in La Paz, Cochabamba, and Sucre.
49. For more information on the Chaco War, see Klein, *Concise History of Bolivia*, 178; Kohl and Farthing, *Impasse in Bolivia*, 45; Hylton and Thomson, *Revolutionary Horizons*, 68–70; and Gotkowitz, *Revolution for Our Rights*, 103–11.
50. Alvizuri, *La construcción de la aymaridad*, 107–10. Alvizuri cites Hilda Reinaga, interview with Verushka Alvizuri, La Paz, Bolivia, July 17, 2005.
51. Yashar, *Contesting Citizenship*, 168. November 14 is the actual date of his death, a day now widely recognized in Bolivia in commemorations of Katari. See del Valle de Siles, *Historia de la rebelión de Tupac Catari*, 315.
52. Dunkerley, *Rebellion in the Veins*, 213.
53. Fausto Reinaga, *La Revolución India* (La Paz: Fundación Amaútica, "Fausto Reinaga," 2014).

54. Ticona, *CSUTCB*, 13. The quote, cited here by Ticona, draws from a phrase in the 1973 Manifesto of Tiwanaku.
55. Hilda Reinaga, interview with the author, La Paz, Bolivia, March 10, 2015.
56. Hilda Reinaga, interview with Pablo Mamani Ramírez, La Paz, Bolivia, January 20, 2011, included in Pablo Mamani Ramírez, "Entrevistas a los luchadores kataristas e indianistas," *Willka* 5, no. 5 (2011): 154. On this topic, also see works by Peruvian intellectual José Carlos Mariátegui: Harry E. Vanden and Marc Becker, eds. and trans., *José Carlos Mariátegui: An Anthology* (New York: Monthly Review Press, 2011); José Carlos Mariátegui, *Seven Interpretive Essays on Peruvian Reality* (Austin: University of Texas Press, 1988).
57. Fausto Reinaga, *Tesis India* (La Paz: Fundación Amaútica "Fausto Reinaga, 2014), 15.
58. José Antonio Lucero, "Fanon in the Andes: Fausto Reinaga, Indianismo, and the Black Atlantic," *International Journal of Critical Indigenous Studies* 1, no. 1 (2008): 16, 18. Lucero quotes Reinaga from Fausto Reinaga, *La Revolución India* (La Paz: Partido Indio Boliviano, 1969), 168.
59. Máximo Quisbert Quispe, "Hay líderes indianistas o kataristas para futuras elecciones presidenciales?" *Willka* 5, no. 5 (2011): 50.
60. García, "Indianismo y marxismo," 159.
61. Constantino Lima, interview with the author, La Paz, Bolivia, October 15, 2014.
62. Constantino Lima, interview with Pablo Mamani Ramírez, El Alto, Bolivia, February 17, 2011, included in Mamani, "Entrevistas a los luchadores kataristas e indianistas," 131-32.
63. Constantino Lima, interview with the author, La Paz, Bolivia, October 15, 2014.
64. Ibid.
65. Tapia, *Ukhamawa Jakawisaxa*.
66. Ibid., 188.
67. Ibid.
68. Ibid.
69. Ibid., 329-73; Pacheco, *El Indianismo*, 21-86.
70. Albó, "From MNRistas to Kataristas," 390-91.

Chapter Two: Kataristas Rising

1. Hurtado, *El Katarismo*, 49. Hurtado notes that the posters of Katari and Sisa were printed by the organization INDICEP and painted by Vargas Cuéllar.
2. Ibid., 31.
3. Ibid., 29, 32.
4. Ibid., 276.
5. Javier Hurtado, "El movimiento aymara contemporaneo 1962-1985," *Temas Sociales*, no. 9 (n.d.). Cited in Pacheco, *El Indianismo*, 36n10.
6. Hurtado, *El Katarismo*, 276.
7. Yashar, *Contesting Citizenship*, 168.
8. Alvizuri, *La construcción de la aymaridad*, 107-10. Alvizuri cites Hilda Reinaga, interview with Verushka Alvizuri, La Paz, Bolivia, July 17, 2005.
9. "Homenaje a Genaro Flores, Universidad UT-K, 1998," disc file 1108, DVD, consulted at the archive of the Museo Nacional de Etnografía y Folklore in La Paz, Bolivia. This is a video produced by the Museo Nacional de Etnografía y

Folklore on a 1998 event organized in homage to Flores and that Flores attended. It covers the marches, celebrations, and speeches and provides a useful audio and visual source on Flores as a speaker and participant in the event.

10.   Hurtado, *El Katarismo*, 266.

11.   Brooke Larson, *Trials of Nation Making: Liberalism, Race, and Ethnicity in the Andes, 1810–1910* (Cambridge: Cambridge University Press, 2004), 237, 253; Klein, *Concise History of Bolivia*, 157. An in-depth look at the Federal War and its aftermath is provided in Forrest Hylton, "Reverberations of Insurgency: Indian Communities, the Federal War of 1899, and the Regeneration of Bolivia" (PhD diss., New York University, 2010). Also see Ramiro Condarco Morales, *Zárate, el "Temible" Willka: Historia de la rebelión indígena de 1899* (La Paz: n.p., 1983).

12.   Hurtado, *El Katarismo*, 266.

13.   Ticona, *Organización y liderazgo aymara*, 51n2.

14.   Hurtado, *El Katarismo*, 267–68.

15.   Albó, "From MNRistas to Kataristas," 391.

16.   Ticona, *Organización y liderazgo aymara*, 53–54. Ticona cites Genaro Flores, interview with Esteban Ticona Alejo, La Paz, Bolivia, 1994.

17.   Hurtado, *El Katarismo*, 30.

18.   Yashar, *Contesting Citizenship*, 170–71. Yashar cites Xavier Albó, "El retorno del indio," *Revista Andina* 9, no. 2 (1991): 312. The statue description is based on a photo of the Katari monument in Centro de Coordinacion y Promocion Campesina "Mink'a," *Mink'a*, no. 7 (1977): 7.

19.   Ticona, *Organización y liderazgo aymara*, 52. Ticona cites Genaro Flores, interview with Esteban Ticona Alejo, La Paz, Bolivia, 1994.

20.   Hurtado, *El Katarismo*, 269.

21.   Ticona, *Organización y liderazgo aymara*, 53–54; Hurtado, *El Katarismo*, 270.

22.   Ticona, *Organización y liderazgo aymara*, 55–56.

23.   Albó, "From MNRistas to Kataristas," 392–93; Hurtado, *El Katarismo*, 271.

24.   Tarrow, *Power in Movement*, 112.

25.   Ibid., 122.

26.   Healy, *Llamas, Weavings, and Organic Chocolate*, 69–70.

27.   For more on INDICEP, see Albó, "From MNRistas to Kataristas," 395; and Healy, *Llamas, Weavings, and Organic Chocolate*, 69–70.

28.   See Choque, *El indigenismo y los movimientos indígenas*; Roberto Choque Canqui, *Historia de una lucha desigual: Los contenidos ideológicos y políticos de las rebeliones indígenas de la pre y post revolución nacional* (La Paz: Unidad de Investigaciones Históricas UNIH-PAKAXA, 2012).

29.   Healy, *Llamas, Weavings, and Organic Chocolate*, 86.

30.   Choque, *Historia de una lucha desigual*, 208

31.   Roberto Choque Canqui, interview with the author, La Paz, Bolivia, October 16, 2014. This interview took place at the La Paz Archives, where Choque worked for many years and continues to conduct much of his research.

32.   Do Alto, "Cuando el nacionalismo se pone el poncho," 28.

33.   Hylton and Thomson, *Revolutionary Horizons*, 85–88. Also see John Dinges, *The Condor Years: How Pinochet and His Allies Brought Terrorism to Three Continents* (New York: New Press, 2005).

34.   Hurtado, *El Katarismo*, 272–73.

35.   Healy, *Llamas, Weavings, and Organic Chocolate*, 64–66.

36.   Hurtado, *El Katarismo*, 58.

37.   Ibid., 58; Healy, *Llamas, Weavings, and Organic Chocolate*, 66.

38.   "Manifesto of Tiwanaku, 1973," in Silvia Rivera Cusicanqui, *Oppressed but not Defeated: Peasant Struggles among the Aymara and the Qhechwa in Bolivia, 1900–1980*

(Geneva: United Nations Research Institute for Social Development, 1987), 169–77. I draw from this version of the Manifesto of Tiwanaku, though it is also available elsewhere, such as, for example, Centro de Coordinacion y Promocion Campesina "Mink'a," "Manifiesto de Tiwanacu," *Mink'a*, no. 7 (1977): 34–40.

39. "Manifesto of Tiwanaku, 1973," 169–77.
40. Ticona, *CSUTCB*, 14; Hurtado, *El Katarismo*, 58.
41. Hurtado, *El Katarismo*, 60; Healy, *Llamas, Weavings, and Organic Chocolate*, 66.
42. Hurtado, *El Katarismo*, 272–73, 60.
43. Tórrez and Arce, *Construcción simbólica del estado plurinacional*, 38.
44. Quisbert, "Hay líderes indianistas," 54.
45. Mink'a, *Mink'a*, no. 3 (1973). Consulted at the library of the Museo Nacional de Etnografía y Folklore in La Paz, Bolivia. This was one of various Katarista and Indianista publications available at the Archives and Library of the Museo Nacional de Etnografía y Folklore. Other Katarista and Indianista documents from the 1970s and 1980s I consulted at this archive and library include the following: Centro de Formación e Investigación sobre las Culturas Indias, *Boletín Chitakolla* 3, no. 23 (1985); Centro de Formación e Investigación sobre las Culturas Indias, *Boletín Chitakolla*, no. 29 (1986); Ofensiva Roja de Ayllus Kataristas, *Propuesta de tesis política al III Congreso de la CSUTCB* (Cochabamba: Ediciones Ofensiva Roja, 1987); Colección de Folletos Para La Formación Indianista, *Algo sobre el socialdemokatarismo o movikatarismo* (Chukiyawu: Ediciones "Muju," 1985); and *Viva el Glorioso Katarismo Revolucionario* (n.p.: Ediciones Ofensiva Roja, n.d.). I consulted additional primary sources published by various Katarista and Indianista groups at the National Archives in Sucre, including *Aymar marka: Vocero del grupo Mallku* 1, no. 1 (1986); *Katarismo: Vocero del eje social nacional*, no. 1 (1986); *Katarismo: Vocero del eje social nacional*, no. 2 (1987); *Q'antati* 1, no. 1 (1985); and Comité Bicentenario Tupaj Katari, *Homenaje a Tupaj Katari* (1981). I also consulted a series of pamphlets at the National Archives in Sucre made up of testimonies with anonymous indigenous campesinos including Editorial Respuesta, "Los derechos y el campesino," *Los Campesinos Opinan*, no. 3 (1979); Editorial Respuesta, "Perspectivas," *Los Campesinos Opinan*, no. 4 (1979); Editorial Respuesta, "Situación económica del campesinado," *Los Campesinos Opinan*, no. 6 (1979); Editorial Respuesta, "Nuestra cultura," *Los Campesinos Opinan*, no. 7 (1979); and Editorial Respuesta, "Oprimidos pero no vencidos," *Los Campesinos Opinan*, no. 8 (1979).
46. Albó, "From MNRistas to Kataristas," 415n15.
47. René Mario Gabriel A., "Los pueblos aymaras y quechuas y el cooperativismo," *Mink'a*, no. 3 (1973): 6.
48. Ibid.
49. Ibid.
50. Centro de Coordinacion y Promocion Campesina "Mink'a," *Ayllu* 1 (1974). Consulted at the library of the Museo Nacional de Etnografía y Folklore in La Paz, Bolivia.
51. Julio Tumiri A., "Pueblo aymara," *Ayllu*, 2.
52. T. Antawalla, "Pido la palabra," *Ayllu*, 4.
53. Centro de Coordinacion y Promocion Campesina "Mink'a," "Tupac Katari y el dia internacional de indio," *Mink'a*, no. 7 (1977): 8–9. Consulted at the library of the Museo Nacional de Etnografía y Folklore in La Paz, Bolivia.
54. Dunkerley, *Rebellion in the Veins*, 210–12. On this massacre, also see Asamblea Permanente de Derechos Humanos de Bolivia, *La masacre del valle: Cochabamba, enero 1974* (La Paz: APBHB, 1979).
55. Rivera, *"Oprimidos pero no vencidos,"* 159–62.

56. CNTCB, "Tesis campesina, 1976," in *Los Campesinos en el Proceso Político Boliviano, Documentos de la CNTCB,* ed. Daniel Salamanca Trujillo (Oruro: Editoria "Quelco," n.d.), 81, 85. (The book is dedicated by Salamanca to Banzer and Busch.) Consulted at the Arturo Costa de la Torre Archives and Library, La Paz, Bolivia.
57. Hurtado, *El Katarismo,* 272–73.
58. Rivera, *"Oprimidos pero no vencidos,"* 164–66.
59. Albó, "From MNRistas to Kataristas," 397.
60. Dunkerley, *Rebellion in the Veins,* 238–41.
61. Ibid., 248–49.
62. Do Alto, "Cuando el nacionalismo se pone el poncho," 31–32.

Chapter Three: The Power of the Past in the CSUTCB Indigenous Campesino Union

1. Jorge Choque Salomé, interview with the author, La Paz, Bolivia, April 4, 2014.
2. Ibid.
3. Kevin Healy, *Sindicatos campesinos y desarrollo rural, 1978–1985* (La Paz: Hisbol, 1989), 9–10.
4. Kohl and Farthing, *Impasse in Bolivia,* 63.
5. Albó, "From MNRistas to Kataristas," 387–88; Yashar, *Contesting Citizenship,* 167n27.
6. Xavier Albó, "And from Kataristas to MNRistas? The Surprising and Bold Alliance between Aymaras and Neoliberals in Bolivia," in *Indigenous Peoples and Democracy in Latin America*, ed. Donna Lee Van Cott (New York: St. Martin's Press, 1994), 55; Yashar, *Contesting Citizenship,* 174.
7. Also see Víctor Hugo Cárdenas, "La CSUTCB: Elementos para entender su crisis de crecimiento (1979–87)," in *Crisis del sindicalismo en Bolivia* (La Paz: ILDIS and FLACSO, 1987), 225; and Iván Arias Durán, "Bolivia: Congreso de la CSUTCB, una lección aprendida," *ALAI Servicio Mensual de Informacion y Documentacion,* no. 107 (1988): 22. Consulted at the library of the Museo Nacional de Etnografía y Folklore in La Paz, Bolivia.
8. Albó, "From MNRistas to Kataristas," 403–4; Rivera, *"Oprimidos pero no vencidos,"* 172.
9. "Inauguración de congreso campesino: Lechín insta a 'romper con el Pacto Militar-Campesino,'" *Presencia,* June 25, 1979, 11.
10. Albó, "From MNRistas to Kataristas," 403–4; and Rivera, *"Oprimidos pero no vencidos,"* 172.
11. Albó, "From MNRistas to Kataristas," 403–4; and Rivera, *"Oprimidos pero no vencidos,"* 172.
12. Yashar, *Contesting Citizenship,* 177–78.
13. Healy, *Llamas, Weavings, and Organic Chocolate,* 71.
14. Ismael Quispe Ticona, interview with the author, La Paz, Bolivia, April 4, 2014.
15. Ibid.
16. Rivera, *"Oprimidos pero no vencidos,"* 172–73.
17. As one audio recording of a June 26, 1987, CSUTCB congress in Cochabamba demonstrates, this gathering began with indigenous music involving pan flutes and drums. See "III Congreso de Unidad Campesina," digital audio file, number 1780, side B, Archives of the Museo Nacional de Etnografía y Folklore, La Paz, Bolivia. Similar scenes occur throughout the recording of a later CSUTCB meet-

ing: "Congreso Campesino," digital video file, number 322, Archives of the Museo Nacional de Etnografía y Folklore in La Paz, Bolivia.
18. Ticona, *Organización y liderazgo aymara*, 105.
19. Durán, "Bolivia: Congreso de la CSUTCB," 22.
20. "III Congreso de Unidad Campesina," digital audio file, number 1766, sides A and B, Archives of the Museo Nacional de Etnografía y Folklore, La Paz, Bolivia.
21. Ibid.
22. "III Congreso de Unidad Campesina," digital audio file, numbers 1780–1785, Archives of the Museo Nacional de Etnografía y Folklore, La Paz, Bolivia.
23. "Marcha por el Territorio y la Dignidad de 1990," digital audio files, numbers 586–593, 01854_1435_04_08_A, Archives of the Museo Nacional de Etnografía y Folklore, La Paz, Bolivia. CSUTCB organizers and participants deployed their historical narratives as strategies for bringing together disparate groups and building a common agenda for change. Similarly, Joanne Rappaport found in her work on historical production in indigenous Nasa communities in Colombia that "in cases in which a broad-based organization is needed, a universal history will begin to surface." Rappaport, *Politics of Memory*, 24; Also see Joanne Rappaport, *Cumbe Reborn: An Andean Ethnography of History* (Chicago: University of Chicago Press, 1994), 5; and Joanne Rappaport and Abelardo Ramos Pacho, "Collaboration and Historical Writing: Challenges for the Indigenous-Academic Dialogue," in Mallon, *Decolonizing Native Histories*, 123.
24. CSUTCB, "Tesis del Campesinado Boliviano," in Hurtado, *El Katarismo*, 332–33.
25. Ibid.
26. Healy, *Sindicatos Campesinos*, 9–10.
27. Bret Gustafson, "The Paradoxes of Liberal Indigenism: Indigenous Movements, State Processes, and Intercultural Reform in Bolivia," in *The Politics of Ethnicity: Indigenous Peoples in Latin American States*, ed. David Maybury-Lewis (Cambridge, MA: DRCLAS/Harvard University, 2002), 271–72; Healy, *Sindicatos Campesinos*, 12–13.
28. Albó, "From MNRistas to Kataristas," 406.
29. Healy, *Sindicatos Campesinos*, 17–20, 31–33.
30. Healy, *Llamas, Weavings, and Organic Chocolate*, 72–73.
31. Ibid., 72.
32. García, Chávez, and Costas, *Sociología de los movimientos sociales*, 504–5.
33. Blanca Muñoz, "La participación de la mujer campesina en Bolivia: Un estudio del altiplano," in *Bolivia: La fuerza histórica del campesinado*, eds. Fernando Calderón and Jorge Dandler (Geneva: UNRISD, 1986), 390–95.
34. Also see Rosario León, "Bartolina Sisa: The Peasant Women's Organization in Bolivia," in *Women and Social Change in Latin America*, ed. Elizabeth Jelin (London: Zed Books, 1990), 138; and Cecilia Salazar de la Torre and Lia van Broekhoven, *Movimiento de mujeres en Bolivia: La Federación Nacional de Mujeres Campesinas "Bartolina Sisa" y los clubes y centros de madres* (La Paz: Servicio Holandés de Cooperación al Desarrollo, 1998), 35.
35. Javier Medina, ed. *Las hijas de Bartolina Sisa* (La Paz: HISBOL, 1984), 68.
36. Ibid., 37.
37. Fanny García Forés, *El proceso de cambio en Bolivia: Una mirada desde las "Bartolinas"* (La Paz: Veterinarios Sin Fronteras, 2011), 81–82.
38. Ibid.
39. For example, "III Congreso de la Federación de Mujeres en Bolivia," September 3, 1988, digital audio file, number 1798–1799, side A and B, Archives of the Museo Nacional de Etnografía y Folklore, La Paz, Bolivia.

40. Anselma Perlacios, interview with the author, La Paz, Bolivia, April 4, 2014.

41. Medina, *Las hijas de Bartolina Sisa*, 17.

42. Ibid.

43. Ibid.

44. "Mujer aymara: Luchas y conquistas," 1990, digital audio file, number 605–606, 01898_1381_01_02_A, Archives of the Museo Nacional de Etnografía y Folklore, La Paz, Bolivia.

45. Rivera, *"Oprimidos pero no vencidos,"* 173–74.

46. Rappaport analyzes Colombian indigenous movement letters to the government that wove histories of centuries-old events from the colonial period with contemporary legal arguments in defense of indigenous territory. In considering Rappaport's analyses of such documents, I realized the CSUTCB was conducting a similar strategic deployment of historical narratives in their 1979 communiqués to strengthen their own legitimacy and claims in a contemporary political struggle. See Rappaport, *Cumbe Reborn*, 101–6.

47. "Confederación Sindical Única de Trabajadores Campesinos de Bolivia, 'Afiliada a la Central Obrera Boliviana,'" *Presencia*, November 10, 1979. Of emphasis here are the ways in which CSUTCB members described how the basic elements and structures of colonialism had remained intact. In this case, CSUTCB members' historical and political analysis reflected what anthropologist Andrew Canessa has argued in his own work on Bolivia. Canessa writes that indigenous people in Bolivia should not be understood simply as "cultural survivors clinging onto a quaint, particular but atavistic culture, but, rather, as inheritors of a colonial situation which has continued over time even though the symbols of power and oppression may have changed considerably." Andrew Canessa, "The Past Is Not Another Country: Exploring Indigenous Histories in Bolivia," *History and Anthropology* 19, no. 4 (2008): 355.

48. "Confederación Sindical Única de Trabajadores."

49. Ibid.

50. Rivera, *"Oprimidos pero no vencidos,"* 173–74.

51. Albó, "From MNRistas to Kataristas," 404.

52. "Campesinos piden comercializar directamente todos sus productos," *Presencia*, December 4, 1979.

53. Albó, "From MNRistas to Kataristas," 404.

54. "Masiva concentración y desfile desaprobó medidas económicas," *Última Hora*, December 5, 1979.

55. "COB plantea anulación de medidas económicas," *Presencia*, December 5, 1979, 1.

56. "Campesinos exigen aumento en los precios de sus productos," *Presencia*, December 4, 1979, 9, 12.

57. "Continuó ayer el bloqueo en carreteras de La Paz," *Presencia*, December 5, 1979, 9.

58. Yashar, *Contesting Citizenship*, 178–79.

59. Healy, *Sindicatos Campesinos*, 13–14.

60. Albó, "From MNRistas to Kataristas," 404–5.

61. Rivera, *"Oprimidos pero no vencidos,"* 175n47.

62. "Confederación Campesina dispuso suspensión temporal de bloqueos," *Presencia*, December 8, 1979, 1.

63. Kohl and Farthing, *Impasse in Bolivia*, 65.

64. Máximo Freddy Huarachi Paco, interview with the author, La Paz, Bolivia, March 24, 2015.

65. Ibid.

66. Felipe Quispe, "La lucha de los *ayllus* kataristas hoy," in *Movimiento indígena en América Latina: Resistencia y proyecto alternativo*, eds. Fabiola Escárzaga and Raquel Gutiérrez (Puebla, Mexico: Benemérita Universidad Autónoma de Puebla, 2006), 73–75.

67. Ibid.

68. CSUTCB, *CSUTCB después de cuatro siglos de opresión: Las conquistas económicas de las mayorías nacionales logradas con la lucha de los explotados del campo* (La Paz: CSUTCB, 1984), 38. Consulted at the library of the Museo Nacional de Etnografía y Folklore in La Paz, Bolivia.

69. James M. Malloy and Eduardo Gamarra, *Revolution and Reaction: Bolivia, 1964–1985* (New Brunswick, NJ: Transaction Books, 1988), 143–47.

70. Dunkerley, *Rebellion in the Veins*, 292–93.

71. Ibid., 295, 298.

72. El Comité Ejecutivo de la CSUTCB, "CSUTCB Tesis Política 1983," in Rivera, *"Oprimidos pero no vencidos,"* 204.

73. Malloy and Gamarra, *Revolution and Reaction*, 148–49.

74. Hylton and Thomson, *Revolutionary Horizons*, 90.

75. Klein, *Concise History of Bolivia*, 239–40.

76. Dunkerley, *Rebellion in the Veins*, 344.

77. Hylton and Thomson, *Revolutionary Horizons*, 90.

78. Healy, *Sindicatos campesinos*, 9–10.

79. Klein, *Concise History of Bolivia*, 241–42.

80. James Dunkerley, *Political Transition and Economic Stabilisation: Bolivia, 1982–1989* (London: Institute of Latin American Studies, 1990), 26.

81. Dunkerley, *Rebellion in the Veins*, 347.

82. Dunkerley, *Political Transition*, 26.

83. CSUTCB, *Bloqueo de caminos* (n.p.: CSUTCB, 1983), 5. Consulted at the Museo Nacional de Etnografía y Folklore in La Paz, Bolivia; El Comité Ejecutivo de la CSUTCB, "CSUTCB Tesis Política 1983," 204.

84. "Huelga y bloqueo de caminos se amplió al departamento de Oruro," *Presencia*, April 1983. Also see CSUTCB, *CSUTCB después de cuatro siglos*; and CSUTCB, *Bloqueo de caminos*.

85. In speeches and communiqués, CSUTCB members regularly made connections between what they perceived as centuries of oppression and their contemporary plight in the 1980s. Similarly, historian Thomas Benjamin argues, regarding the role of shared experience and memory in the Zapatista uprising, that "people who experienced persecution, expulsions, jailing, violence, and worse offenses as a reality of their lives had little difficulty understanding the conquest that their ancestors in the late 1520s suffered." Benjamin, "Time of Reconquest," 445.

86. El Comité Ejecutivo de la CSUTCB, "CSUTCB Tesis Política 1983." This thesis is an excellent example of the type of historical discourses utilized in this period by the CSUTCB. Such narratives and historical analysis were also present in other CSUTCB congress documents and resolutions that I consulted at the Bolivian National Archives including CSUTCB, *Plataforma de lucha de los explotados del campo en su segundo congreso de unidad campesina. 26 de Junio al 1 de Julio de 1983* (n.p.: CSUTCB, 1983); CSUTCB, *V congreso CSUTCB, documentos y resoluciones, Sucre, 26 de junio al 3 de julio de 1992 La Paz, Bolivia* (n.p.: CSUTCB, 1993); CSUTCB, *VI Congreso, documentos y resoluciones, Cochabamba, del 27 de enero al 2 de febrero de 1994, La Paz, Bolivia* (n.p.: CSUTCB, 1994); and CSUTCB, *Conclusiones del 8vo ampliado nacional, Sucre* (n.p.: CSUTCB, 1986), consulted at the Museo Nacional de Etnografía y Folklore in La Paz, Bolivia.

87.   El Comité Ejecutivo de la CSUTCB, "CSUTCB Tesis Política 1983," 195.
88.   Ibid., 194.
89.   Ibid., 198.
90.   Ibid., 205–6.
91.   Ibid., 199.
92.   Ibid., 202–3.
93.   Ibid., 195–96.
94.   Kevin Healy, *Sindicatos campesinos*, 53–54.
95.   CSUTCB, *Ley agraria fundamental, congreso nacional de Cochabamba, del 16 al 20 de enero de 1984* (n.p.: CSUTCB, 1984), 23. Consulted at the Centro de Investigación y Promoción del Campesinado Library in La Paz.
96.   Ibid., 25–26.
97.   Ibid. Also consulted on the CSUTCB work on this agrarian proposal was CSUTCB, *Documentos de trabajo de Coraca* (La Paz: CEDOIN/Ediciones Gráficas "E.G.," 1989). Consulted at the Museo Nacional de Etnografía y Folklore in La Paz, Bolivia.

Chapter Four: The Andean Oral History Workshop

1.   See THOA member Felipe Santos Quispe's overview and analysis of the organization's work: Santos, "Una mirada autocrítica," 169.
2.   Ibid., 161.
3.   Carlos Mamani Condori, *Metodología de la historia oral* (La Paz: Ediciones del THOA, 1989), 22.
4.   The THOA's reasoning behind its embrace of oral history as a source echoes what many other oral history proponents have advocated. British historian Paul Thompson, who played a key role in the spread of oral history collection as a research technique from the early 1970s with the British Oral History Society, argues that oral history "can give back to the people who made and experienced history, through their own words, a central place." Paul Thompson, "The Voice of the Past: Oral History," in *The Oral History Reader*, eds. Robert Perks and Alistair Thomson (London: Routledge, 2006), 26.
5.   Mamani, *Metodología de la historia oral*, 6–7, 9.
6.   Healy, *Llamas, Weavings, and Organic Chocolate*, 87. In this important work on rural development in Bolivia, scholar Kevin Healy provides a brief yet extremely helpful look into the work of the THOA. Healy examines the organization as a part of his wider look at rural development and indigenous politics and organizing in late twentieth-century Bolivia.
7.   Stephenson, "Forging an Indigenous Counterpublic Sphere," 110–11. Stephenson cites Virginia Ayllon S., "Evaluación externa del Taller de Historia Oral Andina. Proyecto: Investigación, formación, y difusión" (report presented to the Inter-American Foundation and Semilla, La Paz, Bolivia, 1993). Stephenson's essay on the THOA is a critical resource on the organization. In it, she argues that the THOA constitutes a "counterpublic sphere" for Aymara intellectuals to collectively promote indigenous histories and political worldviews.
8.   Fundación Para la Investigación Estratégica en Bolivia (PIEB), *THOA: Taller de Historia Oral Andina*. This is a video produced by the Bolivian research organization PIEB on the occasion of its granting the THOA the Premio Nacional de Ciencias Sociales y Humanas "Fundación PIEB," a prestigious annual award. The video provides an overview of the THOA's work and history, and includes interviews with many of the organization's members.

9. Rivera, "El potencial epistemológico," 14–15.
10. Fundación Para la Investigación Estratégica en Bolivia, *THOA: Taller de Historia Oral Andina*.
11. Rivera, "El potencial epistemológico," 15–16.
12. Ibid.
13. Ibid., 18.
14. Healy, *Llamas, Weavings, and Organic Chocolate*, 85.
15. Ticona, *Organización y liderazgo aymara*, 154.
16. Felipe Santos Quispe, interview with the author, La Paz, Bolivia, March 31, 2014.
17. Ibid.
18. Ibid.
19. Healy, *Llamas, Weavings, and Organic Chocolate*, 85–86.
20. Filomena Nina, interview with the author, La Paz, Bolivia, October 16, 2014.
21. Healy, *Llamas, Weavings, and Organic Chocolate*, 86.
22. Marcelo Fernández Osco, interview with the author, La Paz, Bolivia, October 11, 2014.
23. Filomena Nina interview, October 16, 2014.
24. Healy, *Llamas, Weavings, and Organic Chocolate*, 82–83.
25. Martín Cúneo and Emma Gascó, "Bolivia—Taller de Historia Oral Andina: 'Despertamos al descubrir nuestra propia biografía,'" *Upside Down World*, February 3, 2014, http://upsidedownworld.org/main/en-espatopmenu-81/4682-bolivia-taller-de-historia-oral-andina-despertamos-al-descubrir-nuestra-propia-biografia.
26. Healy, *Llamas, Weavings, and Organic Chocolate*, 83.
27. Ibid., 83–84. Healy cites André Gunder Frank, *Capitalism and Underdevelopment in Latin America* (New York: Modern Reader, 1969), 136.
28. Marcelo Fernández Osco interview.
29. Healy, *Llamas, Weavings, and Organic Chocolate*, 85.
30. Ibid., 85–86. An insightful view of this period is also provided by Brooke Larson, *Cochabamba, 1550–1900: Colonialism and Agrarian Transformation in Bolivia* (Durham: Duke University Press, 1998), 322–47.
31. Sergio Di Nucci, "Entrevista con la socióloga e investigadora boliviana Silvia Rivera Cusicanqui: 'La historia escrita no habla del papel indígena en las protestas sociales,'" *Infonews.com*, September 13, 2012, http://tiempo.infonews.com/nota/125763.
32. Cúneo and Gascó, "Bolivia—Taller de Historia Oral Andina."
33. Filomena Nina interview, October 16, 2014.
34. Healy, *Llamas, Weavings, and Organic Chocolate*, 86.
35. "THOA por 30 años recoge la historia oral de los pueblos," *Erbol*, November 22, 2013, http://www.erbol.com.bo/noticia/cultura/22112013/thoa_por_30_anos_recoge_la_historia_oral_de_los_pueblos.
36. Mamani, *Metodología de la historia oral*, 15–16.
37. Ibid.
38. Marcelo Fernández Osco interview.
39. Ibid.
40. Ibid.
41. Felipe Santos Quispe interview.
42. Ibid.
43. THOA members were fundamentally oriented in their work by the communities in which they gathered testimonies. On this topic, also see Audra Simpson, *Mohawk Interruptus: Political Life across the Borders of Settler States* (Durham: Duke

University Press, 2014); Mallon, *Decolonizing Native Histories*; and Smith, *Decolonizing Methodologies*.

44. Carlos Mamani Condori, *Taraqu, 1866–1935: Masacre, guerra y "renovación" en la biografía de Eduardo L. Nina Qhispi* (La Paz: Ediciones Aruwiyiri/THOA, 1991), 7.

45. Marcelo Fernández Osco interview.

46. Filomena Nina, interview with the author, La Paz, Bolivia, April 3, 2014.

47. Selection of THOA audio recordings in archives at the Museo Nacional de Etnografía y Folklore in La Paz, Bolivia. For example, THOA, "Homenaje 45 Aniversario a Santos Marca Tula," (n.d.), digital audio files, 01550_0291_01_03_THOA—01550_0291_03_03_THOA.A, Archives of the Museo Nacional de Etnografía y Folklore, La Paz, Bolivia.

48. Mamani, *Metodología de la historia oral*, 31–32.

49. Ibid., 27.

50. Rivera, "El potencial epistemológico," 21.

51. Ibid., 20–22.

52. Mamani, *Metodología de la historia oral*, 28.

53. Rivera, "El potencial epistemológico," 22.

54. Mamani, *Metodología de la historia oral*, 29.

55. Tomás Huanca L., *Jilirinaksan arsüwipa: "Testimonios de nuestros mayores"* (La Paz: THOA, 1991).

56. Mamani, *Metodología de la historia oral*, 39–41.

57. Huanca, *Jilirinaksan arsüwipa*, 7.

58. Ibid., 9–10.

59. Ibid.

60. Ibid., 11.

61. Ibid., 13.

62. Ibid., 14–15, 78.

63. Carlos Mamani, interview with the author, La Paz, Bolivia, February 5, 2015.

64. Selection of the THOA audio recordings in archives of the Museo Nacional de Etnografía y Folklore in La Paz, Bolivia. For example, THOA, "Homenaje 45 Aniversario a Santos Marca Tula."

65. Felipe Santos Quispe, "La memoria comunal y la historia oral: El caso de la experiencia del THOA," in *XXI Reunión Anual de Etnología* (La Paz: Museo Nacional de Etnografía y Folklore, 2008), 650.

66. Mamani, *Taraqu*, 160

67. Ibid., 12.

68. Stephenson, "Forging an Indigenous Counterpublic Sphere," 108.

69. Mamani, *Taraqu*, 9.

70. Ibid., 9, 12.

71. Stephenson, "Forging an Indigenous Counterpublic Sphere," 109. Stephenson cites "Seminario sobre 'Lucha anticolonial de los comunarios de Taraqu,'" *Presencia*, May 15, 1992.

Chapter Five: Recovering Santos Marka T'ula

1. Alejandro Ilaquita Marka, interview with the author, La Paz, Bolivia, March 25, 2015.

2. Gregorio Barco Guarachi, interview with the author, El Alto, Bolivia, March 25, 2015. Translation from Aymara by Jaime Mejia.

3. Ibid.
4. Ibid.
5. Taller de Historia Oral Andina, *El indio Santos Marka T'ula*.
6. Mamani, *Metodología de la historia oral*, 17.
7. Choque, *Historia de una lucha desigual*, 62. In *Trials of Nation Making*, historian Brooke Larson demonstrates how indigenous people defending themselves from liberal assaults on communal lands in the nineteenth century "tapped into deep customary and legal traditions, *ayllu* history and memory, and sacred meanings of their contested territories." Larson, *Trials of Nation Making*, 54.
8. Klein, *Concise History of Bolivia*, 148.
9. Gotkowitz, *Revolution for Our Rights*, 45–46. In this section of her essential book on Bolivian indigenous movements from 1880 to 1952, Gotkowitz places the struggle of the caciques apoderados as a critical force in the indigenous mobilizations that constituted what she calls the rural "revolution before the revolution" of 1952.
10. Klein, *Concise History of Bolivia*, 147.
11. Gotkowitz, *Revolution for Our Rights*, 45–46.
12. Taller de Historia Oral Andina, *El indio Santos Marka T'ula*, 15–16.
13. Mamani, *Metodología de la historia oral*, 17; Andean Oral History Workshop and Silvia Rivera Cusicanqui, comp., "Indigenous Women and Community Resistance: History and Memory," in Jelin, *Women and Social Change in Latin America*, 153; Roberto Choque Canqi and Cristina Quisbert Quispe, *Líderes indígenas aymaras: Lucha por la defensa de tierras comunitarias de origen* (La Paz: Unidad Investigaciones Históricas, UNIH-PAKAXA, 2010), 27.
14. Choque, *Historia de una lucha desigual*, 62.
15. Gotkowitz, *Revolution for Our Rights*, 43; Waskar Ari, *Earth Politics: Religion, Decolonization, and Bolivia's Indigenous Intellectuals* (Durham: Duke University Press, 2014), 33. Ari provides a fascinating look at the Alcaldes Mayores Particulares (AMP), a group of indigenous activist-intellectuals who defended indigenous land and fought for indigenous education in the decades preceding the National Revolution. The AMP used practices and discourses Ari calls "earth politics," based in native religion and an indigenous relationship with the earth and Aymara gods.
16. Taller de Historia Oral Andina, *El indio Santos Marka T'ula*, 21.
17. Fundación Para la Investigación Estratégica en Bolivia, *THOA: Taller de Historia Oral Andina*.
18. Ibid. For similar cases of grassroots historical research conducted by indigenous intellectuals in Colombia, see Rappaport, *Politics of Memory*; and Rappaport, *Cumbe Reborn*.
19. Olivia Harris, introduction to "The Indian Santos Marka T'ula, Chief of the *ayllus* of Qallapa and General Representative of the Indian Communities of Bolivia," Andean Oral History Workshop, trans. Emma Gawne-Cain, *History Workshop Journal* 34 (1992): 102–3.
20. Choque and Quisbert, *Líderes indígenas aymaras*, 27n14. The authors cite ALP/PC, 1914, *Boletín de actualidad*, December 25, 1913.
21. Marta Irurozqui, "The Sound of the Pututos: Politicisation and Indigenous Rebellions in Bolivia, 1826–1921," *Journal of Latin American Studies* 32, no. 1 (2000): 104.
22. Choque, *Historia de una lucha desigual*, 68.
23. Irurozqui, "Sound of the Pututos," 104.
24. Leandro Condori Chura and Esteban Ticona Alejo, *El escribano de los caciques apoderados* (La Paz: Hisbol/THOA, 1992), 67.
25. Gotkowitz, *Revolution for Our Rights*, 56.
26. Hylton and Thomson, *Revolutionary Horizons*, 60–61.

27. Gotkowitz, *Revolution for Our Rights*, 58–59.
28. Ibid., 61–62.
29. Fundación Para la Investigación Estratégica en Bolivia, *THOA: Taller de Historia Oral Andina*.
30. Ibid.
31. Ibid.
32. Santos, "Una mirada autocrítica," 161–62.
33. Fundación Para la Investigación Estratégica en Bolivia, *THOA: Taller de Historia Oral Andina*.
34. Ibid.
35. Ibid.
36. Rivera, "El potencial epistemológico," 20. Similarly, Larson writes, "Collective peasant memories of rebellion and repression, although discontinuous and latent for much of the nineteenth century, lay buried just under the surface of quotidian consciousness until well into the twentieth century." Larson, *Trials of Nation Making*, 5.
37. Stephenson, "Forging an Indigenous Counterpublic Sphere," 105.
38. Larson, *Trials of Nation Making*, 5.
39. Rivera, "*Oprimidos pero no vencidos*," 86
40. Condori and Ticona, *El escribano*, 64. The spelling of Katari's name here is consistent with the original text.
41. Rivera, "*Oprimidos pero no vencidos*," 86.
42. Taller de Historia Oral Andina, *El indio Santos Marka T'ula*.
43. *Santos Marka T'ula*, directed by Demetrio Nina (Fundación Nina Santos, 2008), DVD. This film, produced in Bolivia, covers T'ula's life and includes many interviews with THOA members and dramatizations of T'ula's struggle.
44. Ibid.
45. Choque and Quisbert, *Líderes indígenas aymaras*, 195.
46. Gregorio Barco Guarachi interview.
47. Taller de Historia Oral Andina, *El indio Santos Marka T'ula*, 36.
48. Ibid., 20.
49. Andean Oral History Workshop, "Indian Santos Marka T'ula," 103–4.
50. *Santos Marka T'ula*, DVD.
51. Gotkowitz, *Revolution for Our Rights*, 47–48.
52. Taller de Historia Oral Andina, *El indio Santos Marka T'ula*, 21–23.
53. Choque and Quisbert, *Líderes indígenas aymaras*, 195. The authors cite Don Marcos Jimenez de la Espada, "Relaciones geográficas de Indias-Perú," in *Relación de la Provincia de los Pacajes*, Biblioteca de Autores Españoles, vol. 183, Pedro de Mercado de Peñalosa (Madrid, 1965), 334.
54. Taller de Historia Oral Andina, *El indio Santos Marka T'ula*, 19, 21–23.
55. Ibid., 23–25.
56. Mamani, *Metodología de la historia oral*, 20.
57. Ibid. On this topic, also see Jonathan D. Hill, ed., *Rethinking History and Myth: Indigenous South American Perspectives on the Past* (Urbana: University of Illinois Press, 1988).
58. Rivera, "El potencial epistemológico," 19. Rivera cites Silvia Rivera Cusicanqui, *Política e ideología en el movimiento campesino colombiano: El caso de la ANUC (Asociación Nacional de Usuarios Campesinos)* (Bogotá: CINEP, 1982).
59. *Santos Marka T'ula*, DVD.
60. Andean Oral History Workshop, "Indian Santos Marka T'ula," 109.
61. Ibid.
62. Gregorio Barco Guarachi interview.

63. Andean Oral History Workshop, "Indian Santos Marka T'ula," 117.
64. Ibid., 116–17.
65. "THOA por 30 años recoge la historia oral."
66. Esteban Ticona Alejo, *Memoria, política y antropología en los Andes bolivianos: Historia oral y saberes locales* (La Paz: Plural Editores, 2005), 86–87.
67. Ibid.
68. Ibid., 87.
69. "THOA por 30 años recoge la historia oral."
70. Stephenson, "Forging an Indigenous Counterpublic Sphere," 106.
71. Fundación Para la Investigación Estratégica en Bolivia, *THOA: Taller de Historia Oral Andina.*
72. Ibid.
73. Healy, *Llamas, Weavings, and Organic Chocolate*, 87.
74. Stephenson, "Forging an Indigenous Counterpublic Sphere," 106–7.
75. Marcelo Fernández Osco, interview with the author, La Paz, Bolivia, October 11, 2014. For more information on the THOA's 1990s work, see E. Gabrielle Kuenzli, *Acting Inca: National Belonging in Early Twentieth-Century Bolivia* (Pittsburgh: University of Pittsburgh Press, 2013), 136–38.
76. Mamoru Fujita, "Radionovelas aymaras entre la oralidad y la escritura," in *Anales de la Reunión Anual de Etnología I, La Paz XXV* (La Paz: Museo Nacional de Etnografía y Folklore, 2011), 575–76. Fujita cites Vera Gianotten, *CIPCA y poder campesino indígena: 35 años de historia* (La Paz: CIPCA, 2006), 70–71.
77. Carlos Mamani, interview with the author in La Paz, Bolivia, February 5, 2015.
78. Fujita, "Radionovelas aymaras entre la oralidad y la escritura," 576.
79. Genaro R. Condori Laurta, "Experiencias comunicacionales de la Asociación de Radioemisoras Aimaras de La Paz," in Ticona, *Los Andes desde los Andes*, 83.
80. Carlos Mamani interview.
81. Ibid.
82. Filomena Nina, interview with the author, La Paz, Bolivia, April 3, 2014.
83. Ibid.
84. Marcelo Fernández Osco interview.
85. Stephenson, "Forging an Indigenous Counterpublic Sphere," 107. Stephenson cites Esteban Ticona Alejo and Xavier Albó, with Roberto Choque Canqui, *Jesus de Machaqa: La marka rebelde*, vol. 3 (La Paz: CIPCA and CEDOIN, 1996), 255.
86. Felipe Santos Quispe, interview with the author, La Paz, Bolivia, March 31, 2014.
87. Ibid.
88. THOA, "Homenaje 45 aniversario a Santos Marca Tula," (n.d.), digital audio file, 01550_0291_01_03_THO, Archives of the Museo Nacional de Etnografía y Folklore, La Paz, Bolivia.

Chapter Six: The Enduring Ayllus

1. Tomás Saqueli Huaranca, interview with the author, La Paz, Bolivia. April 1, 2014.
2. Nilda Rojas, interview with the author, La Paz, Bolivia, March 29, 2014.
3. Raúl Prada, "La fuerza del acontecimiento," in *Tiempos de rebelión*, eds. Álvaro García, Raquel Gutiérrez, Raúl Prada, Felipe Quispe, and Luis Tapia (La Paz: Comuna / Muela del Diablo Editores, 2001), 112–13.

4.   I present a brief sketch of centuries of ayllu history here, based on secondary literature, to trace certain general changes and continuities in ayllu organization and traditions. John V. Murra's pioneering work in the 1960s and 1970s on the ayllu and "vertical archipelagos" in the Andes set the stage for much of the scholarship to come on this topic. See John V. Murra, *The Economic Organization of the Inka State* (Greenwich, CT: JAI Press, 1980). Scholars have explored the nature of reciprocity between ayllus, how power distribution between communities varied, and ayllus' diverse adaptations to both Incan and Spanish rule. For more, see David Lehmann, ed., *Ecology and Exchange in the Andes* (Cambridge: Cambridge University Press, 2007); Karen Spalding, *Huarochiri: An Andean Society under Inca and Spanish Rule* (Redwood City, CA: Stanford University Press, 1988); Brooke Larson, Olivia Harris, and Enrique Tandeter, eds., *Ethnicity, Markets, and Migration in the Andes: At the Crossroads of History and Anthropology* (Durham: Duke University Press, 1995); William Carter and Xavier Albó, "La comunidad Aymara: Un miniestado en conflicto," in *Raices de América: El mundo aymara*, ed. Xavier Albó (Madrid: UNESCO, 1988), 451–92; Florencia Mallon, *The Defense of Community in Peru's Central Highlands: Peasant Struggle and Capitalist Transition, 1860–1940* (Princeton: Princeton University Press, 1983); Nils Jacobsen, *Mirages of Transition: The Peruvian Altiplano, 1780–1930* (Berkeley: University of California Press, 1993); and Herbert Klein, *Haciendas and Ayllus: Rural Society in the Bolivian Andes in the Eighteenth and Nineteenth Centuries* (Stanford: Stanford University Press, 1993).

5.   Larson, *Cochabamba*, 19.

6.   Steve J. Stern, *Peru's Indian Peoples and the Challenge of Spanish Conquest: Huamanga to 1640* (Madison: University of Wisconsin Press, 1993), 6.

7.   Larson, *Cochabamba*, 21–23. On this topic also see Thomas Abercrombie, *Pathways of Memory and Power: Ethnography and History among an Andean People* (Madison: University of Wisconsin Press, 1998).

8.   Stern, *Peru's Indian Peoples*. Stern cites Diego González Holguín, *Vocabulario de la lengua general de todo el Perú llamada qquichua o del Inca*, ed. Juan G. N. Lobato (1608; rep., Lima, 1901), 41. Also see Xavier Albó, *Desafíos de la solidaridad aymara* (La Paz: CIPCA, 1985); and Frank Salomon, *The Cord Keepers: Khipus and Cultural Life in a Peruvian Village* (Durham: Duke University Press, 2004).

9.   Carter and Albó, "La comunidad aymara," 454. Also see Taller de Historia Oral Andina, *Ayllu: Pasado y futuro de los pueblos originarios* (La Paz: Editorial Aruwiyiri, 1995), 19.

10.   Klein, *Concise History of Bolivia*, 34; Gonzalo Lamana, *Domination without Dominance: Inca-Spanish Encounters in Early Colonial Peru* (Durham: Duke University Press Books, 2008); Nathan Wachtel, *The Vision of the Vanquished: The Spanish Conquest of Peru through Indian Eyes, 1530–1570* (New York: Barnes and Noble, 1977); Spalding, *Huarochiri*; Jeremy Ravi Mumford, *Vertical Empire: The General Resettlement of Indians in the Colonial Andes* (Durham: Duke University Press, 2012); Ricardo A. Godoy, "The Fiscal Role of the Andean Ayllu," *Man* 21, no. 4 (1986): 723–41; Ricardo A. Godoy, "State, Ayllu, and Ethnicity in Northern Potosí, Bolivia," *Anthropos* 80 (1985): 53–65.

11.   Carter and Albó, "La comunidad aymara," 454.

12.   Klein, *Concise History of Bolivia*, 35–36. Also see Mumford, *Vertical Empire*.

13.   Carter and Albó, "La comunidad aymara," 454.

14.   See Mumford, *Vertical Empire*.

15.   Lucero, *Struggles of Voice*, 40.

16.   Larson, *Cochabamba*, 304–5. Larson draws from the work of Tristan Platt; see Tristan Platt, *Estado boliviano y ayllu andino: Tierra y tributo en el norte de Potosí* (Lima: Instituto de Estudios Peruanos, 1982); and Platt, "The Role of the Ande-

an *Ayllu* in the Reproduction of the Petty Commodity Regime in Northern Potosí (Bolivia)," in Lehmann, *Ecology and Exchange*.

17. Platt, "The Role of the Andean *Ayllu*," 30–35.

18. Carter and Albó, "La comunidad aymara," 454–55.

19. Also see I. S. R. Pape, "Indigenous Movements and the Andean Dynamics of Ethnicity and Class: Organization, Representation, and Political Practice in the Bolivian Highlands," *Latin American Perspectives* 36, no. 4 (2009): 101–25.

20. Choque and Mamani, "Reconstitución del *ayllu*," 155.

21. Lucero, *Struggles of Voice*, 66, 158. For the history of Jesús de Machaca, also see Roberto Choque Canqui, *Jesús de Machaqa: La marka rebelde*, vol. 1, *Cinco siglos de historia* (La Paz: CIPCA, 2003); and Esteban Ticona Alejo and Xavier Albó, *Jesús de Machaqa: La marka rebelde*, vol. 3, *La lucha por el poder comunal* (La Paz: CIP-CA, 1997).

22. Xavier Albó, *Movimientos y poder indígena en Bolivia, Ecuador y Peru* (La Paz: CIPCA, 2008), 55. Also see Choque, *Cinco siglos*; and Ticona and Albó, *La lucha por el poder comunal*.

23. Carlos Mamani, interview with the author, La Paz, Bolivia, February 5, 2015.

24. Ibid.

25. Silvia Rivera Cusicanqui y Equipo THOA, *Ayllus y proyectos de desarrollo en el norte de Potosí* (La Paz: Ediciones Aruwiyiri, 1992), 102, 114–16, 121.

26. Taller de Historia Oral Andina, *Federación de Ayllus—Provincia Ingavi: Estructura Orgánica* (La Paz: Ediciones Aruwiyiri, 1993), 7.

27. Lucero, *Struggles of Voice*, 117–18. Also see Choque, *Cinco siglos*; and Ticona and Albó, *La lucha por el poder comunal*.

28. Klein, *Concise History of Bolivia*, 261. The office of Vice President Víctor Hugo Cárdenas notably collaborated in the production of a special issue of *Memoria* magazine in 1996 that focused on a gathering of ayllu communities in the department of Chuquisaca, Bolivia. In this issue, Cárdenas touts his government's new legislature, which aided ayllu reconstitution efforts. In his introduction to coverage of this regional gathering of ayllu leaders and members, Cárdenas writes, "The ayllu is the principal cell, one of the foundations for the construction of a multiethnic and pluricultural democracy." Víctor Hugo Cárdenas, "El encuentro de los ayllus de San Lucas," *Memoria*, 1996, 2.

29. Healy, *Llamas, Weavings, and Organic Chocolate*, 94.

30. Klein, *Concise History of Bolivia*, 261. Also see Pablo Regalsky, "Territorio e interculturalidad: La participación campesina indígena y la reconfiguración del espacio andino rural," in *Movimientos indígenas y estado en Bolivia*, eds. Luis Enrique López and Pablo Regalsky (La Paz: Plural Editores, 2005), 107–41. One issue of the small pamphlet *El Ayllu* was dedicated to promoting information about the LPP, including reprinted newspaper articles from *Presencia* on the basic functions of the new law. *El Ayllu* 4, no. 9 (1994). Consulted at the Archivo y Biblioteca Nacionales de Bolivia, Sucre, Bolivia.

31. Lucero, *Struggles of Voice*, 134–37.

32. Ibid., 166–67.

33. Robert Andolina, Nina Laurie, and Sarah A. Radcliffe, *Indigenous Development in the Andes: Culture, Power, and Transnationalism* (Durham: Duke University Press, 2009), 106. The authors cite Vicente Flores's quote from Patricia Almaraz, *Las tierras comunitarias de Orígen, son un instrumento para recuperar el derecho sobre sus tierras* (CIPCA working paper, 2005).

34. Carlos Mamani interview.

35. Andolina, Laurie, and Radcliff, *Indigenous Development in the Andes*, 106.

36. Kohl and Farthing, *Impasse in Bolivia*, 100.
37. Lucero, *Struggles of Voice*, 124–25. Also see Gustafson, "Paradoxes of Liberal Indigenism."
38. Lucero, *Struggles of Voice*, 168.
39. Pablo Mamani, "Reconstitución y cartografía"; Carlos Mamani, "Memoria y politica aymara," in *Aruskipasipxañasataki: El siglo XXI y el futuro del pueblo aymara*, ed. Waskar Ari Chachaki (La Paz: Editorial Amuyañataki, 2001): 47–65.
40. Stephenson, "Forging an Indigenous Counterpublic Sphere," 112.
41. Mamani, "Reconstitución y cartografía," 124–26. Mamani cites an interview with Eusebio Pizarro conducted by Pablo Mamani Ramírez in Sucre, Bolivia, July 11, 2007.
42. Cancio Rojas, interview with the author, La Paz, Bolivia, February 11, 2015.
43. Carlos Mamani interview.
44. Choque and Mamani, "Reconstitución del *ayllu*," 163.
45. Filomena Nina, interview with the author, La Paz, Bolivia, April 7, 2014.
46. Stephenson, "Forging an Indigenous Counterpublic Sphere," 111.
47. María Eugenia Choque, "La reconstitución del ayllu y los derechos de los pueblos indígenas," in *Las sociedades interculturales: Un desafío para el siglo XXI*, ed. Fernando García (Quito: FLACSO, 2000), 28. Another type of grassroots historical recovery of ayllu history is illustrated in a small pamphlet produced by Martín Callisaya C. in collaboration with local students on the history of the rural community of Ch'ama in the province of Ingavi. This twenty-six-page booklet covers the history of the town from the precolonial era up to the time of its publication in 1990. While it is difficult to say the extent to which this text was used in the national ayllu reconstitution efforts, the tone and style of the history echoes other similar publications produced by the THOA and the CONAMAQ. Indeed, it cites the work of the THOA and Aymara historian Roberto Choque Canqi. Martín Callisaya C., *Ch'ama: Nuestra fuerza invencible (breve relato histórico)* (n.p: 1990). In another sign of the importance of ayllu history during this decade, the Bolivian government's National Secretary of Popular Participation and the government of Denmark supported the publication in Bolivia of a small, accessible booklet in Spanish on ayllu history in the northern region of the department of Potosí. Produced by British anthropologist Olivia Harris, this work includes drawings accompanying text on ayllu history and traditions, and cites the THOA as well as the work of Tristan Platt and Xavier Albó. "Somos los hijos de los ayllus," *Historia y Actualidad Norte de Potosí*, no. 7 (1997). Both documents were consulted at the Archivo Histórico de La Paz in La Paz, Bolivia.
48. Carlos Mamani interview.
49. Taller de Historia Oral Andina, *Ayllu: Pasado y futuro*, 14–15.
50. Elizabeth López, interview with the author, La Paz, Bolivia, October 16, 2014.
51. Stephenson, "Forging an Indigenous Counterpublic Sphere," 113.
52. Healy, *Llamas, Weavings, and Organic Chocolate*, 119; Roger Neil Rasnake, *Domination and Cultural Resistance: Authority and Power among an Andean People* (Durham: Duke University Press, 1988).
53. Mamani, "Reconstitución y cartografía," 126–27; Also see Waldemar Espinoza, *Temas de etnohistoria boliviana* (La Paz: CIMA, 2003); and "El memorial de Charcas (1582)," *Ciencia y Cultura*, no. 27 (2011): 37. On related questions of utilizing the past and memory for the political needs of the present, see Jennifer Cole, *Forget Colonialism? Sacrifice and the Art of Memory in Madagascar* (Berkeley: University of California Press, 2001); Ajay Skaria, *Hybrid Histories: Forests, Frontiers and Wildness*

in Western India (Oxford: Oxford University Press, 1999); Donna Lee Van Cott, "Indigenous Struggle," *Latin American Research Review* 38, no. 2 (2003): 220-33; and Sawyer, *Crude Chronicles*. Thomas Abercombie looks at how myth and social memory were preserved largely through oral traditions in the k'ulta indigenous community in the Bolivian altiplano. See Abercrombie, *Pathways of Memory and Power*.

54.   Stephenson, "Forging an Indigenous Counterpublic Sphere," 113.
55.   Choque and Mamani, "Reconstitución del *ayllu*," 165, 147-49.
56.   Stephenson, "Forging an Indigenous Counterpublic Sphere," 113.
57.   Choque and Mamani, "Reconstitución del *ayllu*," 166.
58.   Taller de Historia Oral Andina, *Federación de Ayllus*, 5. I focus on the Estructura Orgánica here as it is an excellent source on the objectives and organizational vision of the ayllu reconstitution efforts at this time. On this topic, I also consulted a 2009 CONAMAQ statute that was meant to provide a similar model for ayllus across its network during this period: CONAMAQ, *Estatuto modélico para autonomías indígenas originarias campesinas* (La Paz: CONAMAQ, 2009). Consulted at the Biblioteca Fundación Xavier Albó in La Paz, Bolivia.

59.   Stephenson, "Forging an Indigenous Counterpublic Sphere," 113.
60.   Choque and Mamani, "Reconstitución del *ayllu*," 165.
61.   Taller de Historia Oral Andina, *Federación de Ayllus*, 70-85.
62.   García, Chávez, and Costas, *Sociología de los movimientos sociales*, 323; CONAMAQ, *Plan estratégico del CONAMAQ, 2008-2013* (La Paz: CONAMAQ, 2008), 37.
63.   García, Chávez, and Costas, *Sociología de los movimientos sociales*, 338-39.
64.   CONAMAQ, *Plan estratégico*, 37. Regarding the organization and proposals of the CONAMAQ in later years, see CONAMAQ, *Bases de la constitución del estado plurinacional* (n.p.: CONAMAQ, 2005). Consulted at the Biblioteca Fundación Xavier Albó in La Paz, Bolivia.
65.   Fidel Condori, interview with the author, La Paz, Bolivia, April 2, 2014.
66.   García, Chávez, and Costas, *Sociología de los movimientos sociales*, 326.
67.   Marcelo Fernández Osco, ed., *Estudio sociojurídico: Práctica del derecho indígena originario en Bolivia* (La Paz: UPS Editorial, 2009), 62.
68.   Ibid., 62-64.
69.   Elizabeth López interview.
70.   Renán Paco Granier, interview with the author, Potosí, Bolivia, February 26, 2015.
71.   Elizabeth López interview.
72.   Mamani, "Reconstitución y cartografía," 104-5.
73.   Gregorio Choque, interview with the author, La Paz, Bolivia, March 24, 2015.
74.   Choque and Mamani, "Reconstitución del *ayllu*," 159.
75.   Hylton and Thomson, *Revolutionary Horizons*, 99.
76.   Kohl and Farthing, *Impasse in Bolivia*, 84-85, 88.
77.   Charles Hale, "Does Multiculturalism Menace? Governance, Cultural Rights and the Politics of Identity in Guatemala," *Journal of Latin American Studies* 34, no. 3 (2002): 507. Also see Mark Goodale and Nancy Postero, eds., *Neoliberalism, Interrupted: Social Change and Contested Governance in Contemporary Latin America* (Redwood City: Stanford University Press, 2013); Edward Fischer, introduction to *Indigenous Peoples, Civil Society, and the Neo-liberal State in Latin America*, ed. Edward Fischer (New York: Berghahn Books, 2009), 1-18; Kay B. Warren and Jean E. Jackson, eds., *Indigenous Movements, Self-Representation, and the State in Latin America* (Austin: University of Texas Press, 2003); Warren, *Indigenous Movements and the Crit-*

ics; and Charles Hale, *Resistance and Contradiction: Miskitu Indians and the Nicaraguan State, 1894–1987* (Redwood City, CA: Stanford University Press, 1994).

78.   Nancy Grey Postero, *Now We Are Citizens: Indigenous Politics in Postmulticultural Bolivia* (Stanford: Stanford University Press, 2007), 16.

79.   See John-Andrew McNeish, "Beyond the Permitted Indian? Bolivia and Guatemala in an Era of Neoliberal Developmentalism," *Latin American and Caribbean Ethnic Studies* 3, no. 1 (2008): 34, 45–46. On the related question of political recognition and decolonization in indigenous movements in Canada, see Glen Sean Coulthard, *Red Skin, White Masks: Rejecting the Colonial Politics of Recognition* (Minneapolis: University of Minnesota Press, 2014).

80.   Postero, *Now We Are Citizens*, 6. Also see McNeish, "Beyond the Permitted Indian?," 53.

81.   Saturnino Tola, "Discurso con motive de la visita del Sr. Presidente y del Sr. Vicepresidente de la República a Jesús de Machaqa, 12 de marzo de 1994," in Ticona and Albó, *La lucha por el poder comunal*, 283, 368–69.

Conclusion: "Looking Back, We Will Move Forward"

1.   Translation of Aymara phrase, *Qhiparu nayraru uñtas sartañani*. See Mamani, *Los aymaras frente a la historia*, 14.

2.   Marxa Chávez, interview with the author, La Paz, Bolivia, February 19, 2015.

3.   An in-depth look at the uprisings in the early 2000s and the MAS government is beyond the scope of this work. However, for readers seeking more information, much has been written on this period. Literature on the movements of the 2000s in Bolivia and the MAS era includes Dangl, *Price of Fire*; Pablo Mamani Ramírez, *Microgobiernos barriales: Levantamiento de la ciudad de El Alto (Octubre 2003)* (El Alto: Centro Andino de Estudios Estratégicos, 2005); Raúl Zibechi, *Dispersing Power: Social Movements as Anti-state Forces* (Oakland: AK Press, 2010); Hylton and Thomson, *Revolutionary Horizons*; Gutiérrez, *Rhythms of the Pachakuti*; Oscar Olivera, *Cochabamba! Water War in Bolivia* (Cambridge, MA: South End Press, 2004); García et al., *Tiempos de rebelión*; Jeffery Webber, *From Rebellion to Reform in Bolivia: Class Struggle, Indigenous Liberation, and the Politics of Evo Morales* (Chicago: Haymarket Books, 2011); Thomson et al., *Bolivia Reader*, 541–72; Esteban Ticona Alejo, ed., *El Pachakuti ha empezado* (La Paz: Ediciones Yachaywasi, 2006); Carwil Bjork-James, "Claiming Space, Redefining Politics: Urban Protest and Grassroots Power in Bolivia" (PhD diss., City University of New York, 2013); and Jason Tockman, "Instituting Power: Power Relations, Institutional Hybridity, and Indigenous Self-Governance in Bolivia" (PhD diss., University of British Columbia, 2008).

4.   On the relationship between Bolivia's diverse movements and the Morales administration, see Dangl, *Dancing with Dynamite*.

5.   For overviews of Bolivia under the Morales administration, see Linda C. Farthing and Benjamin H. Kohl, *Evo's Bolivia: Continuity and Change* (Austin: University of Texas Press, 2014); Farthing, "Evo's Bolivia: The Limits of Change," *The Next System Project*, August 7, 2017, https://thenextsystem.org/learn/stories/evos-bolivia-limits-change/; and Nancy Postero, *The Indigenous State: Race, Politics, and Performance in Plurinational Bolivia* (Berkeley: University of California Press, 2017).

6.   See Benjamin Dangl, "Victories in the Andes: The Recent Past and Near Future of Bolivia under Evo Morales," *Juncture* 21, no. 3 (2014): 238–41.

7.   See Pablo Solón, "Algunas reflexiones, autocriticas y propuestas sobre

el proceso de cambio en Bolivia," *América Latina en Movimiento*, February 25, 2016, http://www.alainet.org/es/articulo/175633.

8. For past and ongoing coverage of such topics and others related to politics and social change in Bolivia, see outlets such as *Upside Down World*, *NACLA Report on the Americas*, *Andean Information Network*, and *Rebelión*.

9. Benjamin Dangl, "An Interview with Evo Morales on the Colonization of the Americas," *Counterpunch*, December 2, 2003, https://www.counterpunch.org/2003/12/02/an-interview-with-evo-morales-on-the-colonization-of-the-americas/.

10. Ibid.

11. Nilda Rojas, interview with the author, La Paz, Bolivia, March 29, 2014. Also see Benjamin Dangl, "The Politics of Pachamama: Natural Resource Extraction vs. Indigenous Rights and the Environment in Latin America," *Upside Down World*, April 25, 2014, http://upsidedownworld.org/archives/international/the-politics-of-pachamama-natural-resource-extraction-vs-indigenous-rights-and-the-environment-in-latin-america/.

12. Ibid.

13. Bill Weinberg, "Indigenous Anarchist Critique of Bolivia's 'Indigenous State': Interview with Silvia Rivera Cusicanqui," *Upside Down World*, September 3, 2014, http://upsidedownworld.org/archives/bolivia/indigenous-anarchist-critique-of-bolivias-indigenous-state-interview-with-silvia-rivera-cusicanqui/. Also see Silvia Rivera Cusicanqui, *Ch'ixinakax utxiwa: Una reflexión sobre prácticas y discursos descolonizadores* (Buenos Aires: Tinta Limón y Retazos, 2010).

14. Ibid.

15. On this theme, see Esteban Ticona Alejo, ed., *Bolivia en el inicio del Pachakuti: La larga lucha anticolonial de los pueblos aimara y quechua* (Madrid: Ediciones Akal, 2011); Tórrez and Arce, *Construcción simbólica del estado plurinacional*; Nicolas and Quisbert, *Pachakuti*; Postero, "Andean Utopias"; Svampa and Stefanoni, *Bolivia: Memoria, insurgencia*; Farthing and Kohl, "Mobilizing Memory"; Marisol De La Cadena, "Indigenous Cosmopolitics in the Andes: Conceptual Reflections beyond 'Politics,'" *Cultural Anthropology* 25, no. 2 (2010): 334–70; and Edward Fabian Kennedy, "The Politics of Representing the Past in Bolivia," (PhD dissertation, University of California, San Diego, 2009).

16. Nicolas and Quisbert, *Pachakuti*, 172.

17. Ibid.

18. Félix Cárdenas Aguilar, interview with the author, La Paz, Bolivia, February 11, 2015. Also see Benjamin Dangl, "Bolivia: A Country That Dared to Exist," *TeleSur*, March 16, 2015, https://www.telesurtv.net/english/opinion/Bolivia-A-Country-That-Dared-to-Exist-20150316-0022.html/.

19. Elisa Vega Sillo, interview with the author, La Paz, Bolivia, October 14, 2014. Also see Benjamin Dangl, "Decolonizing Bolivia's History of Indigenous Resistance," *TeleSur*, February 17, 2015, https://www.telesurtv.net/english/opinion/Decolonizing-Bolivias-History-of-Indigenous-Resistance-20150217-0042.html/.

20. Pablo Mamani Ramírez, interview with the author, El Alto, Bolivia, February 2, 2015.

ARCHIVES AND LIBRARIES CONSULTED

Archivo del Taller de Historia Oral Andina
Archivo Histórico de La Paz
Archivo y Biblioteca del Museo Nacional de Etnografía y Folklore
Archivo y Biblioteca Nacionales de Bolivia
Biblioteca Fundación Xavier Albó
Biblioteca Pública Municipal de La Paz
Biblioteca y Archivo Arturo Costa de la Torre
Biblioteca y Archivo Histórico de la Asamblea Legislativa Plurinacional

LIST OF INTERVIEWS CONDUCTED

Ancieta Orellana, Juanita (Federación Nacional de Mujeres Campesinas de Bolivia "Bartolina Sisa"). La Paz, Bolivia. October 14, 2014.

Ávila, José Oscar (Federación de Juntas Vecinales–El Alto). El Alto, Bolivia. February 2, 2015.

Barco Guarachi, Gregorio (Son of Santos Marka T'ula). El Alto, Bolivia. March 25, 2015.

Burgos, Isabel Elena (Lawyer). La Paz, Bolivia. January 20, 2015.

Calisaya, Oscar (Investigación Social y Asesoramiento Legal Potosí). Potosí, Bolivia. February 25, 2015. ISALP group interview.

Cárdenas Aguilar, Félix (Vice Minister of Decolonization). La Paz, Bolivia. February 11, 2015.

Castro, Marco Antonio (Investigación Social y Asesoramiento Legal Potosí). Potosí, Bolivia. February 25, 2015. ISALP group interview.

Chambilla Mamani, Beatriz (Taller de Historia Oral Andina). La Paz, Bolivia, October 16, 2014. THOA group interview.

Chávez, Marxa (Sociologist). La Paz, Bolivia. February 19, 2015.

Choque, Gregorio (Consejo Nacional de Ayllus y Markas de Qullasuyo). La Paz, Bolivia. March 24, 2015.

Choque Canqui, Roberto (Historian). Archivo de La Paz, La Paz, Bolivia, October 16, 2014.

Choque Salomé, Jorge (Confederación Sindical Única de Trabajadores Campesinos de Bolivia). La Paz, Bolivia. April 4, 2014. La Paz federation group interview.

Colque, Gonzalo (Fundación Tierra). La Paz, Bolivia. January 27, 2015.

Condorena, Cristóbal (Taller de Historia Oral Andina). La Paz, Bolivia. March 30, 2015.

Condori, Fidel (Consejo Nacional de Ayllus y Markas de Qullasuyo). La Paz, Bolivia. April 2, 2014, and October 10, 2014.

Cruz Canaviri, Paulino (Consejo Nacional de Ayllus y Markas de Qullasuyo). La Paz, Bolivia. October 14, 2014.

Fernández Osco, Marcelo (Taller de Historia Oral Andina). La Paz, Bolivia. October 11, 2014.

Guarachi Morales, Joel (Confederación Sindical Única de Trabajadores Campesinos de Bolivia). La Paz, Bolivia. April 3, 2014.

Guarayo, Humberto (Nación Yampara). Sucre, Bolivia. February 24, 2015.

Gutiérrez, Agustín (Taller de Historia Oral Andina). La Paz, Bolivia. March 25, 2015 (THOA group interview), and March 30, 2015.

Huarachi Paco, Máximo Freddy (Confederación Sindical Única de Traba-
    jadores Campesinos de Bolivia). La Paz, Bolivia. March 24, 2015.
Huata Manza, Alberto (Traditional medicine practitioner). La Paz, Boliv-
    ia. October 10, 2014.
Ilaquita Marka, Alejandro (Taller de Historia Oral Andina). La Paz, Boliv-
    ia. March 25, 2015. THOA group interview.
Lima, Constantino (Indianista thinker and leader). La Paz, Bolivia. Octo-
    ber 14, 2015.
López, Elizabeth (Advisor to Consejo Nacional de Ayllus y Markas de
    Qullasuyo). La Paz, Bolivia. October 16, 2014.
Mamani, Carlos (Taller de Historia Oral Andina). La Paz, Bolivia. Febru-
    ary 5, 2015.
Mamani, Pablo (Sociologist). El Alto, Bolivia. February 2, 2015.
Nina, Filomena (Taller de Historia Oral Andina). La Paz, Bolivia. April 3,
    2014, and October 16, 2014. THOA group interview.
Ortega, Isabel (Vice Minister of Indigenous Justice). La Paz, Bolivia. Jan-
    uary 19, 2015.
Paco Granier, Renán (Consejo Nacional de Ayllus y Markas de Qulla-
    suyo). Potosí, Bolivia. February 26, 2015.
Peralta, Justino (Vice Ministry of Decolonization). La Paz, Bolivia. March
    9, 2015.
Perlacios, Anselma (Federación Nacional de Mujeres Campesinas de Bo-
    livia "Bartolina Sisa"). La Paz, Bolivia. April 4, 2014.
Portugal, Pedro (Editor of *Pukara* magazine). La Paz, Bolivia. March 31,
    2014, and October 14, 2014.
Quisbert, Rodolfo (Taller de Historia Oral Andina). La Paz, Bolivia. April
    7, 2014, October 16, 2014 (THOA group interview), and March
    12, 2015.
Quispe, Zenón (Historian). El Alto, Bolivia. January 19, 2015.
Quispe Ticona, Ismael (Confederación Sindical Única de Trabajadores
    Campesinos de Bolivia). La Paz, Bolivia. April 4, 2014 (La Paz
    federation group interview), and January 22, 2015.
Quito Mamani, Apolinar. (Confederación Sindical Única de Trabajadores
    Campesinos de Bolivia). La Paz, Bolivia. April 4, 2014. La Paz
    federation group interview.
Reinaga, Hilda (Fundación Amautica Fausto Reinaga). La Paz, Bolivia.
    March 10, 2015.
Rojas, Cancio (Consejo Nacional de Ayllus y Markas de Qullasuyo). La
    Paz, Bolivia. February 11, 2015.
Rojas, Nilda (Consejo Nacional de Ayllus y Markas de Qullasuyo). La Paz,
    Bolivia. March 29, 2014.
Santos Quispe, Felipe (Taller de Historia Oral Andina). La Paz, Bolivia.

March 31, 2014, October 16, 2014 (THOA group interview), and February 20, 2015.

Saqueli Huaranca, Tomás (Consejo Nacional de Ayllus y Markas de Qullasuyo). La Paz, Bolivia. April 1, 2014.

Valencia Zentero, Juan Carlos (Central Obrera Regional–El Alto, Bolivia. February 11, 2015.

Vega Sillo, Elisa (Vice Ministry of Decolonization). La Paz, Bolivia. October 14, 2014.

Villalobos, Vique (Taller de Historia Oral Andina). La Paz, Bolivia. October 16, 2014. THOA group interview.

INDEX

Page numbers in *italic* refer to illustrations. "Passim" (literally "scattered") indicates intermittent discussion of a topic over a cluster of pages.

A

Agrarian Fundamental Law (proposed). *See* Fundamental Agrarian Law (proposed)

Agrarian Reform Law (1953), 24, 61, 69, 79, 82

agriculture, 24–31 passim, 44, 45, 50, 61, 69, 164; ayllus and, 25–27 passim, 139–43 passim; prices, 68, 75, 76; Toledo Reforms, 140

Alavi Patzi, Zenovio, 136

Albó, Xavier, 48, 75, 135, 142

Alcaldes Mayores Particulares (AMP), 191n15

Allende, Salvador, 49

Amaru, Túpac, 3

Andean Oral History Workshop. *See* THOA (Taller de Historia Oral Andina)

Apaza, Julián. *See* Katari, Túpac

Arce Gómez, Luis, 79

Argentina, 50, 79, 80

Ari, Waskar, 191n15

Arze, René, 98

Asamblea Popular. *See* Popular Assembly

Association of Aymara Professors, 50

audio recordings. *See* sound recordings

Ayllon, Virginia, 91

ayllus, 8–9, 10, 16, 19, 36, 54, 127, 134–61 passim; bibliography, 194; Cárdenas on, 195n28; reconstruction, 8–9, 37, 53, 85, 91, 101, 136, 138, 142–52 passim, 157, 161; replacement with unions, 25, 26, 27, 31; rotational leadership in, 42. *See also* suyus

Aymara language, 3, 96, 104, 177–78n61; Manifesto of Tiwanaku, 52; publications, 18, 91, 104–9 passim; radio, 32, 117, 131–35 passim

Aymara people, 5–8 passim, 13, 32, 42, 54, 60–62 passim, 67; AMP and, 191n15; caciques, 99; Choque, 48–49; coca use, *137*; conceptions of time, 17; dress, 60, 65; El Alto, 21; La Paz, 22, 31–37 passim, 43, 44, 48, 51, 95, 96; Manifesto of Tiwanaku, 50–52; oral history and, 89–96 passim, 101–5 passim, 117, 135, 151, 160–61; protests and direct action, 5, 6, 159; reciprocity and mutual aid, 16, 53–54; suyus, 153; Tambo, 43; Tapia, 39. *See also* Katari, Túpac; Mamani, Carlos; T'ula, Santos Marka; Willka, Zárate

Aymara Professors' Association. *See* Association of Aymara Professors

ayni, 53, 139

Ayo-Ayo, 3, 42–46, 56; statues, *21*, *45*

B

Ballivián, Hugo, 23, 24

Banzer, Hugo, 49–50, 51, 55–57, 63, 81, 84, 133–34

Barbie, Klaus, 79

Barco, Celestina, 133

Barco Guarachi, Gregorio, *115*, 116, 129, 131–32, 133

Barrientos, René, 23, 28–30

Bartolinas. *See* Federación Nacional de Mujeres Campesinas de Bolivia "Bartolina Sisa" (FNMBC-BS)

BCI (Bloque Campesino Independiente), 29, 64

Bechtel, 162

Benjamin, Thomas, 187n85

Blanco, Bertha, 71

blockades. *See* road blockades

AK Press is small, in terms of staff and resources, but we also manage to be one of the world's most productive anarchist publishing houses. We publish close to twenty books every year, and distribute thousands of other titles published by like-minded independent presses and projects from around the globe. We're entirely worker-run and democratically managed. We operate without a corporate structure—no boss, no managers, no bullshit.

The Friends of AK program is a way you can directly contribute to the continued existence of AK Press, and ensure that we're able to keep publishing books like this one! Friends pay $25 a month directly into our publishing account ($30 for Canada, $35 for international), and receive a copy of every book AK Press publishes for the duration of their membership! Friends also receive a discount on anything they order from our website or buy at a table: 50% on AK titles, and 20% on everything else. We have a Friends of AK ebook program as well: $15 a month gets you an electronic copy of every book we publish for the duration of your membership. You can even sponsor a very discounted membership for someone in prison.

Email friendsofak@akpress.org for more info, or visit the Friends of AK Press website: https://www.akpress.org/friends.html

There are always great book projects in the works—so sign up now to become a Friend of AK Press, and let the presses roll!

BENJAMIN DANGL has a PhD in Latin American history from McGill University and has worked as a journalist throughout Latin America for over fifteen years, covering politics and protest movements for outlets such as *The Guardian*, *Al Jazeera*, *The Nation*, *Salon*, *Vice*, and *NACLA Report on the Americas*. He is the author of *The Price of Fire: Resource Wars and Social Movements in Bolivia* and *Dancing with Dynamite: Social Movements and States in Latin America*, both published by AK Press. Dangl edits TowardFreedom.org, a progressive perspective on world events, and teaches at Champlain College.

Website: BenDangl.com